ROGER MANVELL

FILM

PENGUIN BOOKS

HARMONDSWORTH · MIDDLESEX

FIRST PUBLISHED 1944
REPRINTED 1944
REVISED EDITION 1946
FURTHER REVISED 1950

To my father and mother

(WHO TAUGHT ME TO GO TO THE PICTURES)

To John Grierson

(WHO TAUGHT ME TO LOOK AT THEM)

To my students and friends

(WHO TAUGHT ME TO DISCUSS THEM)

MADE AND PRINTED IN GREAT BRITAIN
FOR PENGUIN BOOKS LTD
BY HAZELL WATSON AND VINEY LTD
AYLESBURY AND LONDON

Contents

Illustrations

Tributes in Passing

THE moving picture, although a growth of only a few years, is boundless in its scope and endless in its possibilities. . . . The task I'm trying to achieve is above all to make you see.—D. W. GRIFFITH.

What sort of films do the public wish to see? . . . Type does not matter. . . . Take any subject under the sun, treat it right, and the public will like it.—EXHIBITOR IN BRITISH TRADE JOURNAL.

The cinema, like the detective story, makes it possible to experience without danger all the excitement, passion and desirousness which must be repressed in a humanitarian ordering of life.—C. G. JUNG.

It is the more dangerous to muddle along in an industry in which the difference between showmanship and racketeering is often slight and may pass in the confusion unnoticed.—F. D. KLINGENDER AND STUART LEGG.

That was the ending I wanted for *Blackmail*, but I had to change it for commercial reasons.—ALFRED HITCHCOCK.

Cinema needs continued repression of controversy in order to stave off disaster.—LORD TYRRELL, LATE CHAIRMAN OF THE BRITISH BOARD OF FILM CENSORS.

The cinema in the hands of the Soviet power represents a great and priceless force.—JOSEPH STALIN.

Between the natural event and its appearance upon the screen there is a marked difference. It is exactly this difference that makes the film an art.—V. I. PUDOVKIN.

Let the cinema attempt the dramatisation of the living scene and the living theme, springing from the living present instead of from the synthetic fabrication of the studio. . . . We believe that the cinema's capacity for getting around, for observing and selecting from life itself, can be exploited in a new and vital art form.—JOHN GRIERSON.

The film is the most vigorous art form today.—CONSTANT LAMBERT.

Slanted for the nabe market, it should hit the hinterland jackpot and do yeoman service elsewhere on the lower shelf. An exposé of arson methods, the story includes standard measure of romance, rugged rough-stuff and righteousness triumphant.—AMERICAN TRADE REVIEW.

Note on this New Edition

THIS book in its original form was first discussed with Allen Lane on the Isles of Scilly in the summer of 1941. I asked him why there was no book on films in his Pelican list, and he said no one had got around to writing one. I suggested that what was wanted was a book which showed something of the artistic and social importance of the film, written in a way which would provoke discussion among people who liked talking. The result was the first edition of FILM, published in 1944. If it was provocative, it was also often inaccurate, and in many ways innocent of the real complexities of the film world.

Its success, not only in this country but abroad, was due largely to its cheapness and accessibility, and to the virtual absence of any competition. No other parallel survey of the cinema had been attempted, and most of the best books on this or that specialised aspect of the subject were either out of print or twenty times the price. Meanwhile, I learned a great deal more alike from film-makers, exhibitors and audiences, and in 1945 revised the book considerably, trying to make it more complete factually and more useful, without altering in any way the original idea that it was written to direct people's attention to the problems of the subject and to provoke discussion of them.

Of course it is partly true to say that the more you know the duller you get. If this book has lost its first innocence whilst exploring the complicated film world, I hope it still discusses with honesty most of the far-reaching problems involved. You cannot consider the art of the film without taking into account the fact that it is also an industry, and you cannot discuss either of these aspects without realising its considerable influence upon our present-day civilisation. The film is a new technique of expression that has become more widely influential than reading.

In this new edition the whole text has been revised to bring it into line with more recent developments in film studios.

The main change, however, is the introduction of a Third Part to the book, which gives an outline of the work done in the chief film-producing countries of the world since 1945. Conditions have so altered since the War and so many new artists have become important that I felt this survey would be useful if only for the perspective it gives. But the film world changes more quickly than books about it can be written and printed; keeping such a book as this up to date is always a problem, a problem equal to that of obtaining accurate facts about the film industry. The Lists of Books and Films have been revised, and the Indexes made much more comprehensive than they were in the last edition. An extra section of illustrations has been added, with a selection of stills from the post-war films of many countries.

The number of people who realise the importance of the film and its great artistic potentialities has grown considerably during the past five years. I hope they will find this book useful. It was written to help them and to increase their numbers.

R. M.

London, 1949

Acknowledgements

No excuse is made for the heavy quotation in this book: it is part of its purpose to let as large a number of film-makers and critics as possible raise their own dust. But the debt must gladly be acknowledged to all writers and publishers whose works have been most freely drawn on in the text.

The following publishers have generously granted permission for quotation to be made from books published by them:

Peter Davies Ltd. (*Footnotes to the Film*, edited by Charles Davy).

Faber & Faber Ltd. (*Documentary* by Paul Rotha, *Film* by R. Arnheim and *Film Music* by Kurt London).

George Newnes Ltd. (*Film Technique* by V. I. Pudovkin).

Jonathan Cape Ltd. (*Film till Now* by Paul Rotha and *Garbo and the Night Watchmen*, edited by Alistair Cooke).

Lawrence & Wishart Ltd. (*U.S.S.R. speaks for Itself: Culture and Leisure*).

George Allen & Unwin Ltd. (*History of the Film* by Bardèche and Brasillach).

Permission has also been given to quote from the following periodicals:

Documentary News Letter (Film Centre).

Sight and Sound (British Film Institute).

Kinematograph Weekly (Kinematograph Publications Ltd.).

I would also like to thank David Lean and Cineguild for permission to quote from the script of *Great Expectations*.

This book also contains 240 stills, a third of which are new in this edition. I would like to thank the following organisations and individuals for their help in collecting these photographs: the National Film Library, the Central Office of Information, the Edinburgh Film Guild, the Cinémathèque Française, the Soviet Film Agency, the Centro Sperimentale di Cinematografia of Rome, the Czech Film Archive, the Academy Cinema, the Curzon Cinema, Studio One, London Films, the J. Arthur Rank Organisation, the International Film Bureau, H. H. Wollenberg, Hans Richter, Thorold

Dickinson and all the many production companies individually acknowledged in the credits of each still.

In previous editions I have acknowledged my debt to certain outstanding writers on the film whose work has helped me considerably, in particular V. I. Pudovkin, Lewis Jacobs, Rudolf Arnheim, Paul Rotha and John Grierson. The number of these writers is now slowly increasing, and I would like to add to them the names of Dilys Powell, Richard Winnington, Georges Sadoul and Ernest Lindgren. I also have the inestimable advantage of working closely at the British Film Academy with many of the leading British film-makers, as well as frequently discussing film with film-makers either abroad or when they visit us here. As in all discussion of the arts, one's debt grows wider and deeper the more people one knows.

I very warmly thank those correspondents who have generously taken the trouble to write to me to point out errors of fact in the last edition. In the relatively undocumented history of the cinema, some errors at this stage seem inevitable in a book so full of facts as this. I hope readers will draw my attention to any further points they think require correction or checking.

Finally, I would like to thank my wife for her untiring and patient help throughout the long task of revision and fact-finding which, I hope, makes this edition a little more useful than its predecessors.

Introduction

SURVEY FOR A STUDY

THIS year is the half-centenary of the cinema. In fifty years the mechanical contrivances of Marey, Reynaud, the Lumières, Friese-Greene, Paul and Edison have developed into cameras and projectors capable of entertaining the world, whose population is estimated to buy 235,000,000 seats a week. Mr. Cecil Hepworth, a pioneer of British cinema, spent £7:13:9 in 1905 making a neat seven-minute film called *Rescued by Rover* which was an outstanding success. In 1945 Mr. J. Arthur Rank spent over a million and a quarter pounds on a film version of Bernard Shaw's *Cæsar and Cleopatra*, and the normal cost of any major production in British, American or French studios is £100,000 to £150,000.

The statistics of cinema attendance and the balance-sheets of production and box-office receipts are a fascinating subject for discussion. No one believes that the work of Mr. Fred MacMurray was worth £104,700 in a year, or that the technicolor musical we saw last week deserved to cost a million dollars. But the fact remains that the public demand in terms of expenditure on film-going permitted both Mr. MacMurray's salary and the million-dollar investment in the picture.

It is a good time to take stock. Motion pictures have entered their second half-century, which will see the full development of colour, the third dimension and television in the cinemas. The end of the war has forced the film industries of the world, and especially of America, Britain, France and Italy, to take stock of their position, both economically and culturally. They are determined that the cinema-habit which alone constitutes sound box-office should be maintained and extended. They have therefore to estimate public tastes and needs in entertainment during the age of atomic peace upon which we have now entered.

The cinema as an entertainment medium now outclasses any other in the scope of its provision. Cinema attendance in Britain is fifty times greater than is attendance at the professional theatre.[1] The cinema offers certain unique features to its patrons which are of great significance socially and artistically. We can make a list of them something like this:

The cinema offers the services of its greatest artists and technicians to the remotest audience with a suitably equipped theatre or with a hall to accommodate a road-show.

The cinema offers a common level of performance to all audiences. All that is required is adequate equipment and efficient operation.

The cinema is capable of offering a wide range of entertainment facilities on the same premises, with change of programme as often as patronage demands.

The cinema is capable of offering entertainment on an international scale in the form of films from foreign sources which can be titled or given new sound tracks in the home tongue.

The cinema with its newsreels, documentaries and record films can open the narrow windows of a remote locality until they overlook all the countries of the world, with its peoples, its events and its discoveries.

This is no mean service for a few pounds or dollars a year. All the cinema asks is the widest possible patronage at prices which few people regard as excessive.

The problem for everybody lies in the scale of the undertaking. Civilisation is partly the story of unusual things becoming usual, or new experience becoming common experience. The service of the arts to humanity lies in the discovery and evaluation of human experience and emotion. In the simpler life of the past the arts served the community directly and were produced by the community. With the development of wealth and patronage the professional artist learned to serve the specialised needs of specialised people, and the work of great artists has often become the exclusive property of those who can afford to buy it or have the leisure to learn appreciation of it. With the development of the complex material interests

[1] One good pre-war source of statistics on Hollywood is Leo Calvin Rosten's *Hollywood* (Harcourt Brace, 1941). The British industry is summarised in *Tendencies to Monopoly in the British Film Industry* (Stationery Office, 1944): there have been some changes since its publication.

which take up the bulk of our attention to-day, the finer points and values of living are lost in the crash of mechanised transport, in looking after cars and radio sets, or in watching over our complicated possessions. Art has become the preoccupation of the few who have salvaged sufficient culture out of the academic machine of school-leaving examinations, matriculations and degrees to have any feeling left for anything, beyond casual amusement and sport, which does not offer a fee, a bonus or a spot of graft.

The cinema was invented out of the machine-world, and was at once the subject of patent-wars, and the money-struggling of the modern world. Only a few people in those early days after 1900 realised its possibilities, and set about their development. The greatest of these people was D. W. Griffith. He spent $110,000 on *Birth of a Nation* and $1,900,000 on *Intolerance*. But the money was necessary to provide the personnel and the raw materials out of which he made his cinematic vision come true for his world audiences.

The film industry shows the clash between economic and artistic issues in one of the most openly-contested struggles of the commercial world. The people who finance films say:

We cannot make films with the necessary standard of technical excellence in acting, setting and recording without spending ten times as much as it costs to produce a major stage production, and five hundred times as much as it costs to publish a well-produced book.

We cannot retrieve our money and get in addition the necessary profit which we and our shareholders demand for our imperilled capital without the widest public support. We want a public of a 100 million people for our film. We have to make our film so that 100 million people will pay to see it. We take our public as it is, and give it what past box-office records have shown it was prepared to buy. We are not philanthropists: we are business men. We sell entertainment in the biggest market, that is all.

In order to make films pay we make use of modern business methods. We monopolise the services of the stars whom our business acumen and our publicity methods have turned into assets with a scarcity value. There is only one Bette Davis or one James Mason. Their abilities as represented in our screen stories are unique. Our contracts with them are framed accordingly. It is the business of ambitious film stars to assist us to make themselves unique. The modern world is more interested in personalities than in stories, in clothes and luxury than in art. We make our films accordingly, and we give untold value for the money any individual member of the public pays for our type of entertainment.

If you want an " art " cinema, it is up to you to finance it yourself and build your own cinemas and your own public. But we shall take all legitimate business steps to prevent you building your cinemas near ours (and ours are everywhere) and to prevent you getting enough of the public from our cinemas into yours. In any case, we make " art " films ourselves, and we know just about how much our public is prepared to take in that line. We advise you to keep out, or if we think you are good enough we will contract you into our own studios to work for us: there you will learn the difficult process of keeping public taste on a dead level which can be successfully forecast and exploited.

On the other hand the directors, technicians and actors who make the films say:

Most of us went into pictures originally because we were excited by the idea of having something to do with films. They are so much in the public eye. To be a success in films is to be a big success with big money – while it lasts.

Some of us went into pictures because films are the most important medium of our time. It is a twentieth-century art, an art almost everyone loves. Its possibilities have begun to be demonstrated by men like Griffith, Chaplin, Pudovkin, Eisenstein, Lubitsch, Lang, Renoir, Vigo, Rotha, Ford, Welles, Rossellini. We in Britain have at last established a fine and exciting new type of cinema during the War, and we have created what is perhaps the finest documentary tradition in the world. We have gone with excited anticipation at night to see the best American and foreign-language films after long days in the studios. We reckon to talk more shop in our leisure time than any other artists and technicians. We know we are working in a medium where the latest film may contain the germs of some new technique, some new means to hold and move our audiences.

Some of us are embittered in our fight for recognition for our schemes and ideas. A large number of us have settled down to make good money better by turning out the routine job which always pays until it suddenly doesn't. But then there's always another routine job to take its place. Some of us are still waiting for a break. There is always the gamble that they will try out that new idea of ours, that new device, in the next picture.

A few of us have reached a sufficient level of responsibility that new ideas are accepted from us with respect. Our films are watched for: we have a huge public, but we serve also the few among that public who recognise our capabilities and our sensitiveness to the art of the film. The power to express ourselves in film is peculiarly satisfying: it is of all the arts the widest in range. It can call the architect, the painter and the musician to its aid. It can remake the world in its own image. We are the poets of a new art, the poets who combine sight and sound into a new poetry which belongs to our time and to our society.

But there are other voices too: those of the distributors who rent the films, the exhibitors who show them, the critics who write about them and the public who pays to see them. Of these the smallest voice of all is the last, although in Britain there are little short of 20 million regular film-goers and in America little short of 60 million. They buy in Britain some 30 million seats each week, and in America some 100 million. But they seldom speak, and the box-office receipts remain their single recorded vote. This huge silent army pays and endures, for it cannot know if it will not like a film until after it has bought it, or discussed it with someone who has already paid to find out. To alter the popular routine of habitual film-going with an almost unvocal mass public is extremely difficult. For the cinema is now so much a part of social life itself that men, women and children will go with little thought about the chances of excep-

tional enjoyment. Films are like meals: occasionally you get a
good one: but you must go on eating regularly just the same.

That is why mass-entertainment, like mass-feeding, is a
modern industry. It is far easier and quicker to see a story
visually than to read it. Public Library statistics show that only
a minority of the population uses reading as a subsidiary experience to living, though there is a large market for sensational pulp literature and for the cheaper Sunday press. But
this represents glance-reading for those whom a too-curtailed
education conducted along unfortunate lines has made culturally under-privileged, and so too easily satisfied with rosy
dreams of sex and crime compiled by hacks to literary formulas.
The film was born into a world already prepared to receive it
in these terms, and it took the popular dream-market by a
storm from which the film itself has never been able to recover.
The miracle lies in the number of beautiful and brilliant films
which have been made for sale in such an impossible market,
made by men with sufficient faith to convince the financial
powers they were worth a try-out. For now the elder generation
of Hollywood showmen is passing, the film financiers and
executive producers are becoming somewhat more aware of
the social responsibilities of their medium, and of the need to
compete with each other for prestige as well as for money.
Experiment within limits is therefore encouraged, since out of
experiments like *Citizen Kane* there may be long-term results
of commercial usefulness. New thoughts and styles, provided
they are not *too* new, keep the market alive and attractive.

This, however, is not the end of the story. By no means all
films are produced from a commercial factory interested only
in profit. After the first World War the German government
subsidised the German film industry and founded a national
school of cinema which was an important element in the
development of the art. It is represented by the early work of
Fritz Lang. In 1919 the Soviet film industry was nationalised,
and the study and development of film technique subsidised.
The results are represented by the work of all the great Soviet
directors up to the present day. In Britain there has been some
twenty years of continuous work in documentary film, almost
entirely independent of commercial production and exhibition.

In the smaller industries of countries like Sweden and Czechoslovakia and in occasional productions of Belgium, Holland and Switzerland new types of cinema have emerged, closely linked with the national life of the producers. Although made for commercial exhibition, these films are often so much part of national artistic expression that they escape the stigma of the box-office. They link up with what I have called the prestige pictures of the commercial producers of Hollywood, and of those unusual producers and artists in America who are able to get by with films made in a highly individualised style which are also successful with the public. Chaplin, Lubitsch, Disney, Capra, Dieterle, Ford, the Marx Brothers, Sturges, Milestone, Wellman and Wilder belong to this category of successful men who have also been artists of cinema.

Similarly in France. The peculiarly independent structure of the French film industry allows a freer rein there to experiment and individuality. In no other country with a commercialised cinema could Jean Vigo's *Zéro de Conduite* have been financed and produced. It was in France that a school of cinema developed in the fifteen years before the war which led the world for sensitiveness of characterisation and poetry of theme and treatment. It is represented by the work of Vigo, Carné, Clair, Pagnol, Duvivier, Jean Renoir, Benoit-Lévy and Feyder. It was France, too, that produced the early *avant-garde* movement, the most extreme of the experimental schools of film-makers apart from the work of the more advanced Russian directors. The sound film is too expensive a medium to encourage the lone worker of the type represented by Bartosch: the output of the *avant-garde* tended, therefore, to be for the most part during the silent period of cinema, except in America.

There is also the more recent British school of cinema inspired by the War and by the vision of pioneer producers and directors. These men had fought before 1939 for a British film industry of integrity in the face of the overwhelming competition of Hollywood, and the despicable productions of entrepreneurs made to meet the legal quota obligations of British exhibitors. The British film industry before the War at the highest peak of its production produced only a fifth of the programme needs of British cinema, and a bare tenth of that fifth was worth playing. During the War British producers were able to provide less than a sixth of British programme needs, but the product of their studios reached a sufficiently high artistic standard in a considerable number of films to justify a hope, which has not yet been fulfilled, that we should found a national school of feature film-making equal to that of America, pre-war France or post-war Italy. British documentary, after ten years of regular non-commercial production on a high level before the War, has since been developed under official sponsorship until it has become a recognised part of the public information and educational services. When the post-war economic problems of the industry are solved, and the production rate is expanded without loss of standards, there is no reason why British films, both feature and documentary, should not play a permanent part in world cinema.

It is this work, and what it stands for collectively as an indication of future developments as well as a record of achievement in the past, that has made the cinema exciting. It revealed a new international art, easy to export and import, to share and enjoy. Because of its basis in visual narrative its essential spirit is less easily lost on foreign screens than is that of translated drama on foreign stages. It is a medium capable of extremes of realism and of fantasy, and it has claimed its audiences in every developed country of the world. If its public is largely without self-expression because of its size, those film-critics who watch with excited anticipation for the sequence which will reveal the new artist, or consolidate the reputation of the old, try to represent the best in that public to the limit of their ability. Though the bulk of the hundreds of films they have to see each year leave them washed-up or wild, they watch the innumerable bad and mediocre films faithfully on the look-out for the occasional good one which will bring their sense of human and artistic values into play.

The last voice therefore belongs to the critics. It joins that of the artists and technicians. It says:

> We are on your side. If you make the film your way and not the box-office way, we will commend you. We want to make your way the box-office way too. Chaplin and Disney have done this, why not you? But if you sell out we shall condemn you, unless we ourselves have sold out first.

We do not ask for a continuous stream of masterpieces.

That is unnatural in the evolution of any art. We ask for honest craftsmanship with honest entertainment values. We ask for honest stories which do not lie their way to a foregone conclusion. We want the musical, the detective story and the romance to be honest in their own right. We do not want all films to be highbrow, but we do want the rare artist when he emerges to be allowed to make the rare film his way.

We ask for theatres on a world scale where the rarer films will find their natural audiences, and in so doing their own box-office. We recognise that films are expensive even when economically made. We recognise but do not exaggerate the place of the box-office. But so long as the masterpiece has to please a public come only to see the successor to last week's musical, it will not please them. It has been proved in cities like London that the specialised theatres have a large public. If there were enough specialised theatres organised internationally the masterpieces would pay for themselves. We know there is a sufficient public internationally to support them.

We ask you, not as philanthropists but as artists, to raise the standards of the ordinary film-goer. A public taste maintained on a dead level of consumption is the dead taste of a dead public. In the long run it is a waning public, ready to turn to the next phenomenon of entertainment in an age of quick and phenomenal discoveries. We ask you, because like you we love the cinema, to keep it alive and new by developing, however gradually, the taste of your difficult and conservative public towards finer emotional discrimination and more spiritually exciting demands. The routine dope, the standard measure of romance, crime, sex and sadism, leads to ever slower public reaction. Entertainment, we feel, should reinvigorate and recreate its customers. We look for the pictures which serve such recreation.

Part One
THE FILM AS A NEW ART FORM

1. INTRODUCTION:
The Peculiarities of the Fine Arts generally

EVERYONE has continual contact during his life with the variety
of experience known as art. This experience ranges from the
craft level found in the design and execution of the practical
things of life – utility articles, furniture and clothes – to the
more imaginative, because less material, level required for the
enjoyment of music, painting, sculpture and literature. In the
fine arts human creativeness is no longer concerned with producing an object which will be required for use anyhow, whether
it be beautiful or not, but with providing a stimulus for the
satisfaction of human emotion in its various levels of manifesta-
tion. The majority of human beings, since they are culturally
under-privileged, are satisfied if their emotions are roused easily
and volcanically by the more simple emotional reflexes – by
dance music, by the easily identified references of cinema-organ
sentimentalities, by the picture with a story or easily assimilated
moral, and by the simple violent plots of the cheap magazine or
commercial novel.

The culturally privileged demand a more complicated satisfaction. They require, because they are educated to assimilate
it, the æsthetic aspect of the arts, the highly complex form behind
the Shakespearean play and the Shakespearean verse, the beauty
of composition in the Greek vase or statue, the carefully balanced
æsthetic and psychological values of Renaissance portraiture,
and the investigations into the associative values of language in
T. S. Eliot and James Joyce.

The old and established arts, whether they be crafts or fine
arts, have evolved in the course of time a tradition which governs
their various forms and the legitimate and illegitimate use of
their various mediums – words, paint and canvas, wood and
stone, the variety of musical sounds. The long and elaborate
history of these arts is the story of the young artists in revolt
against the tradition established by their elders and predecessors,

from which rebellion further tradition is developed to add to that already practised.

The success of an artist depends largely on his facility in the medium he has chosen. This is partly native to him, partly acquired by practice and experiment. It also depends largely on whether he has sufficient valuable human experience in him which demands expression, and so forces him to undertake the labour of practice and experiment in his medium in order that he can convey this experience satisfactorily to his fellows. To use another language of criticism, he must be not only inspired but also in technique a master of his art.

Tradition, which has much to be said against it when it overwhelms the new vitality of a growing artist, has this advantage, that it gives dignity to the creator and guidance in his first attempts to pursue his art. So long as he is not subjugated by it, he may succeed largely through its example.

To the person who can discern the work of a good artist, a great part of his satisfaction is derived from " the sense of difficulty overcome." Enterprising human beings like to set themselves problems and achieve the solution with the minimum of time and effort: the less enterprising enjoy watching the others. This is as true of a crowd at a football match as of a professor enjoying a poem by Horace. The difference lies only in the quality of human skill and emotion involved.

All works of art, therefore, are successful because of, not in spite of, the limitations their form imposes on them. A painter must achieve vitality and depth through the colour and composition of his picture, which is none the less two-dimensional and static; the composer must communicate a sense of complex human experience, without the assistance of words or pictures, by the encompassed dynamic of sound; the poet must solve an enigma of experience within the sparse framework of a sonnet. A dramatist must achieve his purpose on the bare boards of a stage within the time an audience is willing to sit his drama out. The film director must achieve his aim by means of a succession of flat though mobile pictures photographed on celluloid and joined together in a long sequence. In all these arts the sense of triumph lies not merely in the humanity of the subject or the story, but also in the skill with which the artist moves freely within his self-imposed limits.

2. *The Peculiarities of the Film in particular*

The film reached its maturity in about the same time as it takes some human beings to reach theirs, that is, twenty years. The motion picture was a sideshow for fairs in 1900, but by 1920, despite the upheaval caused by the 1914 War, the habit of cinema-going had spread sufficiently for all cities and most small towns to have their continually growing number of cinemas. Some five years earlier D. W. Griffith had greatly added to the prestige of the film by making *Birth of a Nation* and *Intolerance*. These films can be seen now sympathetically only by an audience specially devoted to cinema. Their greatness would be overlooked by an unselected audience, which would merely be embarrassed by the crudity of the emotions, situations and much, though not all, of the acting. Griffith's early films are like the plays of the period preceding Shakespeare: they revealed every so often the great artistic potentialities of a medium which before had been merely crude and primitive. The Babylonian episode and parts of the modern story in *Intolerance* belong to the classic repertoire of the student of film art.

Cinema, being mute, had to make its appeal visually. There was as yet no place for subtlety, for innuendo, for discussion before action. Emotions had to be obvious, and the situations in which the characters were involved had to be clear-cut and usually violent. The acting, based on mime and gesture, had to convey, by the exaggerated use of the face and body, the reaction of the characters to their situations. Small wonder, therefore, that educated people left the cinema to their maid-servants, as the country squire still does today.

Almost from the start, however, the cinema has meant good money for those who learnt how to exploit it. From the beginnings of its history to the present day the initial cost of film-making has been heavy. Outlay on plant as well as on executive, technical and acting staff runs high for a feature film, but none the less the returns are good, since once the film is completed these returns are locked up in a few thousand feet of negative. A film which is capable of an infinite number of reproductions in positive prints at low cost can then be shown by a comparatively small staff to a succession of large audiences wherever the commercial set-up on the exhibitors' side of the trade allows. The money pours back, and some of the most inflated salaries in industry are received at the production end of the film trade, if only by a few people.

In its earlier days, therefore, the cinema was almost entirely in the hands of men whose sense of financial gain controlled their discussions at the conference table. Neglected by that section of society which could have brought other values to bear in the making of films, the earlier American cinema stormed the public leisure of two continents and aimed at the lower levels of quick emotional satisfaction by a succession of thousands of films dealing with violence, feud, murder, veiled adultery and virtue rewarded with a girl for prize. Exhibitions of wealth and vulgarity were to be had for less than a shilling, and substitutes for sexual indulgence could be obtained by an hour spent in watching the bathing belles and sirens of the silent screen.

This spread of easy satisfaction through the debased practice of the arts was equally true elsewhere—in literature and music, aided by the cheap press, gramophone and radio.

In spite of all this, the film, because it has a unique appeal to the quick-thinking technical mind of our industrialised twentieth-century society, absorbed into its factories men and women who became technicians, executives and actors, and who were not satisfied with the crass emotionalism of the normal film. These people, artists by inclination though not always aware of it, have come gradually to influence the standards of commercial production. They have gained sufficient prestige as directors and actors to influence the watchful financial powers. Intelligent experiment and a more finely balanced emotion have informed many films made in recent years. Films of artistic excellence have frequently been made during the past twenty years within the seemingly unfavourable framework of commercial production, not only in America and Britain, but especially in France, Italy and Sweden. Similarly, the ideological limitations accepted by Russian film-makers have not prevented their making many outstanding films.

For the film, in spite of its origin in the studio-factory, is as capable as poetry and letters of achieving beauty and distinction; there is no aspect of human emotion which the sound film cannot present, and its qualities are equally well adapted to wit and humour. But, unlike the novel which is written by one man or the picture which is painted in seclusion, the film is the result of conferences and staff-work in which it might be thought that the sensitive artist would become lost among a welter of executives. But this is not so. The twentieth-century artist of the film – the director – is a man who combines sensitiveness with leadership, who can convey to his cameramen, his electricians, his scenic designers and builders, his costumiers and his property-men, the spirit of the film as a whole and of the sequence on which they are working in particular. The film is a co-operative art, but, as in all creative work, a single mind with a single purpose must dominate the whole. The names on the credit titles are the names of those who have served under the leadership of the director to create the unified though composite achievement of the film.

Behind every large-scale film there lies, therefore, the financial conference, the staff-work for camera, lighting, sets, costumes, make-up and finally cutting, together with the discussions of producer, director, scenarist, cameraman, editor and actors. Collectively they stand or fall. Many good films have been vitiated because the best interests of the theme and story were not served, or because the director himself was indifferent to them. Many good films have been created because their best interests managed to survive the board-room and the director was loyal to his own artistic conscience.

3. Essentials of Film Art: First Principles

It is best to start with a description of the film from the purely mechanical standpoint. The sound film consists of a series of photographs printed on a celluloid strip 35 mm. wide, and photographed by the motion camera at twenty-four pictures a second. The film is similarly projected at twenty-four pictures a second by the film-projecting apparatus. The sound is supplied from a band running down the side of the pictorial series on the celluloid. This is called the sound-track, and registers the vibration of sound in terms of light.

The 35 mm. width of celluloid is known as the standard gauge, and is used by all cinemas. There are various substandard gauges, normally 16, 9·5 and 8 mm. Sound can be obtained on the 9·5 gauge, but the most popular and satisfactory substandard gauge for sound film is 16 mm.

Film is measured in reels, 1000 feet (35 mm. standard), 400 feet (16 mm. substandard) and 300 (9·5 mm. substandard). The playing time of a reel of any gauge is about ten minutes.

From the spectator's point of view the essential medium of a moving picture, still black and white more often than coloured, with accompanying reproduced sound. It is important that the picture is flat or two-dimensional. It is also important that it is viewed with the body of the theatre in darkness, so that, from a visual point of view, the spectator's attention is not distracted from the screen. A good many painters, whose work is exhibited among the distractions of a picture gallery, would give a great deal for so concentrated a setting. This brilliantly lit picture in an otherwise darkened hall exercises a distinct hypnosis upon the audience. Lovers may explore private interests, but their eyes at any rate are seldom distracted from the show.

It was previously stated that one of the principles of the successful practice of art is the artist's skill in exploiting the limitations of his medium as distinct from the three-dimensional, all-talking, all-smelling, all-tasting, all-feeling chaos which is the inartistic affair called the experience of life. It is wrong to try to make art too life-like: it becomes released from its limitations, and so loses its sense of form and proportion. No one expects a picture to be without a boundary or frame: but life itself has neither boundary nor frame. No one should want a good two-dimensional picture to be three-dimensional: we can get that effect far better by keeping our two eyes open together in contemplation of the same object. The best pictures, in common with the worst, have all had an enclosing edge to them; they have always been flat and two-dimensional. The artist therefore has to decide where to impose the edge of his picture (a difficult decision); he has to decide its size, and the scale of reduction or expansion from life-size of the people and objects he portrays. The sum-total of these, and certain other decisions affecting the lay-out and colour of the whole work, can be called the picture's composition.

So far the film, except that the picture is projected on to the screen instead of being directly applied to it, shares the artistic limitations of a painting. The film has a frame, in that it has always to fit into the rectangle of the screen; it is two-dimensional, so that it cannot affect the spectator three-dimensionally like his view of the room in which he is sitting. Composition is all-important: everything photographed becomes a two-dimensional pattern.

Look at the room in which you are sitting with one eye closed. After a moment open the closed eye and the room will spring into three-dimensional perspective. What you were looking at with one eye closed was a flat two-dimensional picture little better than a photograph from the point of view of judging how to move about in it.

The first principles of film art are therefore those belonging to the two-dimensional picture within a boundary or frame. The duty of the film artist is to exploit these principles for artistic effect. Director and cameraman do this by choosing the most effective part of the scene to be photographed and excluding the less effective parts by banishing them outside the artificial boundary of the frame. Obvious examples are the close-up of a face where the rest of the body is excluded: only the face matters. In the normal close-up the background is put out of focus and becomes a blur: again only the face matters. Lights are carefully placed so that the contours of the face are brought out by the use of high-light and shadow: for this picture the face matters more than ever, so much more that an elaborate lighting system unknown in real life is carefully prepared for the photograph. If the face does not most effectively reveal the emotion of the person in the story, the hand or foot may. The close-up can then exclude the irrelevant face and concentrate on the significant hand or foot.

A good director tells his film story from the most telling series of selected viewpoints. The good art director assists him by building a set which, when photographed in two dimensions, will form a striking two-dimensional pattern in keeping with the atmosphere of the action in the foreground. The use of shadows, of simple, bold structural designs, of soft lights and shades—the girl dancing in the dusty, empty Regency house in *St. Martin's Lane,* the hard black and white of the palace in *The Private Life of Henry VIII*, or Hitchcock's dramatic use of pronounced backgrounds like the windmill in *Foreign Correspondent* and the Statue of Liberty in *Saboteur*. The remarkable sets and lighting in Eisenstein's *Ivan the Terrible* emphasise the claustrophobic sense of terror pervading a place where so many factions seemed housed in one building with its Muscovite halls, rooms, corridors, steps and low stooping entrances. Even in films where the settings are the ordinary backgrounds of every-day existence (as in Billy Wilder's *The Lost Weekend* or William Wellman's *The Ox-bow Incident*) they can become, by compositional arrangement and the emphatic use of shadows designed by imaginative lighting, strangely significant and influential in the creation of atmosphere. So too can the sudden use of distorted perspective. The two-dimensional steeply sloping photographs looking up at a person or building from below can, when suddenly presented to an audience, give a powerful sense of shock which assists the sense of climax.

Not all directors exploit this visual power of the film in the way that the great directors of silent films in Germany and Russia used to do. Many, in their hurried search for realism, are content with the uninteresting, and fill the picture with details irrelevant enough to rival life itself. But the principle of good art always has been the principle of significant selection, and to clutter up a picture, already severely limited to the rectangle, with the transitory and unnecessary is like packing all the knick-knacks from the mantelpiece into the week-end case.

A study of still photographs exhibited in the better photographic exhibitions will reveal the importance of all aspects of composition in black-and-white photography. The art has reached a high level, and the technician places at the artist's disposal a variety of devices for improving on nature. It is the director's duty to know these devices and to develop their capabilities with appropriate imagination.

The film shares with the still picture the values of two-dimensional composition, but it progresses beyond it by making that composition mobile. The film moves; the design moves; the lighting varies as the objects and persons move. The girl coming down the huge staircase, the boat passing over the moonlit sea, the barge gliding through the mist, the wheat waving diversely against the black and white of a cloudy sky —all these things move within the frame of the picture. The composition is therefore mobile. And although because it moves the film is closer to real life than the still picture, it none the less shares the limitations of the still picture because the movement takes place within the two-dimensional frame. The hand creeps *diagonally* across the frame to switch off the light, the girl falls *diagonally* across the framed-in patch of grass, the ship sails across the frame at a different *angle* from the path of the moonlight, the sun's rays fall across the wall at an *angle* to the table where the man bends into its light. All this movement inspires composition, but it is a mobile and progressive composition, often not complete until the movement in the shot is finished. The pleasure of watching a well-shot film can be greatly increased by sharing this delight in mobile composition with a director and cameraman who are capable of creating it.

Furthermore, the structure of the film leads to another stage in mobile composition. The film is made up of a succession of photographic shots, each of which though mobile in itself has an added compositional quality through its relations to the preceding and succeeding pictures. A sharp movement to the left may be harshly succeeded in the next shot by a sharp movement to the right. A slow diagonal movement may be followed by a beautifully-timed expanding movement from the centre to the boundaries of the frame. Shots, aided by the devices of fading and mixing, may blend into one another with remarkable effect. For example, a series of shots dealing with movement down a river would lend itself to this. A succession of harsh movements might presage a quarrel, where an æsthetic clash in the composition combines with an emotional clash in the action. These examples are all crude: this technique is capable of increasingly subtle development in the hands of a good artist. It can be learnt only by practice: it can be enjoyed only by skilful and practised watching. The person most concerned with this type of composition is the film editor, who is responsible for the final assembly of the shots into the sequence which the audience sees, and who must be the person most aware of the timing of shots in their duration on the screen and in their general relation to each other.

EXAMPLES

1. TARGET FOR TONIGHT: (Crown Film Unit, 1942.
   British.   Director, Harry Watt)

Two sections of this film showed a remarkable sense of the co-ordination of mobile composition, the values of darkness and the gradations of black and white, and the relations of sound to mobile visual composition. The first is the sequence of the taking-off of the bombers, all shot, with natural sound, from different angles emphasising in turn the giant size of the planes against the dark qualities of the night sky. The crashing and roar of the engines were interspersed with fragments of formal speech, and the dark looming shots of the planes were cut in with the remarkable picture of the head of the squadron leader illuminated in his observation dome as he times his pilots out. The whole sequence of picture and sound accumulated into a climax of excitement and tension to match that of the action with which the film was concerned. The second example occurs later when F for Freddie flies through the graceful swelling clouds, shot after shot following the plane with its forward steady movement as the music swells and sweeps with the composition of the pictures.

2. THE LONG VOYAGE HOME: (United Artists, 1940.
   American.   Director, John Ford)
The opening of this film should rank high in American cinema. Dark shots emphasise the fragmentary gleam of the moonlight on the torsos of the seamen still confined to their ship as they listen with tense impatience to the sounds of the native women preparing to meet them. Here, cutting, photography and sound combine to impress the audience with the sensual need of the men and the warm anticipation of the women.

3. EXAMPLE FROM RUSSIAN CINEMA.
Pudovkin, one of the earliest creative imaginations in Russian cinema, writes the following passage in his book " Film Technique." This passage shows precisely how the artist is prepared to exploit every device of which his medium is capable to get the effect he needs. After watching a man scything wet grass in the sunlight, he describes how he would re-create this action in terms of cinema:

  " When the director shoots a scene, he changes the position of the camera, now approaching it to the actor, now taking it farther away from him, according to the subject of his concentration of the spectator's attention – either some general movement or else some particularity, perhaps the features of an individual. This is the way he controls the spacial structure of the scene. Why should he not do precisely the same with the temporal? Why should not a given detail be momentarily emphasised by retarding it on the screen, and rendering it by this means particularly outstanding and unprecedently clear? Was not the rain beating on the stone of the window-sill, the grass falling to the ground, retarded, in relation to me, by my sharpened attention? Was it not thanks to this sharpened attention that I perceived ever so much more than I had ever seen before?

" I tried in my mind's eye to shoot and construct the mowing of the grass approximately as follows:

" 1. A man stands bared to the waist. In his hands is a scythe. Pause. He swings the scythe. (The whole movement goes in normal speed, i.e. has been recorded at normal speed.)

" 2. The sweep of the scythe continues. The man's back and shoulders. Slowly the muscles play and grow tense. (Recorded very fast with a ' slow-motion ' apparatus, so that the movement on the screen comes out unusually slow.)

" 3. The blade of the scythe slowly turning at the culmination of its sweep. A gleam of the sun flares up and dies out. (Shot in ' slow motion.')

" 4. The blade flies downward. (Normal speed.)

" 5. The whole figure of the man brings back the scythe over the grass at normal speed. A sweep—back. A sweep—back. A sweep. . . . And at the moment when the blade of the scythe touches the grass—

" 6. —slowly (in ' slow motion ') the cut grass sways, topples, bending and scattering glittering drops.

" 7. Slowly the muscles of the back relax and the shoulders withdraw.

" 8. Again the grass slowly topples, lies flat.

" 9. The scythe-blade swiftly lifting from the earth.

" 10. Similarly swift, the man sweeping with the scythe. He mows, he sweeps.

" 11. At normal speed, a number of men mowing, sweeping their scythes in unison.

Tchekov, Aristophanes and Sean O'Casey are men of dramatic speech, and actors succeed or fail on the stage because they are or are not artists of the spoken word. They combine with this quality movement and gesture, qualities to be seen, but they are subsidiary.

The film comes closest in structure to the novel, from which, judging from some screen adaptations, it seems most divided. The novel has the quality of free narration, of directing the reader's attention wherever it is most necessary for the good of the story or the emotion, of ranging backwards or forwards in the time sequence of the plot, of stressing this and eliminating that. It parts company from the film, however, at the point where the emotions of a character are described, not shown objectively in terms of outward signs or action, and again in its discursiveness owing to the fact that a novel may be taken up and put down by the reader at any time, whereas the film, to succeed in its effect, must be seen continuously from beginning to end.

Perhaps it is with the ballet that the film can find a kindred technique. The ballet with a story implies its narrative by movement and gesture, to which the music acts in precisely the same creative capacity as the sound track of the film. Whereas the favourite themes of the ballet are fantastic, those of the film are realistic. But too little has been done to create a special choreography for the screen, like the ballets in *Cover Girl* and *The Red Shoes,* or the Indian film *Kalpana.*

4. *Essentials of Film Art: Further Principles—Shot; Sequence; Editing*

It is worth while repeating the elementary fact of cinema which few of its patrons, sitting a solid two hundred and thirty-five million a week, bother to realise, namely that twenty-four photographs on celluloid are flashed at them every second on the screen. In silent days only sixteen photographs a second were necessary.

In order to achieve a smooth transition from each single picture to the next slightly different picture, the screen is blacked-out for one forty-eighth of a second while it is replaced. That is, for one-half of the time an audience is seeing a film it is sitting in total darkness without knowing it. If we estimate the number

" 12. Slowly raising his scythe a man moves off th
the dusk.

" This is a very approximate sketch. After actual s
ing, I edited it differently—more complexly, using
taken at very various speeds. Within each separate s
were new, more finely graduated speeds. When I saw
result upon the screen I realised the idea was sound.
new rhythm, independent of the real, deriving from
combination of shots at a variety of speeds, yielde
deepened, one might say remarkably enriched, sense
the process portrayed upon the screen."

These examples, together with a few critical visits to
pictures, should be sufficient to prove that the film is essentia
something to be seen. Sound, though an integral part of fil
art, is normally subsidiary in its hold over the attention of th
spectator. This does not stop the film being used for purel
auditory purposes, as in a picture poorly shot and dully pu
together, but with a sound track full of brilliant wisecracks
This is using the medium of the film just to put across the wisecracks. It is very efficient for this purpose, just as words are
efficient to describe how somebody wishes to leave his property.
But these same words can be used by poets and dramatists with
a fuller knowledge of their artistic possibilities. In the same
way the film can be used to its full potentialities only by men
who have the imagination to do so. The average director is
satisfied with average results. So is the average public. But
the average public is pleasantly surprised when the more-than-
average artist arrives and shows the possibilities of the medium
in a new light. Shakespeare and Shaw did this for the average
public of the theatre. Griffith, Pudovkin, Eisenstein, Chaplin,
Disney, von Stroheim, Lubitsch, Pabst, Hitchcock, Capra, Ford,
Welles and some others have done this for the average cinema
public.

The film has its links with most of the major fine arts, but
retains its own artistic individuality very strongly. Its alliance
with the work of the painter and still photographer ends where
its essential beauty, mobile composition, begins. Its alliance
with the drama is very superficial, since the best drama is in the
first place something to be heard, with sight as the subsidiary
function. Shakespeare and Shaw, the Greek tragedians and

of man-hours spent in the cinema each week as seven hundred million, over three hundred million of them are spent seeing nothing. If the camera cannot lie, a projector can. The sound track, however, is continuous. This should act as a deterrent to readers who were contemplating asking for half their money back.

Cinemas use banks of projectors—that is, projectors and spares for breakdown lined up in series. Each projector in use projects two reels of film (about twenty minutes' showing time) and is then replaced by its twin. The change-over from one machine to the next is carefully synchronised so that the audience is seldom aware of the transition. The momentary appearance of a black circle on the top right-hand corner of the picture acts as a cue for the operator on the new machine to effect the change-over.

The formula for making a film is therefore as follows:

Take twenty-four pictures a second for as long as you want the image to last on the screen. Call the pictures " frames ", and one complete image on the screen a " shot." We have already seen that the combination of shots which make up a complete film is divided by the natural development of the story into sequences or stages in the narrative.

Shots can last a long or short time on the screen, as required to convey their contents to the audience. They may be mere flashes, or they may last, though they seldom do, two or three minutes. Visual variety is one of the main technical features of film-making, and a five-minute conversation between two people in one place, unbroken on the sound track, will probably be most athletic on the part of the camera. The art of shifting camera position is to be varied without being restless. A rest-less camera distracts from the conversation: a varied camera builds the conversation from a few reproduced words to signifi-cant, pointed drama.

Just as sentences are punctuated by the , ; : —() and ., and reading speed consequently controlled in relation to the sense-divisions of the word-group, só a film is punctuated by various devices:

1. By direct cut. One shot immediately succeeds the next.
   Impression: speed. If well done, clean, efficient con-tinuity. If badly done, slight to serious visual shock, and sense of restlessness and jerky continuity.

2. By fade-in and fade-out. The gradual emergence of a shot from a black frame, and its opposite. The direct cut is a kind of comma; the fade-out, if quick a semi-colon, if long a full stop. Any film will produce a variety of fades used for a number of types of punctuation.

3. By dissolve. The gradual change from one scene to another by superimposition of the images, the end of the first shot being carefully timed in relation to the emergence of the next. This can be used merely as a technical trick instead of a direct cut or fade, or it can be used with artistry. Its virtue lies in its power of suggestion, the soft, almost imperceptible link it can imply between the two shots momentarily married on the screen.

4. By wipe. The effect of a wipe has been described as if an invisible roller were passed over the screen horizontally or vertically, wiping out one picture and revealing the next. It is used most in newsreels and quota quickies. It implies pep. It takes a sensitive viewer a moment to recover from the shock to his illusion of the depth and pattern of the shot. It is violent, inartistic and destructive compared with the direct cut. Whilst the roller rolls, neither shot is of any value to the audience. It has no psychological value parallel to the dissolve.

5. By continuity title. Words cease on the sound track and either silence or music ensues. Words appear as titling on the screen, as in the old silent days. This effect is excellent for paragraphing an episodic film, or for journalistic headings, as in *The March of Time*. Its value is emphasis. Salient points of introduction or fact can be imparted in this specialised manner: it is more pointed than emphasis in the spoken commentary because it is different and because it is visual. Its abuse is over-use. It is excellently handled in *The March of Time* series and in the better-edited newsreels.

6. By other camera devices, not involving a cut, dissolve or fade. The technical elaboration of the modern studio encourages a director to stop at nothing for effect. Instead of a simple cut from outside to inside a building, the camera offers him legs and wings. It can appear to

climb steps and steal like a ghost in and out of public buildings and private flats. It can run up a skyscraper and slide in through a window to intercept the last few sentences of the gangster's plot. It can behave with or without sympathy when trying to see life steadily and see it whole on behalf of intoxication. It can swing through the air with the greatest of ease. It can pass away from a lady as she starts to undress, and swing back when she is robed again, so that the various Boards of film censors shall be spared a morality conference. It can tilt down the slender calves as the underclothes fall and climb up thousand-dollar legs to meet the on-coming nightdress.

All these devices save cutting and take their place in the field of film punctuation. Their value is obvious: they assist in smoothness of continuity and variety of effect. They can be used for their true purpose, to put the story across pointedly and economically, or they can be used to show themselves off at the film's expense—technics for technique's sake. Audiences enjoy the fun at first, but in the end they have a date with the story, not the camera.

We are now gradually reaching a point from which we can appreciate the position of the scenario writer getting down to his script. He is given a story and has to prepare a treatment. The treatment must conform to the basic principles and limitations of the art of the film. It must use what the film has to offer in the way of technique to make the subject effective through the medium of the screen. Broadly speaking, sight must come first and sound second. They cannot, of course, be treated separately in a sound film, but the predominant sense enjoyed is sight, and to starve it for the sake of beautiful or even witty dialogue, or for a breezy-up-to-minute-hundred-per-cent.-wisecracking commentary, is eventually to sell out as far as the future of cinema is concerned. Cinema-goers prefer a Hitchcock or a Capra to a quota quickie however packed with badly-handled thrills. It is rare for a first-class film to fail to get its audiences. Occasionally a good film may pull ahead too far from the grasp of mass audience comprehension or acceptance, such as *The Grapes of Wrath, Citizen Kane* and *The Ox-bow Incident*. But even these advanced films held large audiences taken in the aggregate, although requiring for their appreciation rather more resilience of imagination than the average public queueing up after work has been able to acquire.

The scenarist, using various methods peculiar to himself as an artist, sets out to group the action into shots and sequences. He translates story into pictures with sound. He is a good artist in so far as he does this brilliantly and with full regard for the capacities of camera and microphone; a competent artist in so far as he does this faithfully but without more than ordinary skill; a mediocre artist in so far as he cares little for the story in film terms but earns his living to the best of his mediocre imagination; and a bad artist in so far as he is careless of his medium and conscienceless over his duty to his story. He may be helped or hindered by good or indifferent producers, directors, cameramen and actors. A large number of the best brains in the world are in the daily service of the screen. It is because of this that it is rare to see a technically bad film these days in a good-class cinema: what one sees more commonly is a pedestrian story competently handled. The significance of this from the cultural and social point of view will be discussed later in the book.

Both the competent and the brilliant artist are aware first of all of the mobility of the camera. They realise that the advantages they have over the dramatist are that the camera as a recording instrument can be placed successively in the ideal positions to see the action, and the microphone in the ideal positions to hear it. The difference between competence and brilliance lies in the degree of imaginative interpretation and reconstruction of the action into terms of cinema which the artist can bring to bear.

The competent worker watches continuity, clean camera-work, efficient subjection of the story into sequence-groups and economic timing of all movement and acting to make sure no essential element clarifying the story is missed out. He will tolerate no obscurity in his shots, no poor acting by star or super, no unnecessary pictures. His work is finally cut with precision, and, if the running time is ninety-three minutes, the story could not have been told more efficiently in the manner intended in less than ninety. There is little room for criticism of his work technically; producer, distributor, exhibitor and audience are alike well-off in pleasure or in pocket. This competent treatment is the staple of good box-office.

The brilliant artist, on the other hand, is prepared to take risks which he may or may not sell to his public, or for that matter to his producer. His films are often too long (like the Russian epics), too intense or obscure (like *L'Atalante*), too episodic (like *The Grapes of Wrath*), or too technically preoccupied (like *Citizen Kane*). They may overbalance by allowing too much predominance to dialogue at the expense of the camera (like *La Femme du Boulanger* or *Les Enfants du Paradis*), or to music at the expense of dialogue (as in *Brief Encounter*). They may put too great a stress on sheer beauty of camerawork and decor (like *La Belle et la Bête*). They may develop any number of faults for the critics, brought up on competence, to pick out for wisecracks to the neglect of the salient virtues of a picture worth a hundred competent marvels. They may be fortunate, like Hitchcock and Lang, because their stories in any case appeal to all comers, who may not be able to appreciate the skill and beauty with which these stories are presented. Or they may have the advantage which the late Sergei Eisenstein possessed of permanent State support for long-term experiments and technical research in the art of film-making. Or they may merely have to take a risk like Disney in *Fantasia*, Welles in *Citizen Kane*, Ford in *The Grapes of Wrath*, Chaplin in *Modern Times*, Powell in *The Edge of the World*, Capra in *Mr. Deeds Goes to Town*, Santell in *Winterset*, Wilder in *The Lost Weekend*, Flaherty in *Nanook* and Vigo in *L'Atalante* or *Zéro de Conduite*. Films like these are of variable value in recent cinema history, but all are significant and many of permanent distinction in the period to which they belong. The average film of today has grown, as always, out of the more-than-average film of yesterday, and the production boss and the public who look to scoff remain to pay.

Some technical points are worth watching at the cinema with the query in one's mind: Is the treatment of the action just competent or is it occasionally or continuously brilliant?

1. THE SHOT

The use of variable set-up for the camera. Taking a given object mounted on a glass floor and a camera with the standard variety of lenses (including telephoto), there seem to be few limitations placed upon the cameraman as to the set-up which can be adopted to photograph the outside of the object. If the object is too small to be seen easily, then a photomicrographic shot will magnify it (as in *The Secrets of Nature*). The only limitation appears to be lighting, which again is under the control of the cameraman, or the unwillingness of the object to be photographed on a glass stand, such as an untamed lion in an African jungle. In practice, leaving the glass floor to the director of revue with legs to look for, the camera can work indoors from floor to ceiling, or outdoors from ground to stratosphere. To be original, pointed and economic with such variety of opportunity is far more difficult than finding a needle in a haystack. To find the most apt out of the many adequate camera-angles is the act of genius over competence.

The film is, after all, a collection of camera-angles consciously selected and purposely limited within the frame. Each shot has to be labelled telephoto shot, distance shot, long shot, medium shot, close-up, photomicrographic shot, with all their various intermediates. If the camera moves it must either tilt, which means move upwards and downwards; pan, which means move sideways; fly on a crane, or track on a wheeled base. It may even sway on a pendulum as in Vertov's *Three Songs of Lenin*, though one hastens to add that this should be for exceptional effect only.

Out of all these possibilities the right shot must be chosen. The competent director will be satisfied with clean well-lit shots taken at near eye-level from distance shot to close-up, varied sometimes by a shot taken from above or low on the ground (pity the poor locomotive). The undershot, however, was used with culminating effect in *Winterset*, when Trock's confederate arrives as from death itself after being filled with lead and thrown into the river.

The brilliant director will take more chances and usually be right. René Clair shot a wedding-group kissing one another from six feet over their bare bald heads and ducking feathered hats in *The Italian Straw Hat*. Some director or other, probably a Russian in the earlier post-war silent days, realised the psychological value of the distortion achieved by photographing dominant capitalist figures and military bullies from two yards in front of their feet, tilting up. Fritz Lang in *M* saw the psychological value of shooting the chase of his demented victim from a roof-top looking down where four streets meet in the lamplight, with the lonely figure rushing hysterically from side to side as the pursuit closes in. A wonderful long tracking shot slowly passes down the line of St. Joan's clerical inquisitors with white habits and cruel, repressed, other-worldly expressions as the camera relentlessly leaves one for the other and then the next in *La Passion de Jeanne d'Arc*. The line of military jack-boots steps down with brutal grace and trained precision on to the step along which the eye of the camera is looking from foot-level: the spectator is prone before the White Guards, like the dead bodies that sprawl over the Odessa steps in *The Battle-ship Potemkin*. In *Un Carnet de Bal*, one of the few French films widely shown in the provinces of Britain on a commercial scale, the sequences dealing with the epileptic doctor were shot aslant with macabre effect, culminating in a dissolve from the man struggling in a paroxysm as he shoots his wife, to a picture of the crashing, clanking cranes which work interminably outside the tenement consulting-room.

The invention of these things, the initial conception which realises they are the right thing to do before they have been done, is the work of a fertile visual imagination. Two are from sound, three from silent films. The visual experiment of the mature silent film is of the greatest value to the later sound film.

Lighting.—Lighting is all-important to the shot. It is rare to see a flat white light in any modern film. Lit from various angles, actor, furniture, property and set can be induced to make the shot pictorially impressive. The sense of pattern can be developed by the sharpness of high-light and shadow, or the sense of mystery deepened by the use of misty half-light produced by the device known as soft focus or an image slightly blurred. This, one may feel in retrospect, particularly suits close-ups of beautiful women and scenes in docks or railway stations at night. Even squalor can be made beautiful if shot in half-light. The German silent cinema specialised in the beauty of slums, backwaters and fairgrounds.

Close-up.—Finally, in sizing up his shot in his mind's eye, the scenarist or the director, or both in conference, must decide on the correct and sparing use of the close-up. In all films a small proportion of shots must be in close-up and even big close-up. The use must be sparing, because the emphasis in point of size is overwhelming, and few actors and actresses survive the close-up with distinction. Details of facial expression can easily be seen in the medium or half-length shot, and there should be a genuine reason for the appearance of a close-up in the shooting script. In some films it is flogged mercilessly whilst large face speaks to large face in an unrelenting succession of unnecessary intimacies. Used in early primitives without much thought, it was used creatively by Griffith. The untrained audiences at first cried out for the actor's legs. No harm would be done now if they called out sometimes for the actress's.

Close-up, with its supreme power of emphasis, can be used to enforce the full attention of the audience upon facial acting at a crucial moment in the story (remember among others the remarkably expressive faces of Laughton, Dietrich, Garbo, Bette Davis, Agnes Moorehead, Louise Rainer, Celia Johnson, Fonda, Edward G. Robinson, Cherkassov, Gabin, Baur, Raimu, Michel Simon, Jean-Louis Barrault and Arletty), or direct attention to detail necessary to the development of the story— in melodrama, the hand feeling the automatic in a pocket; in drama, the hand on the door knob; in comedy, the hand finding the dime on the pavement; in tragedy, the hand falling still in death. The close-up is part of the mobility of the camera now expected by a generation of trained cinema-goers, but they complain when they get too much of it. For facial acting, only highly developed actors can survive this terrific magnification with more than momentary success. The case of the close-up in documentary, where the non-professional actor is used, is rather different, as we shall see. So also is the obvious importance of close-up in the instructional film, where processes are being explained and emphasised.

Other Devices.—Before proceeding from shot to sequence, certain devices can be used to bring added value to the narrative presentation. First is distortion. Soft focus is a form of this, but the distortion can be much more violent and serve a definite artistic purpose. It is deliberately used, for instance, in *In which we Serve* to link the sequences of the men machine-gunned in the water with the scenes depicting their past individual experiences. The shot of the raft and the men distorts like an image reflected in disturbed water and then dissolves into the new sequence at home. The slanting shots in *Un Carnet de Bal* are distortions within the frame. So are many shots in *Citizen Kane,* which will be discussed later. Second is slow motion. The shot in Pudovkin's *Deserter* of the suicide who jumps into a river is taken in semi-slow-motion, and so the man appears to be sucked down into the water which splashes round him in a great fan of enclosing waves. The values of quick-motion for farcical effects are obvious. All these devices are psychologically justified if used with judgment and artistry.

What is Left Out.—We have seen earlier that the film must exploit its own limitations for artistic effect, and that one of these limitations is that comparatively small area which the camera-lens can cover compared with the wide-angled lens of the human eye. The artist can make use of this limitation with excellent effect. It is obvious in every film that dialogue is often carried on without the camera shooting the speaker. The effect of what is said is seen in the faces of the hearers. The person responsible for the filmic treatment of narrative or documentary has to work out how time may be saved and the treatment tightened by letting the sound track do one job while the visual track does another. Whilst Mr. Barrett of Wimpole Street prays to his God, Flush, fresh from earthly preoccupations, passes his master's dining-room door with a shrug of contempt and sidles upstairs to his mistress. A good deal can be learned from this in less than thirty seconds. Bette Davis in *The Letter* begins the film by standing on the steps of her Malayan residence and shooting her revolver off-screen. The body of the man she shoots, irrelevant at this stage when everything that matters is herself, is never even seen. In the old German film *Variety,* which made Emil Janning's reputation as an actor in America, the scene where the two men struggle on the floor with a knife is shot at a level above the fight, with only a drab hotel bedroom to look at while you wait in a state of tension for the face of the man who is to be left alive to rise up into the frame. In the French film *Remous* the sensual wife of the civil engineer rendered impotent by a car accident during their honeymoon preens herself whilst she is inspecting a large dam built under her husband's direction. Eventually we are allowed to see why: a virile workman is admiring her in smiling silence.

From then on the theme of the film is set without word and almost without action.

This last example leads us naturally to consideration of the sequence, since no shot in a film can be considered by its single self as complete: it requires to be seen in conjunction with what went before and what succeeds.

2. THE SEQUENCE.

The sequence is the paragraph of the film. It may consist of a few shots naturally linked together and lasting only a minute, or it may plan out an almost indefinite length of time as in *The Petrified Forest,* when the scene remains the same and the characters are hardly regrouped for a considerable period. A short sequence was given in detail above from Pudovkin's book on film technique. Consideration of the sequence at once gives rise to the consideration of editing, or, as it used to be called in earlier and more æsthetic days, " montage."

Editing is the art of putting the film together shot by shot from the celluloid strips themselves. Documentary directors often do their own editing and attach as much importance to this process as they do to the actual shooting. Russian directors frequently adopted the same attitude, and so did Flaherty in *Man of Aran* and in previous films shot on lone locations. The common practice, however, is to employ a highly paid technician to edit the film carefully from the shooting script. The director, whether he takes part in the actual process of editing or not, cannot fail to take an interest in it. The effect he has aimed at on the studio floor can be ruined by careless or unsympathetic editing. The skill required to edit a competent film with a clean shooting script and a routine sense of efficient timing and slick continuity is obviously less than is required to assemble films like *L'Atalante* and *The Grapes of Wrath* from their component shots. A film playing an hour and a half may contain as many as three, four or five hundred separate pictures. The editor has to choose the beginning and end of each of these, as well as reject the material which never actually reaches the screen. Many directors do not shoot economically, but shoot to waste with many versions of the same scene, one of which has to be chosen and the rest junked. The editor's task is a formidable one, helped though he may be by his director and his assistants.

But it should not be forgotten that in America most directors are not permitted either to prepare or edit their films on their own initiative. They are required to shoot them point by point on the floor of the studio. The producer, not the director, is the arbiter of what should or should not be done with what the director creates from the camera. The director himself rarely begins or ends the creative treatment of the film he is supposed to complete.

The problem as to whether or not he should edit his own films is best left to the opinions of two eminent directors, one Russian and one English:

"Editing is the language of the film director. Just as in living speech, so, one may say, in editing: there is a word—the piece of exposed film, the image; a phrase—the combination of these pieces. Only by his editing methods can one judge a director's individuality." (PUDOVKIN, "Film Technique", p. 72.)

"With the help of my wife, who does the technical continuity, I plan out a script very carefully, hoping to follow it exactly, all the way through, when shooting starts. In fact, this working on the script is the real making of the film for me. When I've done it, the film is finished already in my mind. Usually, too, I don't find it necessary to do more than supervise the editing myself. I know it is said sometimes that a director ought to edit his own pictures if he wants to control their final form, for it is in the editing, according to this view, that a film is really brought into being. But if the scenario is planned out in detail, and followed closely during production, editing should be easy. All that has to be done is to cut away irrelevancies and see that the finished film is an accurate rendering of the scenario." (HITCHCOCK, in Davy's "Footnotes to the Film", p. 5.)

The editing of the earliest primitives was a matter merely of expediency, not artistry. The first man to sense the creative power in his hands was David Wark Griffith. To Griffith is due the elementary principle of slow and quick cutting: the development of tempo and rhythm. Slow cutting induces a gentle mood: quick cutting induces excitement and tension. Griffith, who brought the close-up into artistic prominence, also shot the ice-flow sequence in *Way down East* and the last-minute reprieve in *Intolerance*. These required the build-up of tension in the audience by alternating between shots of the approaching rescue and the plight of the victim. Chaplin developed economy: shorts like *Easy Street* and *The Cure* were masterpieces in the cutting away of inessentials without sacrifice of comic detail.

In the German cinema we find an entirely different development immediately after the War. Although German film-makers by no means confined themselves to macabre and sombre subjects, their artistic isolation during the First World War and their æsthetic and spiritual needs after defeat turned their imaginations in the direction of mysterious, horrific and other-worldly subjects, often with medieval settings or wrapt in timeless periods when men were prone to meet allegorical figures or speak with Death himself. *Destiny, Caligari, The Golem, Siegfried, Warning Shadows, Dracula* or *Mabuse* are only a few of the titles which haunted the German screen and founded a reputation abroad for German film art. Siegfried Kracauer, in his book, "From Caligari to Hitler," traces the psychological reasons for German cinema taking the shape it did during the twenties. Design, photography and character-acting all combined to create the sense of terror when man is subjected to the forces of destiny.

Caligari was the first of these films to become world-famous. Wiene gathered together his little group of actors and theatrical scene designers and made *The Cabinet of Dr Caligari*, the reconstruction of a madman's fiction woven round his fellow inmates at an asylum. Out of a little lath and canvas, and by the use of ingenious lighting which is never elaborate, he produced a series of beautiful sets and moving images in the expressionist manner. The film has been called decadent and primitive, but it can still be received today in absorbed silence by a discerning audience. Shots remain in the memory—the lovely shadows across the frame as Caligari opens the sleep-walker's upstanding coffin on the trestle stage in the fairground; the hanging draperies round the sleeping girl, and the tall oncoming figure of the sleep-walker, played with an early feeling for cinematic detail by Conrad Veidt; the same black figure with arm upstretched against the wall creeping through the fantastic courtyard to stab the sleeping girl; the flight up the sharp angles of the roof-tops and across the weird foreshortened bridge when the pursuit draws close.

This film was the most advanced piece of art the cinema had yet seen except for Griffith's epics and Chaplin's one-reelers in a very different manner. It founded no school and led nowhere, for expressionist sets do not suit the film, which is an art based on the realistic approach to the material of life. Its contribution was solely that of lighting, the subtle development of visual atmosphere, and evidence of a true conception of screen-acting in the work of Werner Krauss and Conrad Veidt. There is much still to be learnt from it by the competent director, since it was the product of real feeling and devotion to a new and relatively untried medium and was an undoubted success within its own limits. It was shown widely in this country in the early twenties, and was revived by many film societies in the early thirties.

But neither *Caligari* nor the succeeding tradition of U.F.A. added pace or subtle timing to the practice of editing. These films progress with a steady slowness, the atmosphere depending on each shot or on the genius of occasional actors like Veidt, Krauss and Jannings. There is elementary cutting in the manner of Griffith as Siegfried approaches the watching dragon through the tall trees and sloping shadows of the great forest, or in the hectic dance scene in *Metropolis*, and great feeling for tempo in the last reel of *Variety*. For the German film pondered and dwelt where the American cut and ran, whilst the Russian became a symphony of movement and design. It was the Russian film which took film æsthetic a full stage farther during the silent days of cinema.

The Russian cinema industry was nationalised in 1919. In the same year the Moscow State School of Cinematography was founded. In the early twenties experiment in camera-angles was carried out by Vertov (his theory being that the camera has an eye which can go anywhere), and in cutting by Kuleshov, who, from the Russian point of view, brought editing to a prominence undreamed of by Griffith, though derived from him, with acknowledgments, by Pudovkin. Here at last was a country which put the film first and the box-office afterwards, and encouraged its brilliant directors to experiment at the State expense whether they made mistakes or not. In return it expected the Russian revolution in all its phases, past, present and future, to be their guiding theme, and asked for masterpieces to be produced at reasonable intervals to educate both the literate townsman and the illiterate peasant in the new economy and the new ideology. Russian cinema obtained, as a result, the greatest series of films of the silent period, and world cinema obtained its first æsthetic, Montage.

Montage is a French word which cannot be translated without losing some of the meaning. It means what Pudovkin so lucidly explains in his book " Film Technique," a collection of papers on the subject ably translated by Ivor Montagu and published here in 1929. This book, together with Arnheim's " Film ", which attempts a German synthesis of film æsthetic based mainly on the silent period, was one of the first constructive attempts to analyse the creative impulse behind film-making. It is clear that just as the teens of the century saw the flowering of creative film-making in America more than elsewhere, the twenties saw the flowering of film æsthetics in Europe more than elsewhere. Film-makers and students of the cinema joined together to write for the advanced journals (such as *Close-Up*, founded in 1926, or the magazines of the French avant-garde artists), and discussion of the film and its artistic potentialities became the fashion of the time, coincident with the founding of the specialist cinemas, like those in Paris, and the film societies, like the London Film Society.

The books of Pudovkin (there is another on " Film Acting ") and of Arnheim should be read by everyone who is prepared to take the cinema seriously as an art. Pudovkin's book is full of a progressive and captivating enthusiasm: he is discovering as he writes. Arnheim's book, more august, more comprehensive, more philosophic and more German, was the first complete æsthetic between two covers that film criticism had yet produced, though writers like Canudo, Moussinac and Delluc had already begun creative criticism.

PUDOVKIN

Pudovkin explains that to the director-editor separate shots are like separate words: their meaning is built up in their context.

" I claim that every object, taken from a given viewpoint and shown on the screen to spectators, is a dead object, even though it has moved before the camera. The proper movement of an object before the camera is yet no movement on the screen, it is no more than raw material for the future building-up, by editing, of the movement that is conveyed by the assemblage of the various strips of film. Only if the object be placed together among a number of separate objects, only if it be presented as part of a synthesis of different separate visual images, is it endowed with filmic life." (PUDOVKIN, "Film Technique", pp. xiv, xv.)

Before setting out to make his film, the director-scenarist must consider his work in three stages. First, the theme, that is the general subject of the film (the October Revolution, the conquering of peasant opposition to mechanised farming, the mutiny of the battleship "Potemkin"). Second comes the action and its treatment (the story which is the bare outline that will at once contain an illustration of the theme and form the staple entertainment value of the film). Third comes the cinematographic planning of the action (the preparation of the story for the camera in the form of a shooting script in which the values of individual shot and constructive editing are balanced in accordance with the visual genius of the director).

Pudovkin[1] speaks of the selection of proper plastic material. This is not a dead theoretical phrase, but a vital part in the invention and building process of his film. The selection of what is to be photographed and what excluded, how the material is to be placed in front of the camera, even the shape and movement of an actor's face and limbs, and the relation of them to the pattern of the set, the properties and the desired angles of light-shadow; this is the process of using the proper plastic

[1] Career: V. I. Pudovkin, born 1893. Educated at Moscow; studied chemistry at the University; volunteered 1914; German prisoner; during captivity studied languages and drew pictures; after the Revolution met Kuleshow and studied cinema technique with him; also worked as an actor. Outstanding films include—silent: *The Mechanism of the Brain,* 1925 (for Pavlov); *Mother,* 1926; *End of St. Petersburg,* 1927; *The Heir to Genghiz Khan* (*Storm over Asia*), 1929; sound: *Deserter,* 1933; *General Suvorov,* 1941; *Admiral Nakhimov,* 1946. Lecturer in the State Academy of Motion Pictures. Two books translated into English by Ivor Montagu: "Film Technique" (Gollancz, 1929; Newnes, 1933), and "Film Acting" (Newnes, 1935).

terial. Everything in the picture is significant in the early
ussian masterpieces.

The development of a sense of tension is derived by Pudovkin
rom Griffith, whom he acknowledges to be his master.

> " During work on the treatment the scenarist must always
> consider the varying degree of tension in the action. This
> tension must, after all, be reflected in the spectator, forcing
> him to follow the given part of the picture with more or
> less excitement. This excitement does not depend on the
> dramatic situation alone, it can be created or strengthened
> by purely extraneous methods. The gradual winding-up
> of the dynamic elements of the action, the introduction of
> scenes built from rapid, energetic work of the characters,
> the introduction of crowd scenes, all these govern increases
> of excitement in the spectator, and one must learn so to
> construct the scenario that the spectator is gradually
> engrossed by the developing action, receiving the most
> effective impulse only at the end. The vast majority of
> scenarios suffer from clumsy building up of tension."
> (PUDOVKIN, " Film Technique ", p. 18.)

He summarises the work of the director-scenarist in these
terms :

> " Hence an important rule for the scenarist : in working
> out each incident he must carefully consider and select each
> visual image; he must remember that for each concept,
> each idea, there may be tens and hundreds of possible
> means of plastic expression, and that it is his task to select
> from amongst them the clearest and most vivid. Special
> attention, however, must be paid to the special part played
> in pictures by objects. Relationships between human
> beings are, for the most part, illuminated by conversations,
> by words; no one carries on conversation with objects, and
> that is why work with them, being expressed by visual
> action, is of special interest to the film technician. Try to
> imagine to yourself anger, joy, confusion, sorrow, and so
> forth expressed, not in words and the gestures accompany-
> ing them, but in action connected with objects, and you will
> see how images saturated with plastic expression come into
> your mind. Work on plastic material is of the highest
> importance for the scenarist. In the process of it he learns

to imagine to himself what he has written as it will appear upon the screen, and the knowledge thus acquired is essential for correct and fruitful work.

"One must try to express one's concepts in clear and vivid visual images. Suppose it be a matter of the characterisation of some person of the action—this person must be placed in such conditions as will make him appear, by means of some action or movement, in the desired light. Suppose it be a matter of the representation of some event —those scenes must be assembled that most vividly emphasise visually the essence of the event represented." (PUDOVKIN, "Film Technique", pp. 30, 31.)

The art of editing, or montage, develops out of the results of this creative labour. The scenarist edits on paper; the film is conceived, organised, shot: the rushes are in the director-editor's hand, and probably round his neck. Out of all this celluloid divided into hundreds of separate strips, and guided only by his shooting script and his filmic sense, he must begin the final process of montage.

Pudovkin divides editing for the silent screen into:

(1) The simplest form: the art of the attentive observer. The camera moves around and over the action so that by the process of long, medium and close-up shots the story is told action by action from the best of all possible viewpoints. The viewpoints are then linked together into the sequence.

(2) The more complex form of cutting parallel action. This is the form of cutting developed by Griffith when dealing "with simultaneity of actions in several different places." The editor cuts from one to the other action, building his tempo to suit the excitement or degree of tension. Pudovkin points out the psychological nature of this treatment:

"There is a law in psychology that lays it down that if an emotion gives birth to a certain movement, by imitation of this movement the corresponding emotion can be called forth. If the scenarist can effect in even rhythm the transference of interest of the intent spectator, if he can so construct the elements of increasing interest that the question, 'What is happening at the other place?' arises and at the same moment the spectator is transferred whither he wishes to go, then the editing thus created can really excite the spectator. One must learn to understand that editing is in actual fact a compulsory and deliberate guidance of the thoughts and associations of the spectator. If the editing be merely an uncontrolled combination of the various pieces, the spectator will understand (apprehend) nothing from it; but if it be co-ordinated according to a definitely selected course of events or conceptual line, either agitated or calm, it will either excite or soothe the spectator." (PUDOVKIN, "Film Technique", p. 45.)

(3) *Relational Cutting.*—Various devices can be used to heighten the effect required :

(*a*) *Contrast.*—Shots of starvation cut in with shots of gluttony.

(*b*) *Parallelism.*—This is a development of contrast. Pudovkin's illustration uses the situation of a condemned worker under the old regime and a drunken, callous factory-owner. The condemned man is to be executed at 5 a.m. Scenes of preparation in the prison are timed, not by the prison clock, but by the wrist-watch of the capitalist as he lolls in untidy drunken sleep.

(*c*) *Symbolism.*—In Pudovkin's film *Mother* the procession of the strikers advancing to meet the White cavalry is symbolised by cutting-in shots of a huge ice-flow breaking itself against the parapet of a bridge. The movements are carefully related in speed.

(*d*) *The Simultaneous.*—Cutting with increasing tempo from the growing plight of the victim to the dash of the rescuer. Used by Griffith.

(*e*) *Leit-motif* (reiteration of theme).—The repetition of the same shot in a film to emphasise a theme.

Pudovkin takes a strong view of the dictatorship of the director. He alone is the key-man in the production; his assistants contribute only according to his will. His actors, though requiring to have plasticity of expression, act only under his guidance. He is the final arbiter of the disposition of his strips of celluloid, which, free in his own space-sense and his own time-sense, he links into a final pattern of movement by which he controls the mood of his audience.

"Between the natural event and its appearance upon the screen there is a marked difference. It is exactly this difference that makes the film an art. Guided by the director, the camera assumes the task of removing every superfluity and directing the attention of the spectator in such a way that he shall see only that which is significant and characteristic." (PUDOVKIN, " Film Technique ", p. 58.)

" When we wish to apprehend anything, we always begin with the general outlines, and then, by intensifying our examination to the highest degree, enrich the apprehension by an ever-increasing number of details. The particular, the detail, will always be a synonym of intensification. It is upon this that the strength of the film depends, that its characteristic speciality is the possibility of giving a clear, especially vivid representation of detail. The power of filmic representation lies in the fact that, by means of the camera, it continually strives to penetrate as deeply as possible, to the mid-point of every image. The camera, as it were, forces itself, ever striving, into the profoundest deeps of life; it strives thither to penetrate, whither the average spectator never reaches as he glances casually around him. The camera goes deeper; anything it can see it approaches, and thereafter eternalises upon the celluloid." (PUDOVKIN, " Film Technique," pp. 62, 63.)

" The work of the director is characterised by thinking in filmic pictures; by imagining events in that form in which, composed of pieces joined together in a certain sequence, they will appear upon the screen; by considering real incidents only as material from which to select separate characteristic elements; and by building a new filmic reality out of them. Even when he has to do with real objects in real surroundings he thinks only of their appearances upon the screen. He never considers a real object in the sense of its actual, proper nature, but considers in it only those properties that can be carried over on to celluloid. The film director looks only conditionally upon his material, and this conditionality is extraordinarily specific; it arises from a whole series of properties peculiar only to the film." (PUDOVKIN, " Film Technique ", pp. 69, 70.)

EISENSTEIN

The greatest names of the Russian silent film are Kuleshov, Vertov, Dovzhenko, Alexandrov, Ermler, Protasanov,

Trauberg, Turin, Pudovkin, Eisenstein,[1] Alexander Room and Mikhail Romm. Sequences linger in the visual memory from the work of some of these directors, especially Eisenstein and Pudovkin. It is impossible to forget the handling of the lock-out and the strikers' march in *Mother,* the tractor and milk-separator sequences in *General Line,* and above all the Odessa-steps sequence of *Potemkin,* which is a classic sequence of silent cinema and one of the most influential few minutes in cinema history. It illustrates the theory of montage in Pudovkin's book, and was the model from which Grierson and the British documentary directors received their first education in cinema technique. It is made up as follows:

Theme. The Russian Revolution of 1905.

Story and Treatment of Action.

The sailors of the " Potemkin " have mutinied and killed their tyrannical officers. They put in to the port of Odessa, which, though held by the White Guards, is full of sympathetic working-class and bourgeois people, who, after sending gifts of food in little sailing ships, throng the huge flight of stone steps leading down to the water's edge to wave to the distant battleship.

Plastic Material.

Major: the steps, the crowd, the White Guards. Detailed: (persons), the cripple, the elegant lady with the parasol, the children, the mother with the dead child, the nurse, the elderly bourgeois lady; (objects), the parasol, the jackboots and rifles of the soldiery, their shadows on the steps, the perambulator, the smashed spectacles on the sabred face of the elderly lady.

[1] S. M. Eisenstein, 1898–1948. Engineer, architect and artist. In the Red Army 1918. Worked for the theatre and on crowd pageants during early twenties. Interest in epic and crowd work took him into the cinema 1924. Chief films with the distinguished cameraman Eduard Tissé are: silent, *The Battleship Potemkin,* 1925; *October (Ten Days that Shook the World),* 1928; *The Old and the New (The General Line),* 1929; sound, *Thunder over Mexico,* 1932 (with Alexandrov, but commercial American editing and sound track of Mexican folk songs); *Alexander Nevski* (with Vassiliev), 1938; *Ivan the Terrible,* 1944–6. Writing to be found chiefly in the form of articles and interviews in " Close-up," " Film Art," etc., and his works, " The Film Sense " (Faber, London, 1943) and " Film Form " (Harcourt Brace, 1949).

Types of Shot.

Whole range from distant to close-up.

Location and Cast.

The steps themselves; the people themselves; a contingent of the Red Army in the uniform of the Whites.

Editing or Montage.

General shots introduce the audience to the crowd on the steps facing out into the harbour, unconscious of the threat to their lives behind them at the top of the long wide flight of stone stairs. Individuals involved in the subsequent attack are introduced in shots of smiling sympathy for the mutinous sailors. Then, with the title " Suddenly," the sequence itself opens:

(*a*) A series of impressionist shots, some long, some of only a fraction of a second's duration, launches the attack. A girl is killed in close-up, her hair falling forward over her gaping mouth; a legless cripple heaves himself to safety; the parasol of the bourgeois lady lunges forward into the camera. The steps as a background appear at different angles as shot follows shot. Distant shots alternate with varieties of close-up. One shot shows the fleeing crowd from over the back of the line of soldiers now advancing steadily down the steps, pausing every so often to aim and fire.

(*b*) An impressionist scene of three shots of a fraction of a second each shows the body of a man tipping to fill the frame, then falling head and arms forward, then with knees caving. Finally a shot lasting two and a half seconds shows him splayed over the steps.

(*c*) Longer shots alternate between the running crowd and the soldiers. Close-ups of various types (worker and bourgeois) in attitudes of fear. A bald man clutches his head. Then the first important element is introduced:

(*d*) The woman and child. She is running down the steps with the crowd. The soldiers fire on the crowd; the child falls. He screams. The mother realises her child has fallen: shots of blood on the child's head are cut in with people still rushing over him. A foot crushes his hand: he is kicked by running feet. The mother's face is stricken with horror. She returns to the body of her child: she is alone, the crowd below, the soldiers above. She picks up the child, and turns to face the camera and the on-coming line of soldiers (off-frame). Cut to

(e) Bourgeois group, harangued by the elderly lady in the black dress. " Go, beseech them," she says (title). But they are too frightened. Cut back to

(f) Shadows of the line of soldiers on the steps. The mother is seen once more, side shot over the steps; she is advancing, the dead child in her arms, to challenge the soldiers. The soldiers are shot from various angles, from above, from the front behind the climbing figure of the woman. Once more she moves into the frame (right) whilst the shadows of the soldiers appear (left) culminating in the uplifted sword of the officer. With rifles just visible they shoot her down: several shots build up to the climax of a close-up. The soldiers descend over the bodies of the mother and child. Cut back to

(g) The fleeing crowds. (The action throughout is prolonged and reduplicated for tragic emphasis. In actuality it would have taken two or three minutes to clear the steps and shoot down the people. It plays, however, some six minutes on the screen.) The crowd is cut off at the base of the steps by mounted soldiers. The second important element appears:

(h) The nurse and perambulator. Several shots show the nurse protecting the perambulator with her own body. The jackboots of the soldiers move down with almost mincing care, step by step. They fire. The nurse's mouth opens in pain. She clutches the buckle on her belt, and leans back against the perambulator. Cut from her hands slowly covered with the blood from her wounded stomach, to the wheels of the perambulator which her falling body gradually pushes down the steps; the action is prolonged for emphasis by cutting and recutting. Meanwhile the soldiers descend, keeping their neat line, firing precisely. The nurse's body is still launching the perambulator on its careering journey down the steps. Gradually shot by shot it is pushed away. Shot from overhead, from angles sideways, the perambulator goes down the steps, watched by the horrified elderly lady, until finally it topples over, throwing the child out. The climax approaches in a succession of shots mostly of variable duration from one to three seconds. All the elements: the crowd, the soldiers, the dead nurse, the perambulator, the bourgeois group are built together with rapid cutting. , The final element arrives.

(*i*) The elderly lady faces a soldier. He slashes at her, the movement of his sword matching the tipping of the perambulator. Her face, in horrid astonishment, is covered with blood behind her shattered spectacles. The sequence is over.

Owing to its difficult economic position, and the enormous number of silent projectors which still cannot be replaced by sound equipment, Russia was slow to take to the sound film. As we shall see later, when the structure of the Soviet Film Industry is considered, in 1937 Richard Ford ("Sight and Sound," Spring, 1937) tells us there were only three thousand sound cinemas for a population of one hundred and sixty million as against some thirty-six thousand silent projectors mostly on the farms. In any case, the early thirties saw something of a crisis between the older and the younger directors. Eisenstein was in London, Paris, Hollywood, Mexico. Pudovkin experimented in sound in *Deserter* (1933). The younger directors disliked the æstheticism of their seniors' work: they preferred socialist realism and a newsreel technique. Symphonies and montage were dead and too much after the fashion of bourgeois art, suitable for history rather than for films dealing with the Five Year Plans, but the new spirit was exemplified with a pæan of triumph in *Chapayev* (Vassiliev Brothers). This film seemed and was notable for developing, with sound, the personality of a character. It had star-value without a star. Its continuity was satisfying and strong, without the poetic and rhetorical delays incident upon the symphonic tradition of montage. It was bright and fresh and clean and realistic. It threw aside the æstheticism of the silent days and solved the problem of how to make a good story about a great Soviet hero in a realistic but not pedestrian manner.

Many films that arrive from Russia today seem pedestrian to those who responded to the great days when Russia stood out as a pioneer of filmcraft. Their excessive dependence on dialogue and long individual harangues, their dead level of

realism and excessive length show a strange lack of imagination, considering the seriousness and urgency of their subjects
from the Soviet point of view. Acting and characterisation on
the other hand are outstanding. Soviet achievement in individual
films since 1930 has been considerable. *The Road to Life* (Ekk,
1931), *Deserter* (Pudovkin, 1933), *Storm* (Petrov, 1934), *The
Three Songs of Lenin* (Dzig-Vertov, 1934), *Chapayev* (Vassiliev Brothers, 1934), *Peasants* (Ermler, 1935), *The Baltic
Deputy* (Zharki, 1937), *The Lone White Sail* (Legoshin, 1937),
Lenin in October (Romm, 1937), *Peter the Great, I and II*
(Petrov, 1937-8), *The Childhood of Maxim Gorki* (Donskoi,
1938), *Alexander Nevski* (Eisenstein, 1938), *Shors* (Dovzhenko,
1939), *Lenin in 1918* (Romm, 1939), *My Universities* (Donskoi,
1940), *General Suvorov* (Pudovkin, 1941), *Lermontov* (Gendelstein, 1943), *Girl 217* (Romm, 1944), *Kutusov* (Petrov,
1944), *The Rainbow* (Donskoi, 1944), *Ivan the Terrible, I and
II* (Eisenstein, 1944-6), *The Vow* (Chiaureli, 1946), *The Turning Point* (Ermler, 1946), *Admiral Nakhimov* (Pudovkin,
1946) represent some of the finest achievement of Soviet
studios at their best during the sound period.

ARNHEIM

Arnheim's book on the film appeared just after the change-
over to sound was assured, and he was able, therefore, to consider the problems of sound more carefully than Pudovkin, who
was in the process of working out *Deserter*. His book emphasises, as we have seen above, the importance of the limitations
within which the film has to work, and its consequent artistic
advantages. With great elaboration, which is characteristic of
the whole book, he works out afresh the principles of montage
in a long analytical scheme. He then deals with the principles
of the selection of fit material for the screen, the problems of
film acting, the mass-produced film and kindred subjects. He
finally reaches the problem of the sound film itself.

5. Essentials of Film Art: Sound

When sound first arrived in the late twenties it was usually
amplified from gramophone recordings synchronised with the
projector. Later the sound track was added to the visual track,
and the manifold problems of synchronisation were solved.

The second reaction of the trade, which hung back conservatively at first, was to jump at this new phenomenon. The house with sound in a provincial town had the pick of the box office irrespective of the quality of the picture shown. As long as it talked and sang, as long as doors banged and telephones rang, the public was happy and the trade scrambled in its wake, because a happy public pays easily with its critical faculties softened.

The discerning film critic, who had watched the gradual maturing of the silent film in America, Russia and Germany, felt at first lost in a welter of showmanship. Paul Rotha, writing at the turn of the decade a book which is full of discernment for what had been achieved so carefully in the silent days, says:

" Now the addition of sound and dialogue to the visual image on the screen will tend to emphasise its isolated significance by reason of the fact that, as the sound and dialogue take longer to apprehend than the visual image, the duration of time that the shot is held on the screen will be determined by the sound and dialogue instead of by the assembling. Dialogue, by very reason of its realism, represents real time and not the filmic time of the visual image. Obviously this is in direct opposition once more to all the dominant factors that have been proved to achieve emotional effect by visual images." PAUL ROTHA, " The Film till Now," p. 307.)

This was precisely true of the type of film at first produced. With the camera trained steadily on the singing fool, the music went on and cutting could be and was forgotten. Whole plays were transferred to the screen, with the camera following the dialogue around the set like a lap-dog terrified of being left alone. It was a depressing return to adolescence and cheap effect. The equipment was expensive, and by God it must be used, and used it was until the directors and the public wearied of it, and decided that, after all, you went to see and not merely to hear a film.

Arnheim and Pudovkin, having time to breathe, set about the problems of this new technical gift. It had, after all, certain obvious advantages. The break-up of the illusion caused by the titles flashed on the screen for as long as it took the slowest reader to spell them out could now be forgotten. The film could speak for itself. It could also score and reproduce its own music. Regardless of its employees, the industry threw thousands of cinema musicians on the streets and recorded its own music when and how it was needed. The old devices, so interesting and so unknown to the public, through which the conductor of the cinema orchestra could keep his music linked to the visuals on the screen above him, were now no longer necessary. The old music libraries, with tunes or movements to match all moods, passed from the hands of the cinema conductor to his more highly paid colleague in the studio.

Arnheim's solution was a perceptive one:

"Sound film—at any rate real sound film—is not a verbal masterpiece supplemented by pictures, but a homogeneous creation of word and picture which cannot be split up into parts that have any meaning separately. (This is the reason why so little is to be expected of dramatists and novelists for sound films.) Even the picture part is meaningless alone. Moreover, in general, speech in sound film will be much more effective if used as a part of nature instead of as an art form. Film speech will have to be more lifelike in the same degree as the film picture is more like nature than the stage picture." (ARNHEIM, "Film," p. 213.)

He also recognised that natural sounds were of equal importance to speech when the process of artistic selection could be brought to bear:

"For this form of acoustic art there would seem to be inexhaustible material—sighs and the sirens of factories, the ripple of water and revolver shots, the songs of birds and snores—and also the spoken word, as one sound among many." (ARNHEIM, "Film," p. 216.)

His recognition of the more transitory nature of sound compared with light is as profound as it is important for the full understanding of the relation sound should have to sight in the well-made film.

"Light waves and sound waves tell us about the conditions of things in the world in which we live—what these things 'are' and what at the moment they are 'doing.' In this manner we arrive without actual contact at a knowledge of these things across space, and actually at a much better and more thorough knowledge than is possible by the direct process of touch. That is what is called sight and hearing.

" Only few of the objects in our surroundings are in the habit of giving off sounds uninterruptedly. Some do it occasionally, most not at all. The sea murmurs unceasingly, a dog barks occasionally, a table never makes a sound. With the help of light, on the other hand, we can, as long as the object exists at all, get information about it. Hence light gives a more complete and therefore more accurate picture of the universe than sound. Light gives us the ' being ' of things, while sound generally only gives us incidental ' doing.' "   (ARNHEIM, " Film," p. 217.)

The subjects of sound may be classified roughly into speech, natural sounds and music. The director can choose at any given moment in his script which he is going to use, and which will most forcibly and inevitably be the right artistic combination with the visual image. Just as we have seen that a director selects his image with an eye to obtaining the most telling visual effect on his audience, so he must select his sound. Raymond Spottiswoode in his " Grammar of the Film " gives a careful classification of the alternatives that lie before a director preparing his shooting script for camera and microphone : examples will help to clarify these alternatives.

Scene : A murderer is about to kill a sleeping man with a knife. He creeps up behind his victim, and pauses a moment to balance himself for the act of stabbing.

Alternatives for Sound :

(a) Non-selective. (i) Every noise is included : soft tread of feet, heavy breathing of sleeper and any other extraneous noise coming from next door, or traffic from the street outside.

(ii) Only extraneous sound used. Complete quiet as far as the visible action itself is concerned. Only the sound of the traffic outside reproduced without conscious selection.

(b) Selective. (iii) Selected sounds originating from the scene only; breathing of sleeper, soft tread of feet.

(iv) Selected sounds from outside the visible action itself. Cry of man murdered, though all we see in the frame is the swift flash of the falling knife.

Artificial though these classifications may seem, they offer alternatives along the lines of which a director must decide what is right for inclusion and what is wrong. Only by examples of what appears to be right selection can one judge the complexity of the new opportunities offered to the director sensible of the powers of sound.

EXAMPLES

1. THE ROAD TO LIFE: (Mezhrabpomfilm, 1931.
   Russian.   Director, Nikolai Ekk)

One of the earliest of Russian sound films, it contained many experiments. Under inspired leadership, a band of vagabond street boys learn Russian citizenship. They build a railway from their Collective to the city. The halt at the end of the journey is gaily decked to receive the first train when the railway is opened. The boys' leader, however, is killed on the lonely track by a reactionary. The body is placed on the cowcatcher of the engine, and the lyrical emotion built up on the completion of the track and the maiden voyage of the train is hushed in the waiting crowd by the sight of the body as the engine draws slowly in. The sound matches this collective emotion by giving only the long dying sighs as the steam escapes slowly from the train when it draws to a standstill. Symbolism and natural sound are matched.

2. KAMERADSCHAFT: (Nerofilm, 1931.
   German.   Director, G. W. Pabst)

A remarkable use of natural sound occurs after the disaster. The distracted grandfather runs through section after section of the empty shafts calling his buried son's name. The voice is distorted in the echoes—Georges, Georges—the last syllable drawn out into an echo of helpless despair.

3. SCARFACE: (United Artists, 1932.
   American.   Director, Howard Hawks, with Paul Muni)

Scarface is a film of murder and callous terror, one of the first gangster pictures. Early in the film the initial murder happens in a deserted bar. The visuals alternate between the silent victim in a telephone kiosk and the shadow on a white wall of a man in a felt hat. The sound of the shot is preceded by the quiet whistling of a popular tune. After the shot there is silence. The shadow moves away and the whistling is resumed.

4. DESERTER: (Mezhrabpomfilm, 1931–33.
   Russian.   Director, Pudovkin)
Pudovkin put all his theoretical knowledge into the making
of this film. In the opening sequence where the visuals are grey
with fog, he used a rhythm of ships' sirens at varying distances:
in the shipbuilding sequences he cut his natural sounds along
with his images.

> " For the symphony of siren calls with which *Deserter*
> opens I had six steamers playing in a space of a mile and
> a half in the Port of Leningrad. They sounded their calls
> to a prescribed plan and we worked at night in order that
> we should have quiet." (PUDOVKIN, " Film Technique,"
> p. 173.)

> " Perhaps a purer example of establishing rhythm in
> sound film occurs in another part of *Deserter*—the docks
> section. Here again I used natural sounds, heavy hammers,
> pneumatic drills working at different levels, the smaller
> noise of fixing a rivet, voices of sirens and the crashing
> crescendo of a falling chain. All these sounds I shot on
> the dock-side, and I composed them on the editing table,
> using various lengths, they served to me as notes of music.
> As finale of the docks scene I made a half-symbolic growth
> of the ship in images at an accelerated pace, while the
> sound in a complicated syncopation mounts to an ever
> greater and grandiose climax. Here I had a real musical
> task, and was obliged to ' feel ' the length of each strip in
> the same spirit as a musician ' feels ' the accent necessary
> for each note." (PUDOVKIN, " Film Technique," pp. 172–3.)

5. STRANGE INTERLUDE: (Metro-Goldwyn-Mayer, 1932.
   American.   Director, Robert Z. Leonard)
This film was based on Eugene O'Neill's play, the technical
feature of which was that the characters spoke their thoughts
in full soliloquy whilst taking their part in conversation. It is
now often used. It has a curious effect when mixed with
direct speech, as in some of the soliloquies in Olivier's *Hamlet*.

6. NIGHTMAIL: (G.P.O., 1935.
   British.   Director, Basil Wright, with Harry Watt)
Special verse by W. H. Auden was used here to run with the

mail train as it crossed the border. The verse reduplicated the rhythm of the train, and the speaker's voice took over from the wheels.

7. PETER THE GREAT: (Lenfilm, Moscow, 1939.
   Russian.   Director, Petrov)

In this film of the Westernisation of the backward Russians by Peter the Great, the beautifully recorded church bells, symbol of the old way of life, act as a recurrent theme throughout, until a climax is reached in the hurling down of the bells with a resounding crash when they are required for gun metal. Bells are also used by Eisenstein to build up the oppressive atmosphere of *Ivan the Terrible.*

8. CITIZEN KANE: (Mercury Productions, 1941.
   American.   Director, Orson Welles)

This film is remarkable for its use of sound in many sequences. Echo is used until the voices are filled out into an unnatural hollowness, particularly when the husband and wife draw more and more apart in the vast cavernous rooms of Xanadu. The sinister echo emphasises the poverty of the servant's story as he conducts the last visitor over the desolate palace.

9. MICKEY'S MOVING DAY: (Walt Disney, 1930)
   and many SILLY SYMPHONIES:
   American.

10. LISTEN TO BRITAIN: (Crown, 1942.
    British.   Director, Humphrey Jennings)

These films are put together because they make great use of natural sound—Disney's for comic effect, *Listen to Britain* to build up a sound-visual commentary on Britain at war by day and night. All have superbly complicated sound-tracks constructed largely in a symphony of music and natural sounds.

11. BRIEF ENCOUNTER: (Cineguild, 1945.
    British.   Noel Coward and David Lean)

Trains are used as part of the montage of many films. In *Brief Encounter* at the little station of Milford Junction they are used with such imaginative skill as poetic imagery that this film could become an example of how to develop a visual cliché into an inspired symbol. The express trains, which never stop, the slow local trains which always shunt usefully in at fixed times, gradually become accepted symbols, the first of the passion which is unattainable by the two lovers because they are already married, the second of the humdrum responsibilities which are only too easily accessible because they are tied to them through marriage itself. In the final train image when Celia Johnson, as the married woman who has just parted for the last time from her lover, rushes out to throw herself beneath the familiar express train, the rush of sound and the staccato flashing of the window lights on her agonised face become a terrifying reminder that she is too old to accept this final surrender to the headlong and insane journey of passionate romance. She does not commit suicide. (Compare the brilliant use of trains in Renoir's *La Bête Humaine*.)

Some of these examples show the result of careful thought as to which particular sounds (or silent periods) will be most effective dramatically to prolong the tension and spell-bind the audience. Others show the development of natural sounds into artificial patterns, or the use of distortions (like echoing sound) to develop the atmosphere inherent in the particular situation. The possibilities of the dramatic use of sound are endless: they depend on the director's integrity of imagination, his common sense and his artistic courage in experiment.

Arnheim has said rightly that the dialogue of sound film must be realistic. It is necessary to distinguish between the efficient, hundred-per-cent talkie and the real sound film. The film, like the drama, consists of its ninety-five-per-cent lowlights and its five-per-cent highlights. We do not banish Marlowe, Shakespeare, Congreve, Sheridan, Wilde and Shaw from our theatres merely because they knew how to write plays better than the four or five hundred dramatists whose names occur in the indices of Professor Allardyce Nicoll's histories of drama. Moreover, some people, possibly highbrow, would maintain that these particular dramatists are popular in their own right and are of great importance to the development of the theatre. When the one-hundred-per-cent-smash-hit-box-office-money-spinners have been enjoyed by us all they are forgotten and replaced by kindred superlative mixtures as before. The ones that remain in memory are those which occasionally gave up talking in order to become films, or, because of some peculiarity in their contents (like the films of the Marx brothers), stand out from the rubbish-heap of subject-matter which the more carrion of scenarists pick over. The Marx brothers, in any case, often knew what a film was, and said it in pictures as well as in wisecracks.

This is the reason why Shakespeare's and Shaw's plays, undiluted and unaltered, cannot become more than hundred-per-cent talkies. Admittedly you can *see* the people *talking* more clearly, but it is a doubtful advantage since the lines were written to be projected orally over a distance, and the broad eloquent phrasing of great drama is lost in the overpowering visual presence of the actor. Many situations in a Shakespeare play, on the other hand, would make excellent cinema (Lear driven out on to the heath by Fritz Lang, the riots in Rome by Eisenstein, the murder of Duncan by Hitchcock), but Shakespeare's words would be cut to nothing and his rhythms lost among visual silences or natural sounds. Shaw, at first a martinet against cutting his lines for film purposes, gave way so that *Pygmalion* and *Major Barbara* became enjoyable partly as sound films and partly as hundred-per-cent talkie Shaw. Olivier's *Henry V*, a beautiful rendering of the play from the theatrical point of view, achieves a certain cinematic quality in the prose scenes where Shakespeare's speech is at its most intimate, idiomatic and realistic, such as Mistress Quickly's story of the death of Falstaff and Henry's scene with the soldiers the night before Agincourt. Agincourt itself is excellent cinema following the classic example of medieval battle in Eisenstein's *Alexander Nevski*. Olivier's *Hamlet* again showed that Shakespeare's verse is too intricate for the predominantly visual medium of the film. In *Cæsar and Cleopatra,* however, Shaw and Pascal have held far too rigidly to the essentially theatrical text of a very theatrical play, and no amount of De Mille-like crowd scenes or amazing sets filmed in Technicolor could save this most expensive of British films from being entirely uncinematic. It became a highly-coloured film record of theatrical eloquence spoken by a distinguished and excellent cast, but not a film. It is rumoured that if he had his time over again Shaw would have written for films, not for the theatre. He began life as a critic of music and art: he has a mobile plastic sense and has turned theatre technique upside down. But as a critic his eloquence sold his ideas to a public unused to hard truth, and

his theatrical experiments were all made in favour of words
and yet more words. Would Shaw have had the reticence
necessary for the screen?

American idiom is clipped and pert, insolent and free,
quickened with imagery and spoken at speed. Good American
talkies, and they are many, register fast, but they shoot a percentage of their dialogue round, not into, the ears of the very
un-American British, who think they speak the same language
properly through their mouths. But reticence is known in
American films (the opening of *The Long Voyage Home* and
The Grapes of Wrath, sequences in *Fury* and *Scarface* when the
visuals are left to sink in on their own), and directors are
obviously doing their damnedest to get that camera around even
whilst the actor does the talking. Comedy particularly—and
the American rhythm of life and rhythm of tongue lend themselves to comedy both foolish and satiric—is often an affair of
slick words, but the skill of the American editor in cutting and
continuity frequently puts a kick into the dialogue by means of
scissors and acetate. Comedy is also a matter of situation,
usually sexual (*Her Cardboard Lover, My Two Husbands, Tom,
Dick and Harry* and a host more excellent stories), and sexual
situations are frequently as much something to spy upon as
listen to. Good cinema takes advantage of this; no film has
lost its box-office appeal because its writer, director and editor
took the trouble to make its action visually exciting.

The following quotations from the early scenes of *Great
Expectations* will show dialogue and natural sounds in their
proper place in relation to the visual action of a film:

> Shot 13. *Ext. Thames Estuary. Sunset.* V.L.S.[1] of a small
> boy—PIP—running LEFT to RIGHT along the bank of
> the Estuary. A wind is blowing and making a high-
> pitched and ghostlike whistling noise. CAMERA TRACKS
> and PANS with PIP as he runs round a bend in the path-
> way and comes towards CAMERA. A gibbet is built on
> the edge of the path CAMERA RIGHT and PIP glances up
> at it as he passes—he continues running and moves
> out of picture CAMERA RIGHT. DISSOLVE TO:
>
> Shot 14. *Ext. Churchyard. Sunset.* M.S. PIP, wearing

[1] The various initials stand for Very Long Shot, Medium Shot,
Medium Long Shot, Medium Close Shot, Long Shot, Close Shot.

long trousers, a short jacket and a woollen scarf tied round his neck. He is carrying a bunch of holly in his right hand. He climbs over a broken stone wall and CAMERA PANS LEFT TO RIGHT with him as he walks past the tombstones and old graves in the churchyard. CAMERA CONTINUES PANNING as he makes his way towards one of the tombstones and kneels in front of it —is now in M.L.S.

Shot 15. M.S. PIP kneeling at the foot of the grave. He pulls up an old rose bush which he throws aside, pats down the earth again and then places his bunch of holly at the head of the grave near the engraved tombstone. The wind is still howling.

Shot 16. M.C.S. PIP kneeling near the tombstone—he looks round nervously towards the CAMERA.

Shot 17. L.S. from PIP's eyeline of the leafless branches of a tree—the wind is blowing them, and to PIP they look like bony hands clutching at him.

Shot 18. M.C.S. PIP looking round at scene 16.

Shot 19. M.S. of the trunk of an old tree from PIP's eyeline—it looks very sinister and to him like a distorted human body.

Shot 20. PIP—he jumps up from the grave and runs away RIGHT TO LEFT towards the stone wall—CAMERA PANS with him, then becomes static as he runs towards CAMERA and into the arms of a large, dirty, uncouth and horrible-looking man; from his clothes and shackles it is obvious that he is an escaped convict. PIP screams loudly.

Shot 21. C.S. PIP; his mouth is open as he screams, but a large, dirty hand is clapped over it, silencing him.

Shot 22. C.S. of the CONVICT—his face is dirty and scowling, his hair is closely cut—he leers down at PIP.
CONVICT: Keep still, you little devil, or I'll cut your throat.

Shot 23. M.C.S. PIP, silent, looking up towards the CONVICT—CAMERA SHOOTING from the line of the CONVICT's right hip. His hands are round PIP's throat.
PIP: No, sir, no.
CONVICT: Tell us your name. Quick.

PIP: Pip, Pip, sir.

The CONVICT shakes PIP vigorously.

Shot 24. M.C.S. CONVICT—the top of PIP'S head is in
the bottom right-hand corner of the screen. He is still
being shaken by the CONVICT.

CONVICT: Show us where you live, point out the place.

PIP leans across the CONVICT and points out of picture,
CAMERA LEFT.

PIP: There, sir, there.

Shot 25. M.S. of the CONVICT as he bends and lifts PIP
—he turns him upside down—CAMERA PANS DOWN the
CONVICT'S body to show PIP'S head upside down, between the CONVICT'S shackled legs—PIP is being
bounced up and down and his head bangs the ground
—he gasps loudly.

Shot 26. C.S. of the soles of PIP'S shoes and legs from
over the CONVICT'S shoulder as he bounces PIP up
and down.

Shot 27. M.C.S. PIP'S head upside down between the
CONVICT'S legs.

Shot 28. M.S. CONVICT and PIP—the CONVICT stands
PIP upright and bends down to pick up an apple which
has fallen from PIP'S pocket.

Well-scripted dialogue remains one of the essentials of good
filmcraft. Scenarists like Robert Riskin who works with Frank
Capra, Dudley Nichols who has worked among others with John
Ford and has been responsible for many excellent scripts such
as *The Informer*, Preston Sturges who is a script-writer turned
director, Jacques Prévert in the earlier films he made with
Marcel Carné, all show that there is such a thing as film-style in
dialogue writing. British script-writing as far as dialogue goes
is not its strongest point. There is a point where simplicity and
directness of speech become a form of poetry: this is seen in the
dialogue of films like *The Ox-bow Incident, The Grapes of
Wrath, The Lost Weekend* and *The Southerner*. Examples of
good scripting in British films are: *Nine Men, San Demetrio
London, The Life and Death of Colonel Blimp, 49th Parallel,
In Which We Serve, This Happy Breed, Next of Kin, The Way
Ahead, The Way to the Stars, Millions Like Us, Passport to
Pimlico, Odd Man Out, The Queen of Spades*. Too many other-

wise good British films still prattle when they should be swift
and precise, or else they produce the effect of theatricalism by
over-writing the words until they do not speak naturally. The
war films on the whole have been the best scripted, and this is
especially true of the feature-scale type of documentary film
for which the directors of the Crown Film Unit have made
themselves famous (*Target for Tonight*, *Coastal Command*,
Close Quarters and *Western Approaches*). American dialogue
at its worst has a horrible banality and gold-digging insincerity
which no amount of gags or slickness or blonde bombshells
can redeem from shame: it is worse than the priggish May-
fair debutante banter which so many of the best homes of
Britain try to copy from novel, stage and screen. If it were
not already called small-talk, it could be called tea-tattle.

Next comes the examination of the importance of film music.

Many of us will remember the girl (out of the piano endlessly
playing) in the half-empty silent cinema during the afternoons
of the twenties, and the films accompanied by full and sometimes augmented orchestras for the packed houses at night.
With characteristic Italian musical ingenuity Giuseppi Becce
compiled a music library called the Kinothek, which he began
in 1919 and developed until thousands of pieces were classified
under headings of mood and playing time. The conductor
could therefore build up a mosaic or pot-pourri of musical
fragments to fit the varying tempos and moods of the film,
taking his cue either mechanically from a visual rhythmonome
synchronised with the picture or from his own skilled sense of
what was going on above him on the screen. Silent pictures
left on the stocks with the coming of sound had similar pot-
pourris added to them either on records or on the sound track,
and so were saved from junking before release.

This type of musical jugglery presupposed that all the music
did was to underline the action with a parallel musical throb and
rhythm. The silent screen, except for its high-spots, always did
seem to lack sound, and the noise of the projectors in any case
required drowning along with the coughs and cat-calls of the
untrained cinema audience. In a few rare instances a special
score was prepared of original music to accompany the film,
such as Meisel's music for Eisenstein's *Battleship Potemkin*
when it was shown in Berlin. But musical acrobatics were the

rule, with the artist following the spotlight instead of the spotlight tracking the artist.

The line of advance was obviously to weld the score into an artistic whole with the picture, rather than to use it as a running commentary underneath it. This meant time, money and imagination. The Russians had the time, the Americans the money, and the French the imagination. In this country Arthur Bliss added point to the visuals of Wells' and Menzies' *Things to Come,* and the music was subsequently arranged as a suite. This music at any rate had the virtue of being composed by a distinguished musician to impregnate the visual passages in a film for which it was specially intended. It was not a hotchpotch of Chopin and Sousa alternately lumping the throat and swelling the breast of a happily victimised audience. Maurice Jaubert (distinguished for his work with René Clair in *Le Dernier Milliardaire* and *Le Quatorze Juillet*) writes of film music :

"We do not go to the cinema to hear music. We require it to deepen and prolong in us the screen's visual impressions. Its task is not to explain these impressions, but to add to them an overtone specifically different—or else film music must be content to remain perpetually redundant. Its task is not to be expressive by adding its sentiments to those of the characters or of the director, but to be decorative by uniting its own rhythmical pattern with the visual pattern woven for us on the screen.

"That is why I believe it to be essential for film music to evolve a style of its own." ("Footnotes to the Film," p. 111.)

Kurt London, in his admirable book on "Film Music," writes as follows :

"The musical accompaniment in a film which is a play with little dialogue appears for long stretches at a time to play the part played by illustration in silent films. But here we have the essential distinction between musical accompaniment in silent and in sound-films : in the latter, there are never more than relatively short lengths of film running 'silent' and having no other sound than the music, whereas the whole of a silent film must inevitably be illustrated. Sound-films need no illustration, but their music has to be the psychological advancement of the action. While, therefore, we may characterise silent-film operetta as a near approach to dumb show, the music accompanying the scenes which are without dialogue in a sound-film is neither illustrative nor mimetic. It is an altogether new mixture of musical elements. It has to connect dialogue sections without friction; it has to establish associations of ideas and carry on developments of thought; and, over and above all this, it has to intensify the incidence of climax and prepare for further dramatic action." ("Film Music," p. 135.)

Again, examples prove the theory:

A. Films using theme songs dramatically:

1. CARNET DE BAL: (Paris Export Film Co., 1937.
     French.   Director, Julien Duvivier)
The waltz is the musical theme of the film. It haunts the day-dream of the young widow until it builds into a grand symphony of illusion with lovely waltzing images in a pattern of luxury. It distorts into regret and lonely thinness as disillusion sets in, and grows cynically dissonant in the episode where the mature woman revisits her former lover, now a criminal doctor crazy with epilepsy living in a quayside tenement.

2. REMOUS: (H. O. Films, 1934.
     French.   Director, Edmond T. Greville)
The theme love-song, sung at the cabaret with wonderful French eroticism by Lyne Clevers, permeates this fundamentally erotic film. It is played frequently on the gramophone and is used for background and incidental purposes until it becomes a leit-motif creeping into the situations in which the characters find themselves involved. (See later comment on the incidental music at the close of the film.)

3. L'ATALANTE: (Gaumont, France, 1933.
     French.   Director, Jean Vigo; Music, Maurice Jaubert)
Jean Vigo died in 1935. He was perhaps the most original and promising of the greater French directors. The story is the simplest possible—the young skipper of a barge on the Seine brings his bride to live on the boat: she is cramped and ambitious for city life even in the docks and slums of Paris where eventually the barge arrives. A momentary quarrel and she is gone. The separated couple yearn for each other (and at its

climax the treatment becomes surrealist). They are eventually brought together again by the grotesque half-mad ship's mate, brilliantly played by Michel Simon. As for the realism of the film, the documentary producer, John Grierson, said he could have found his way about this barge blind drunk on a wet night; and the surrealists claim part of the film as psychologically theirs. Jaubert's music, basically a theme song, appears as leitmotif throughout the film, and, distorted, becomes dominant as the separated lovers dream of each other as though they were searching eternally in a vast sea, swimming under water.

B. Films using music incidentally:

1. THINGS TO COME: (London Films, 1935.
    British.   Director, William Cameron Menzies)
Arthur Bliss composed music for this film which was later arranged as a suite and recorded by Decca. The music was used for bridging the episodes, and underlining some of the more spectacular actions (such as the sequences dealing with the declaration of war, mobilisation and the subsequent pestilence and devastation of the civilised world). The music is impressionist and closely linked with the atmosphere created by the images.

2. MY TWO HUSBANDS: (Columbia, 1940.
    American.   Director, Wesley Ruggles)
This is the type of comedy in which the Americans are at their best. It is chosen as typical of many. It is good throughout, and uses music for comic emphasis when the quarrel between husband and wife is at its height, and he boldly stalks along to a marching tune to settle the matter on the spot, only to be thrown out defeated with the tune distorted.

3. REMOUS: (H. O. Films, 1934.
    French.   Director, Edmond T. Greville)
The final suicide of the paralytic husband, in the face of his wife's sacrifice of her lover to devote herself to him, is anticipated in the heavily-charged atmosphere of the final sequences. This anticipation is confirmed by the ominous staccato throb of the strings which starts almost imperceptibly and leads up to the climax of the shot itself, which is heard while the camera dwells on the emotion of the wife in another room from that in

which the suicide is happening. The terrific sense of tension is undoubtedly impregnated by the subconscious effect of this special score, which might well escape conscious notice in the strength of the visual action.

4. DESERTER: (Mezhrabpomfilm, 1931–33.
   Russian.   Director, Pudovkin; Music, Shaporin)

Music is used ironically in this film when a policeman on point-duty appears to direct the large cars filled with somnolent capitalists to the tune of a waltz. At the climax of the action Pudovkin counterpoints by playing triumphant music throughout whilst the strikers suffer temporal defeat, the music emphasising the spiritual triumph of the action which is visually unapparent.

> " The course of the image twists and curves, as the emotion within the action rises and falls. Now, if we use music as an accompaniment to this image we should open with a quiet melody, appropriate to the soberly guided traffic; at the appearance of the demonstration the music would alter to a march; another change would come at the police preparations, menacing the workers—here the music would assume a threatening character; and when the clash came between workers and police—a tragic moment for the demonstrators—the music would follow this visual mood, descending ever further into themes of despair. Only at the resurrection of the flag could the music turn hopeful. A development of this type would give only the superficial aspect of the scene, the undertones of meaning would be ignored; accordingly I suggested to the composer (Shaporin) the creation of a music the dominating emotional theme of which should throughout be courage and the certainty of ultimate victory. From beginning to end the music must develop in a gradual growth of power. . . . What rôle does the music play here? Just as the image is an objective perception of events, so the music expresses the subjective appreciation of this objectivity. The sound reminds the audience that with every defeat the fighting spirit only receives new impetus to the struggle for final victory in the future." (PUDOVKIN, " Film Technique," pp. 163–4, 164–5.)

5. CITIZEN KANE: (Mercury Productions, 1941.
    American.   Director, Orson Welles)

The music in the opening sequence as the camera glides up
the ironwork of the Kane palace builds the atmosphere as
macabre and terrifying. It continues to build with the images
up to the climax of the sequence, when the crystal rolls from
the dying man's hand and crashes splintering on the floor with
the last word " rosebud " declared from Kane's dying lips.

Many distinguished composers have recognised the importance of music in the film, and have realised the distinction
between the score which merely supplements the visual action
with an accompaniment on the " programme-music " level, and
the composition of music which informs the spirit of the film
with a genuinely creative addition to its artistic effect. The
work of Prokofiev for Eisenstein's films *Alexander Nevski* and
Ivan the Terrible is a fine example of such creative co-operation.
In the sequence when the Teutonic Knights remove their
sinister emblematic helmets and order the massacre of their
victims in the captured Russian town, Prokofiev's music becomes the formalised expression of pain and terror. In
Ivan the Terrible at the ceremony of coronation a resonant
bass voice rises into a great anthem taken up by the choir:
this unaccompanied voice has a curious effect of largeness and
distance and echo, even though the singer is seen in close-up.
British films of recent years have been finely scored by such
composers as William Alwyn (*The True Glory, The Way
Ahead, World of Plenty, Odd Man Out*), Clifford Bax (*Oliver
Twist*), Arthur Bliss (*Things to Come, Men of Two Worlds*),
Benjamin Britten (*Coal Face, Night Mail, Instruments of the
Orchestra*), Leighton Lucas (*Target for Tonight*), Clifton
Parker (*Western Approaches, Children on Trial*), Alan Raws-
thorne (*Burma Victory, Captive Heart*), William Walton
(*Next of Kin, First of the Few, Henry V, Hamlet*), Vaughan
Williams (*49th Parallel, Coastal Command, Joanna Godden*)
and John Ireland (*The Overlanders*). The music has been
magnificently recorded, mostly under the direction of Muir
Mathieson. It is undoubtedly true that the artistic quality
of British films has gained immeasurably by the use of
imaginative music composed especially for them in place of

using a pot-pourri of classical music torn from its emotional roots to serve other gods.

6. *Essentials of Film Art: Acting*

Film acting is fortunately a controversial subject. The first point of controversy has already been put by Pudovkin in a previous quotation dealing with the dictatorship of the director-editor. The actor is so much plastic material in the hands of the only man who knows how the film is to emerge from the studio to the projection room. On the other hand, how does this match up with the legend of Garbo and Dietrich? So much has to be disentangled from the blurb of publicity and the personal silence of most stars and directors.

The second point of controversy arises in the problem of whether the star is acting in the film, or whether the film is merely a vehicle for a star's peculiar and limited talent. The third issue turns on the colossal salaries earned by people without special acting talent but with an ability to look well and dress well in all situations.

The simplest issue is the last. Its social importance will be discussed later. Its importance to the present argument is merely to state once and for all its truth. A proportion of stars, but only a proportion, are good-lookers with or without clothes, and normal men and women will pay to go and see them because it is pleasant to see as much as you can of good-looking women and handsome men. There should be no controversy here on the matter of acting. These people are asked to parade through certain situations before making their bow and collecting their contract money, and they are sold by their publicity allocation as actors and actresses instead of highly paid exponents of beauty and clothes-wear. Their work is not relevant to any study of screen acting, but their existence is of great importance to a study of the social effect of the screen.

The first issue cannot be resolved in words. The relationship between director and actor in the film is far more complex than that between producer and actor on the stage. It is always pointed out, quite rightly, that the stage actor has a run for his money and that the film actor has not. The stage actor's work is progressive. He begins at the beginning and ends at the end. His sense of acting climax is never thwarted. Unless he is hopelessly sunk in his own part at the expense of his colleagues, he has almost as good a sense of the development of the play as a whole as his producer in front. The film actor has this sense of continuity in theory only, since he can never act his part through from beginning to end except in imagination, or over the conference table (if he is allowed there, as he may well never be). The director is the admitted co-ordinator of the actors' work, with the continuity girl killing the details. Shot topside up and sideways round, the actor is hurled from moment to moment in an order dictated by floorspace and technical considerations. After having died, he proceeds to live; after marriage, he starts in to earn his engagement, because the floorspace occupied by the church is required for another show. High-lit and howled at, he is the victim of James Dunne combined with all the surrealists, and it is small wonder that he earns enough in a year to keep him a life-time and retires as soon as possible to the order and calm of the divorce courts.

Pudovkin calls him plastic material, and it sounds true. But where are the signs of all this turmoil in the faces of Gabin, Fonda, Raimu, in the eyes of Bette Davis? How did Fonda ever get into pictures? Why do intelligent and sane stage actors like Donat appear in them when there is reasonably good money in the theatre?

The answer is compromise, skill and patience. The cinema is a hard industry seeking hard cash. Where money changes hands orders are given, and dismissal waits around the corner. But as against this, actors capable of imaginative survival of the racket are rare and hard to come by, and without them there would be no money to change in financiers' hands. So compromise ensues, and the stars themselves gain the power and influence to answer back to capital on their own account. They may also make friends with their producers.

The screen, like the stage, cannot let the technicians banish the temperament. But the stars must control their tempers to co-operate with the technicians. The true answer to the problem is that where there is co-operation and understanding between star, director and technicians there is greater likelihood of artistic achievement.

The secret of screen acting is the secret of the imaginative use of realism and of the quality of detail which accompanies the magnification of the screen. The Americans, the French and the Russians understood this well when they built up a tradition of film-acting. It requires imagination and great self-discipline of body and face to enact subjective feeling in terms of minute objective changes of expression and attitude. Yet this is what the real artists of cinema acting can do. They observe and reproduce the small things. The stage actor, working through space, observes and reproduces the larger movements. For people who like definitions to remember, it might be said that the stage actor, for the most part, acts in the major key, whilst the film actor, for the most part, plays in the minor. Both may effectively reverse the process to obtain certain given effects, but the main part of their work must be conceived in these ways.

This imaginative feeling for the details of expression which suggest character and emotion seems to be the essence of screen acting. Some actors can achieve their object through the careful development of technique. Others, as far as the screen is concerned, are so-called "naturals." This means that they possess naturally, without special technical development, qualities of bearing, voice and expression which fit them for acting in films. These natural actors often give a film verisimilitude (for example, the boy in *Children on Trial* or the sailor in *The Best Years of Our Lives*). But in either case, it is the detailed forms of expression which count.

To understand this one must watch for the details of acting technique. You will see them in the eyes and hips of Bette Davis, the face of Jouvet (whose body is nearly always stiff and still), and apparent expressionlessness of Raimu, whose body was part of his eloquence, the walk of Fonda and the poetic quality of his hesitant voice, the smile of Spencer Tracy, the differing sensuous qualities of face in Garbo and Dietrich (watch the lighting which accentuates this), the commonplace ease of Gabin. You will see these details in the sensitive, intense expression of Jean-Louis Barrault in *Les Enfants du Paradis,* in the signs of neurotic passion which are the strength of Agnes Moorehead's performance in *The Magnificent Ambersons.* You will see them in the curious eccentricities of facial expression and bodily movement with which Michel Simon presents his characters. And you will see them in the use of her eyes as Celia Johnson reveals the intensity of feeling of the heroine in

Brief Encounter, a part very different in kind from her magnificently reticent study of a housewife in *This Happy Breed.* It is difficult to tell where acting stops and the plastic properties of face and body begin. The great stars all have plastic faces, full of vitality however controlled, and with great photogenic qualities. Just so far the director is the master. Just so far the actor. The two main issues are complementary, after all.

There is one further point which requires its place in the argument. Men of the great acting quality of Laughton and Howard are often accused of being themselves at the expense of their parts. It must be recognised that, despite make-up and lighting, the range that a film-actor can cover is relatively less than that of the stage actor, where broader lines of make-up and bodily transformation can be assumed. A man is often chosen for his first lead because he has the right face and physique for the part: Laughton made his film name as Nero and Henry VIII; Alexander Knox as Wilson. Laughton passed through a series of parts for all of which his physique and remarkable face were of great plastic value. He has great versatility within his own range—Henry VIII, Rembrandt, Bligh, Ginger Ted, Ruggles, all different and yet the same photogenic Laughton mannerisms in all. The late Leslie Howard varied still less, but his audiences loved his quiet, superior, confident, kindly charm.

But there are a few actors and actresses whose work raises the issue as to what constitutes great acting anywhere, on stage or screen. It seems to be the power to bring convincing objective life in voice, face and body to any character with which their imagination can come to grips. The true appreciation of their work begins at the point where one is able to distinguish it from that of the merely brilliant or competent stars who have devoted their careers to the experience of playing themselves over and over again. This repetition is the commercial attribute of stardom. But it does not constitute great acting after the manner of the few who remain artists whatever part they play.

7. *The Film: Realism and Fantasy*

" But as soon as speech came in the cinema changed its character. It became, it is, and it remains realistic." (MAURICE JAUBERT.)

" The creative treatment of actuality." (GRIERSON.)

And so on. Everyone has said it sometime. And yet the film retains Disney, the Marx brothers, René Clair, Boris Karloff and many sights which ought not to be realistic even if they look it.

T. E. Hulme in his book " Speculations " has written that there is an eternal antagonism in all the arts between realism and formalism—the urge to make the arts look like life (realism) and the urge to make the arts look like art (formalism). Yet both of these different artistic attitudes are born of a like attitude to the chaos of experiences which is life itself. The realist looks at experience steadily and records it with a view to analysis in the process (later Greek sculpture, Leonardo da Vinci, much of Shakespeare, Goya, Balzac, Dostoevsky, Tolstoy, Joyce, Proust, the French, Russian and American film tradition). The formalist rejects actuality as such except in so far as he can create a permanent form of beauty from it which he may eternalise in the still processes of art and literature (early Greek, Etruscan and early medieval sculpture, much of Shakespeare, much Negro art, much Eastern art, much great music, the German silent cinema, the sets of art directors of many otherwise realistic films,[1] the symphonic element in Pudovkin and Eisenstein).

Hulme goes on to say that certain periods in civilisation prefer the one attitude to art, some the other. This is by main tendency only: civilisation cannot be bounded by the nutshell of a generality, and there is always a fellow in an attic or a dungeon doing the other thing to prove the historian wrong. Shakespeare did both with perfect ease: he was old-fashioned medievalist and Renaissance modernist at once and so gets the best of both worlds and pleases everybody prepared to be pleased at all.

Our present cycle of civilisation is realistic by tendency, but with a strong leaning to formalism to keep the realists awake. There is no date to give for the start of this cycle except to say it began before Shakespeare's time. The realist's urge (to see life steadily, to see it whole, to analyse society and the functions of mankind) began once more with the Renaissance. Against

---

[1] For instance, in a fine, tough, ultra-realistic racketeering film, *The Glass Key*, the art director allows a beautiful symphony of shadows on the wall when the faithful friend visits his political boss in a back room at the attorney's office, where he is held on suspicion of murder.

reactions spiced with romanticism, peppered with idealism, intoxicated by mysticism or stiffened by dogma, our divine curiosity has stood boldly for liberty of speech and enquiry from the voice of Milton to the voice of Shaw.

From the point of view of the subjects and treatment expected of films by the modern audience, the love of realism is undoubtedly the fundamental taste. However glamourised by the impossible, the audience expects the film it pays to see to bear a resemblance to the life it lives, or to be like its conception of the life it thinks the other fellow lives. The film of escape must always be the film of credible escape, and audiences look askance and a little lost when faced with films like the abstract sections of *Fantasia,* because these, however beautiful, belong to a world which rarely impinges on the breadwinner and his family.

The industrial revolution stole the last remnants of beauty out of formalised living. Life, never very clean, grew dirtier, and even the rich and leisured had to become aware of the dangers of another sort of revolution. The study of social welfare by the leisured class grew proportionately, and some positive achievements were contributed by the acts of social amelioration made in the Parliaments of the nineteenth century. Dickens wrote his novels just in time for the middle class to read them with a realistic eye.

The film took up the social theme early in its life. Barely twenty years after its start it was making *Birth of a Nation* and *Intolerance.* Both were three hours long. The first dealt with the racial problem in Southern American history. The second showed the spirit of Intolerance as an evil destroying the great achievements of mankind. Serious-minded people visited the pictures for the first time. This was something to be reckoned with.

Although the cinema has not wholly shirked its responsibility in showing the broader movements of history to the world, it prefers on the whole the more obvious attractions of a story and a personality. It produced in silent days the great French picture *La Passion de Jeanne d'Arc* as a serious contribution to history, but it is more likely to build up its historical personalities round those of the stars who play them. It is more fun to see Fonda as Abe Lincoln and Laughton as King Henry than to see a scholar's dummy. With history as entertainment, a long line of titles could be produced with the stars shining bright in historical circles.

For realism means real people, honest, four-square, lovable, hateful, unambiguous people. Personality, character, individuality, unusual careers, go-getting, living, loving and dying, these are the staple interests of a realistic age. Along with it comes an interest in occupations, jobs, social backgrounds. Films not about high society are usually about people with a definite occupational background, gangsters, actresses, barmen, dancers, shop-keepers, policemen, taxi-drivers, engine-drivers, soldiers, sailors, airmen, schoolmarms, nurses, doctors, miners, bankers, racketeers, businessmen, detectives, inventors, musicians and writers. Though the story may not much concern their occupations, none the less it is good to know the girl marries a man with a job. However foolish, melodramatic, dull or thrilling the action may be, realism is the order of the day from an audience's point of view.

This is not to deny that the film as a technical medium is suited to the fantastic. The most convincing dragon seen by human eye was probably the elaborate model in the German film *Siegfried* which lost its illusion only when its belly ripped like canvas against the warrior's sword. A film ghost is a guaranteed ghost since it is photographically a true one. The film can make all things credible, including traffic running backwards and cars running up walls. Harold Lloyd's film *Safety Last* was a success, not because everyone did not realise it was a trick, but because in spite of this it was so difficult not to believe in it.

The film has been a playground for fantasy from the start when Méliès of France went star-gazing on the moon. Ever since then ghosts and day-dreams, visions of pasteboard heavens and plaster hells have counteracted the steady stream of realism pouring out of the studios. On the whole it is a poverty-stricken mysticism—the sort of thing you cannot take a child to see because it is too like goblins in the dark. Mixed with a spurious religious content came films like *Dante's Inferno, The Four Horsemen of the Apocalypse, Earthbound,* and in more recent times the sort of thing that spoilt *The Great Mr. Handel.* With that dash of puerility which seems to lurk in the most sophisticated film executive, you may at any time find yourself affronted with the primitive visions of religious fantasy pronounced between telegrams into a dictaphone.

But the film remains the expert medium for fantasy—because it is so realistic. Seeing is believing even in *The Invisible Man*. The truer regions of fantasy lie not in the easy technique of superimposed images, but in the fantastic approach to life found in the films of Clair, the Marx brothers and Walt Disney.

The peculiar genius of Clair flourished only in his native France.

Hollywood occasionally produces the genuine fantasy in films like the delightful *Wizard of Oz* or the hilarious *Hellzapoppin*. One has always to distinguish between the high jinks or general tomfoolery and those genuine bursts of fantasy which may be found in many otherwise ordinary pictures, such as some of the dance numbers in *Cover Girl*. Some American comedies, especially those of Garson Kanin, Capra and Preston Sturges, all the time verge on fantasy, though their observation of life is essentially realistic. They exaggerate the absurdities of human behaviour and convention until we realise what a fantastic civilisation we have created to live in.

The peculiar gift of Chaplin to the cinema was two-fold, the supreme art of pantomime where he is approached only by the Marx brothers, and a humane vision which, like that of Griffith, derives from the nineteenth century. Apart from the moments of pantomime, which are always superbly conceived and timed, it is peculiar that one can more easily play one of his old two-reelers to a modern audience than one of Chaplin's greater films of feature length made after 1921. The old two- and three-reelers contained not only wonderful acrobatic and pantomimic shots made with superb economy and projected at great speed (*The Rink, The Cure* and the fights in *Easy Street*), but also imaginatively invented comic business (*The Pawn-Shop, Shoulder Arms*). As Chaplin matured his sense of comic fantasy retreated before the emotionalism of the little man who is downtrodden and rejected most of the time, an essentially old-fashioned conception of the sentimental tramp. This may lead to superb moments in the longer films from a dramatic point of view; for example, the scenes of pathos in *The Gold Rush, The Kid* or *The Circus*. But although this need in Chaplin to express his sympathy with the sentimental character he evolved

must be admired on humanitarian grounds, in the end it is the
insolent, fantastic character of the clown in the commedia del
arte tradition which is at the root of Chaplin's art. This character will never die or grow old-fashioned. The resource, the
ingenuity, the by-play with vice and virtue, the visual innuendoes
of Chaplin survive the old-fashioned sentimentalities found
alongside in *Modern Times* and *The Great Dictator*. These
resources are the products of a superb cinematic imagination.

René Clair began his film life at the age of twenty-five in 1923.
He mingled his interest in absurdity and the fantastic (*Entr'acte*
and *Paris qui dort*) with an interest in that early French experimental school called the *avant-garde*, which played around with
the camera and the scissors. It was perhaps peculiarly French
that the logic of the *reductio ad absurdum* of camera work
should be developed in France while the same studies in Russia
were directed to the ends of propaganda. The advantages of
the *avant-garde* movement were the advantages of freedom to
do what you liked as you looked for material to put through
the gate of the camera. The disadvantages were that the movement was experimental without direction, and on the whole
had little to say. Being experimental you had to stop that
way, and when you were short of ideas you made your material
interesting by shooting upside down or at an angle at which no
one could recognise what you were after.[1]

It is easy to criticise the *avant-garde* now, just as it is easy for
middle-age with cash to criticise the antics of youth without it.
It produced many fine directors for the sound period, and was
to the same immeasurable degree responsible, no doubt, for
the fine spirit of independence which was the glory of the best
French cinema until Fascism blacked it out from the screen,
and jack-booted so much of its genius to territories where it
could be free but no longer French.

Clair, nurtured in this different spirit of cinema, produced his
first distinguished film on French life in *The Italian Straw Hat*,
where he pillories the bourgeois eighteen-nineties with merciless

---

[1] The true workers in French experimental cinema will appreciate that
this is not a criticism of their endeavour to use the medium outside the
normal margins of contemporary technique, but rather of the merely
playboy approach to the camera which too many *avant-garde* films,
made both in France and elsewhere, have tended to show during the
past twenty years.

glee under the pretence of filming a farce by Labiche. *Sous les Toits de Paris* was one of the earliest of sound films, released in 1930, and shown rather later in England. With a memorable theme song, the first line of which was the title of the film (how memorable and emotionally apt these French theme songs are: I can still hum the tunes from *Sous les Toits*, *L'Atalante* and *Remous* after all these years), *Sous les Toits* was realism trans- figured into a world made by the imagination of René Clair, a bolt from the solid earth of the tenements back to the blue of joy and tears and laughter. There was an atmosphere of a totally different kind in the fight with knives in the misty light of the railway embankment: an early experimental use of sound. There was gay fantasy in *Le Million* with its background of the exaggerated passions of the opera-stages, a glorious setting for true-love, and the magnificent chase for the coat which ends up as a football match on the stage and in the wings of the theatre. (Did the Marx brothers see this before making *A Night at the Opera*?) Then follows the grimmer fantasy of *A Nous la Liberté* with the workers' lovely pasteboard paradise into which they escape from the ballet of the factory belt. This fantasy of mass production culminates in the collapse of social formality as the crowd breaks up to scramble for banknotes and dances hilariously through the factory in great streams of movement to a climax of music and montage. Clair has the heart of Chaplin and the social destructiveness of the Marx brothers combined. (Did Chaplin see *A Nous la Liberté* before making *Modern Times*?) *Le Quatorze Juillet*, a beautiful and restrained film, cannot be regarded as fantasy like its prede- cessors, and his last film before leaving France, *Le Dernier Milliardaire*, is more in the tradition of theatrical burlesque.

Clair next came to England and made *The Ghost Goes West*. This witty film seemed to mark a change of style. The films Clair had made in France had a delicacy of touch due to his intimate knowledge of the characters and the places he used in his stories. His fantasies and sentimentalities were all the more refreshing and the more touching because they were rooted in actual French life. *The Ghost Goes West* was a straight comedy-fantasy, a story adapted for the screen and no more than made by a famous French director working abroad. The film had not got similar roots with their delicate veins worked into the soil of Britain. Clair's subsequent films made in America are the same—unique, charming, clever, their humour sweet and never coarse, but without their roots bedded in American ground.

After the War Clair returned to France to make *Le Silence est d'Or*. This slender story of an elderly man-about-town and producer of silent films at the beginning of the century who succumbs once more to the fascination of falling in love with a young girl, was carefree and pretty, tender and human, and its comedy had a flash of the old René Clair working again in his own country.

Into a world of pomp and circumstance, the Marx brothers burst like a wind of relief. They represent all the things one was brought up not to do, but wanted to do. They take the place to pieces with steady glee. They dress like nothing on earth except that their clothes are recognisable in bits and pieces. Groucho wears a painted moustache which no one in the film dreams of querying; he moves with the assured insolence of a ballet dancer who cannot stop dancing off-stage. Every gesture is an act of impertinence; he makes love like a panther, and all women are his prey. He is the great charlatan who when he goes takes the door with him. He would take the kick off a horse.

Harpo is mad until you see he is sane. A harp softens him into a smile and a sense of the people around him. He is a musician who goes mad in his off-time. His wisecracks are gestures. Master of impulse, dressed like the Mad Hatter, he chases a girl before he can see her: he knows his type at psychic speed. Destructive, happy, unfailing and unflinching, he removes the wires from the piano and plays sweet music to please himself. And then he smiles at children and Negroes and simple people who can be happy as he is happy with a harp.

Chico is the nearest sanity. He stands in the middle between Harpo and Groucho and leads them on. He can play the piano and knows it. He has a mischievous finger on the keys which nobody trained but himself. If he had not existed in the Marx family, it would have been necessary to invent him. He keeps the peace and gives Groucho his lead into wisecracks. He looks like a man selling ice-cream at a funeral or betting-slips at a wedding. He could sell anything anytime anywhere.

Straight from music-hall to film, the Marx brothers do not

care a dime about the camera. They treat it like Margaret Dumont, though they know they cannot do without it. Groucho cracks the audience through it. They fill its frame with struggling bodies in a ship's cabin. They stick it in front of them while they wisecrack to each other or at their victims.

Their wisecracks are in the quickest American tradition, and leave the gangsters behind. After a time they let romance in through the back door in order to give the audience a rest. Even Marx brothers sleep and eat. But the romance leaves something to be desired.

Disney provided a folklore for the modern world. We are still a primitive people, but our fears and hopes follow a different line from the remaining races on the globe whom we call primitive to distinguish them from ourselves. Our fears are the rent-collector and the landlord, the job that is too complicated, machinery that goes wrong and clothes that are too tight, and the absence of money. Our hopes are the pretty girl and the cottage, a faithful dog, friendship, good food and good pay. Our metaphysics are the principle of evil which goes from the instinct to bully via Hitler to the big bad wolf himself, and to his partisans the looming spider and the fabulous witch. The average man in this world of good and evil is Mickey Mouse who knows a thing or two once he has been bitten. The lesser sins of sloth and boastfulness are in a dog and a duck. The wise expert on life, remote, watchful, helpful if you handle him right, is a crow or an owl or a cricket. The whole thing is common sense, common decency and a weather-eye on the world at large.

Into this simple philosophy of things, Disney brought a wealth of technical virtuosity and rhythmic dexterity. His timing is unique. So is his sense of sound, which is used for every conceivable comic effect. Because of the relative flatness of his earlier images he was the first director to use colour with effect. His film factory is shown with all its elaboration in *The Reluctant Dragon* and described in detail in Professor Feild's excellent book on Disney. It is amazing that Disney's simple philosophy, which is everyman's philosophy, survived this astonishing mass production, with its graded artists and technical elaboration. Perhaps it was for a time symptomatic of a better world to come in a machine age.

Disney's later films have unfortunately lost much of this appeal. They have ceased to be folklore for a troubled world and have become displays in pyrotechnics. The sentimentality present in his early work, which was acceptable like that of Griffith and Chaplin in a different context, has now become banal. Although many of the cartoons have been vulgar and unimaginative, their technical virtuosity has developed to a point of mechanical perfection which makes them a miracle of calculation. If anyone breaks into the third dimension commercially it ought by the logic of events to be Disney.

Disney's films are not made for children. The people who objected that the witch in *Snow White* was unsuitable were probably frightened themselves. Fright and terror exist in this world, whether under gangsters' lights or fascists' whips. These things are terrible, and there are corresponding experiences in Disney's folklore. In an early Disney a huge black spider crawls with beastly lust over a little dwarfed town. The Soviet war posters represented Hitler this way.

Many of Disney's one-reelers, and much of *Fantasia,* are just a technical *tour de force,* but Disney once knew when to stop and let humanity in. He knew that a man likes to take his watch to bits to see how it works, but he also knew that the same man would rather have his watch going when he sets out to meet his girl. Audiences love the huge swirling movements, the lovely coloured distortions, the fantastic reductions of the animal body to absurdity, the plops and bangs and whangings of anthropomorphised machinery. They love the rhythmic give and take between sound and image. It is all great fun with a technical medium which seems to put no stop to the acrobatics of sight and sound. But Disney's greatest achievement still remains his creation of a people's folklore, not untainted with sentimentality, but full of laughter and energy and defeat of the devil. The wheels of the imagination ran backwards to a standstill when the news came on the screen after the Disney.

The movie camera lends itself to puppets and moving cut-outs. Most audiences have seen Georg Pal's puppets, if only when they advertised Philips' Radio or Ovaltine. They are no more than pleasant and amusing. With an altogether more delicate technique Lotte Reiniger cut out her paper figures and added depth to their antics by filming their backgrounds through shelves of glass. Disney also employs different levels of background to get the exceptional qualities of perspective seen in films like *Fantasia,* using a special multiplane camera. Lotte Reiniger made films of baroque silhouette; the figures bob and dance in attractive patterns.

A single film stands out as a work of art in the medium of the serious drawn film: this is *L'Idée,* by Berthold Bartosch with music by Honegger, a film little seen in this country because of its left-wing political idealism and its attack on capital and clericalism. It plays about half an hour, and is a moving experience which can be seen and reseen both for its action and for its magnificent draughtsmanship.

L'IDEE: (Scenario, Direction, Photography, Berthold Bartosch. France, 1930–34.   Based on Woodcuts by Frans Masereel.
Music by Arthur Honegger.)

Theme: The rich and powerful fear the aspect of truth. They buy the Church and Courts of Justice to enslave truth and rob it of its uncompromising nakedness. Even the poor reject truth in the blindness of their slavery, though the cause of truth is theirs.

Treatment: Truth is represented as a nude woman, the Idea which comes to every creative artist. The film begins with flowing revolving nebulæ from which is born the naked luminous figure of the woman. A worker receives her in diminished form, and carries her in an envelope as a message to the capitalist figures, who fall away shocked even at her diminutive nakedness. They clothe her. She is judged by an Ecclesiastical Court, who examine her only to clothe her again. She passes through the city in search of her interpreter, crossing over the old Pont-Neuf-like bridge of tradition and wealth to the iron bridge symbolic of industrialism. She meets the worker once more. Against an industrialised background of smoke and furnace she addresses the workers through her interpreter. He is arrested, and tried with only the Figure as his protector and guide. He is executed. The workers carry him with long jerky movements in a rough coffin to his grave, where he is interred with only the luminous Figure of Truth to watch over him. A professor attempts to measure her, but she bursts the bonds his theory would impose upon her. Then she finds her medium in the workers' Press. A capitalist wonders how to enslave her: he hopes to buy the Church. He squeezes coins from the dwarf workers in his grasp: but explosions and harsh music result. The march of soldiers counter-flows against the march of workers. Over the soldiers moves the symbol of money: Truth moves over the advancing workers. They clash. The workers die to harsh high music. Like Venus Aphrodite, Truth rises from the blood and slain flesh of the people, and the march of the soldiers counter-flows with the funeral march of the coffined dead. The symbol of the Church debased by money fades before the fiery outline of Truth itself, which merges back once more into the flowing revolving nebulæ of ultimate being.

All these pictures are off the main stream of realistic cinema. About seven hundred feature-length films were released in this country each year between 1935 and the war. Of these not half a dozen could be classified as fantasy in the proper sense of that term. Though most films are films of escape, they are not presented as fantasies, and other problems arise as to their effect on their audiences. These problems will occupy us in the second part of this book.

8. *Documentary*

The medium of the film, like the medium of writing, is so wide in its possibilities of expression that it cannot be classified except very loosely. A relative division into three categories might be made as follows:

(1) The use of motion photography for record purposes.
(2) The use of motion photography for "the creative treatment of actuality."
(3) The use of motion photography for the creation of film fiction.

The term Documentary is often used for all types of film which come within the first two categories, ranging from the newsreel proper to documentary proper in the form of *Western Approaches* or *The World of Plenty*. In between these extremes lie first the simple *Record Films* of scientific experiments (Dr. Doyen's films of surgical operations made as early as 1910 and Dr. R. G. Canti's on the cultivation of living tissues made from

1924 onwards), or films like Herbert Ponting's *With Scott in the Antarctic* (1910–13), and the many films up to the present day which do little more than show a process from the ideal point of view for the spectator (for example, the lung-operation sequence in the British Council's *Surgery in Chest Disease*). Then there are *Instructional Films* which aim at explaining a process so that the audience may learn it for themselves: the training films for the Services and for Civil Defence during the War are examples. They are quite distinct from *Educational Films* made for classroom instruction and demonstration: these are often silent so that the teacher and class can discuss the significance of the moving picture whilst it moves: the concern of the educational film is to provide the teacher with a further aid to demonstration in those subjects where movement in a pictorial form is useful: geography, biology, science, civics, and so on. There is also the *Propaganda Film*: this should induce an emotional impetus which leads to action helpful to the cause from which the propaganda originates, for example, the *Why we Fight* series prepared by Frank Capra for the American servicemen, the Russian atrocity film *Justice is Coming*, films like *Britain can take it*, and Rotha's powerful advocacies for world sanity in food production *The World of Plenty* and *The World is Rich*. The Nazis themselves developed the editing of record films into weapons of war in their propaganda campaign against Europe: they made a film of the defeat of Poland before the might of the Luftwaffe called *Baptism of Fire:* this was exhibited to the officials and where possible the public of the then neutral surrounding countries as a terrible warning against incurring the wrath of Germany. Propaganda can be political, but it can also be an attempt to promote action in any group of people from whom action is needed in matters of health, housing, food, personal safety or service to the community. Where the picture does not lead to immediate personal action, it becomes the *Information Film* of which so many were made in Britain by the documentary movement during and since the War.

All these types of film, except possibly the newsreel itself which dates back to the earliest films known in 1895 and 1896, have been included in the term Documentary, which was adapted by John Grierson from the French word *documentaire* used to describe the travel pictures which were popular in French cinema. It seems to Grierson, writing in the late twenties, a good word to use of Flaherty's films, which, apart from a very few other factual films, were the first notable films of this class to be made. Some other important films of this type had been:

Herbert Ponting: With Scott in the Antarctic. Great Britain, 1913.

J. B. MacDowell and Geoffrey Malin: The Battle of the Somme. Great Britain, 1916; and other War films.

H. Bruce Woolfe and Percy Smith: The Secrets of Nature Series. Great Britain, 1919 onwards.

Dr. R. G. Canti's films on the cultivation of Living Tissue. Great Britain, 1924 onwards.

Schoedsack and Cooper: Grass. U.S.A., 1925.

Leon Poirier: Eve Africaine. France, 1925.

Marc Allegret and André Gide: Voyage au Congo. France, 1925.

Cavalcanti: Rien que les Heures. France, 1926.

W. Ruttmann: Berlin. Germany, 1927.

The newsreel itself started with the first films of Lumière in 1895. After many reels had been shot of particular events (such as Queen Victoria's Diamond Jubilee in 1897 and her funeral in 1901) the regular issue of weekly newsreels was started by Charles Pathé in 1910. These films were of commercial origin and newsreels remain so to this day. The five newsreels of Britain are now (excluding the special B.B.C. newsreel service for television):

Universal News.

Gaumont-British News.

Both these are made by companies under the control of the Rank organisation.

Pathé News.

Made by Associated British and Warner Brothers, a joint British and American company with French affiliations.

British Movietone News.

Made by Twentieth Century Fox (American).

British Paramount News.

Made by Paramount Pictures (American).

The newsreels before the War were mostly dull records of dull events; their fascination lay in their actuality and the speed with which the event in the newspaper was produced again in front of the spectator, who now had a grand-stand view of the Great for the first time in his life. Until the recent War newsreels were scarcely more than strips glued together in chronological order, united only by the vividness of the commentary. Military reviews, society weddings and horse-racing were the staple items, with a dash of royalty. During the War, partly by the fine efforts of their staff cameramen and the liberal provision of Service material, the newsreels became eloquent visual records of notable war events. No one present will forget the scenes on the cinema-screen as Europe was gradually liberated, and the emotion felt by British audiences. Now that peace has made the social problems of the world of the greatest importance most newsreels have slipped back into the easy channel of the race-meeting, the football-match and any other event which avoids controversial issues but which has popular surface appeal.

The Westerns from the earliest days shot more or less real cowboys in the bright American sun, but only for reasons of fiction. It was Robert Flaherty, an explorer using films, who took the camera to real life for real life's sake. The Revillon Frères Fur Company of New York sponsored his *Nanook of the North*. This was in 1922. Paul Rotha writes of this film:

" *Nanook* differed from previous and many later naturalmaterial pictures in the simplicity of its statement of the primitive existence led by the Eskimos, put on the screen with excellent photography (before the days of panchromatic emulsion) and with an imaginative understanding behind the use of the camera. It brought alive the fundamental issue of life in the sub-Arctic—the struggle for food —with such imaginatively chosen shots and with such a sincere feeling for the community interests of these people that it suggested far greater powers of observation than the plain description offered by other naturalistic photographers. Not merely did it reveal the daily struggle for life maintained by the Eskimo people, but it demonstrated that the progress of civilisation depends upon man's growing ability to make Nature serve a purpose and by his own skill to bind natural resources to his own ends. The screen has probably no more simply treated yet brilliantly instructive sequence than that in which Nanook builds his igloo. In short, it established an entirely new approach to the living scene, forming the basis for a method of working which Flaherty has since developed." (PAUL ROTHA, "Documentary Film," pp. 81–2.)

And John Grierson writes:

" *Nanook* was the simple story of an Eskimo family and its fight for food, but in its approach to the whole question of film making was something entirely novel at the time it was made. It was a record of everyday life so selective in its detail and sequence, so intimate in its ' shots,' and so appreciative of the nuances of common feeling, that it was a drama in many ways more telling than anything that had come out of the manufactured sets of Hollywood." (JOHN GRIERSON, " Cinema Quarterly," No. 1, pp. 13–14.)

Flaherty is a great film-maker in his chosen sphere. He has never ceased to be an anthropologist and explorer, and because he sought for his material in distant or romantic places he has often been unfairly criticised as escapist by documentary producers whose main subject-matter has been the social problems to be found at home. But in *The Land* Flaherty made as powerful a documentary about soil erosion in America as any of the social realists could have done.

Nanook was a commercial success. From then on till *Man of Aran* Flaherty suffered for his fame. Sent to the South Seas by the trade, he came back with *Moana* after two years' hard work studying and shooting his material. The film is a study of the ceremonial ritual of pain, the tattoo, inflicted to prove native manhood. The trade released it, writes Rotha, " as the love-life of a South Sea siren, prologued by stripped chorus girls and jangling guitars." After a number of further troubles Flaherty made *Tabu* in the South Seas with Murnau; but was dissatisfied enough to come to Europe after it was finished. In 1934 he made *Man of Aran* for Gaumont-British, and in 1939 *The Land* in America. In 1948 he completed *Louisiana Story*.

The importance of Flaherty to documentary proper is that he was the first film-maker to carry out Grierson's precept, " the creative treatment of actuality." The difference between a newsreel and *Nanook* is that the newsreel is a record of reality, whereas *Nanook* is an interpretation. Flaherty lived with his subjects before he photographed them. He worked with them, studying their ways of life and thought. He watched the struggle with Nature, the fulfilment of tradition, the skill of the craftsman, the rhythm of simple age-long movements. Then he shot what he had seen, unrolling vast quantities of negative in the process, like Eisenstein in Mexico. Then he cut and built his film, using only a fraction of what he had shot so that his observation and its interpretation should be of the best. He was a craftsman studying craftsmen: a romantic recording the great theme of mankind and Nature.

Grierson, however, was concerned with the people around him. He was a young man who had taken a degree in Philosophy at Glasgow University after spending most of the 1914 war on auxiliary patrol and minesweeping in the Navy. He returned to England in 1927 after studying Public Relations for three years in America on a Rockefeller Research Fellowship in Social Science. He joined the staff of the Empire Marketing Board, whose Secretary was Stephen Tallents (now Sir Stephen Tallents), himself one of the most brilliant students of the practice of public relations of the period. Grierson made his first film *Drifters* (1929) very much under the influence of Russian technique with its montage of superimposed shots of, for example, the ship's engines turning over and the swing of the stoker's shovel. *Drifters* demonstrated an important principle: it showed the life of one section of the community (the herring fishers) to the rest. It did not merely record that life as an "interest" short might have done: it set out to re-create the whole pattern of work on the drifters, and the significance of the fishermen's service to the community and their dealings with it when they came to sell their fish after landing the catch.

Grierson worked for the Empire Marketing Board until its dissolution in 1933. He then followed Tallents to the G.P.O., where the famous Unit was founded which developed later into the Crown Film Unit of the Ministry of Information. The Board, however, made many notable films with Grierson as producer. Some of these were

The Country comes to Town (Basil Wright, 1931–2).
O'er Hill and Dale (Basil Wright, 1932).
Windmill in Barbados (Basil Wright, 1933).

Cargo from Jamaica (Basil Wright, 1933).
Industrial Britain (Grierson and Flaherty, 1933).
Granton Trawler (Edgar Anstey, 1934).
Aero-Engine (Arthur Elton, 1934).

Parallel to the work of the Government Units, though perhaps it would be fairer to say developing from that work, was the enlightened sponsorship of film production by industries such as Gas and Oil. The whole idea of public relations as exemplified by film production spread until Imperial Airways, the Travel Association, the Films of Scotland Committee, the Ceylon Tea Propaganda Board, and some British Government Departments were all sponsoring films. Among these were:

Contact (Paul Rotha, 1932).
Song of Ceylon (Basil Wright, 1935).
Housing Problems (Arthur Elton and Edgar Anstey, 1935).
Workers and Jobs (Arthur Elton, 1935).
Enough to Eat (Edgar Anstey, 1936).
From Cover to Cover (Alexander Shaw, 1936).
The Smoke Menace (John Taylor, 1937).
Today we Live (Ruby I. Grierson, 1937).
Children at School (Basil Wright, 1937).
Spanish ABC (Thorold Dickinson, 1938).
The Londoners (John Taylor, 1938).
Dawn of Iran (John Taylor, 1938).
The Face of Scotland (Basil Wright, 1938).
Four Faces (Alexander Shaw, 1938).
Wealth of a Nation (Donald Alexander, 1938).

Gaumont-British Instructional (founded 1933: previously British Instructional Films) made important contributions under the enlightened leadership of Bruce Woolfe, Percy Smith and Mary Field, notably in the *Secrets of Life* series. They specialised in educational films, but also produced many documentaries such as:

The Mine (J. B. Holmes, 1935).
Citizen of the Future (Donald Taylor, 1935).
The Face of Britain (Paul Rotha, 1935).
Shipyard (Paul Rotha, 1935).
Medieval Village (J. B. Holmes, 1936).
The Gap (Donald Carter, 1937).

This was England (Mary Field, 1938).

They made the Land (Mary Field, 1938).

The G.P.O. Film Unit (later Crown Film Unit 1940) had Grierson as Supervising Producer until 1937. It is now controlled directly by the C.O.I., with Donald Taylor in charge of production. The old G.P.O. Film Unit made films notable for their experimental quality, to which Cavalcanti contributed much after his arrival in Britain as guest producer at the invitation of Grierson. Before the War they made such films as:

6.30 Collection (Edgar Anstey, 1934).

Under the City (Arthur Elton and Alexander Shaw, 1934).

Weather Forecast (Evelyn Spice, 1934).

Airmail (Arthur Elton and Alexander Shaw, 1935).

B.B.C.—The Voice of Britain (Stuart Legg, 1935).

Coalface (Grierson, Cavalcanti, Auden, 1935).

Night Mail (Watt, Wright, Cavalcanti, 1936).

We Live in Two Worlds (Cavalcanti, 1937).

North Sea (Harry Watt, 1938).

Other independent and private Units were founded to deal with the increasing demand for documentary film productions: Strand (founded by Donald Taylor and Ralph Keene in 1936) and Realist (founded by Basil Wright in 1937). These were in addition to Gaumont-British Instructional and the Shell Film Unit, which were sponsored Units. Edgar Anstey took charge initially of the Shell Film Unit (1934), which was later supervised for the Asiatic Petroleum Company by Film Centre, itself founded in 1937 as a consultative organisation on the production and distribution of documentary.

From this considerable body of activity a new profession grew up in the film world, and nearly three hundred films were made which were the expression of a new school of film-making. The names of the leading documentary producers and directors became well known, John Grierson, Cavalcanti, Paul Rotha, Basil Wright, Arthur Elton, Edgar Anstey, Ralph Keene, Harry Watt, Stuart Legg and many others. The types of film they made within the field of documentary varied considerably: there was the lyrical beauty of *Song of Ceylon,* the dynamic impressionism of *Shipyard,* the realistic social awareness and directness of approach of *Housing Problems,* the analytic presentation of social problems of *Enough to Eat,* the careful descriptive quality of *6.30 Collection*, the panoramic survey of *Face of Britain* and the scientific breakdown of the subjects explained in the Shell Film Unit's pictures. The men and the subjects created the approach and the style. Within the G.P.O. Unit " experiment " was the watchword, and this ranged from the colour abstracts of Len Lye and the sound tracks of Cavalcanti, Auden and Britten, to the comic fantasy of *Pett and Pott*.

Drifters stands out not merely as Grierson's personal film, but as the first example of the British school of documentary. He made *Drifters,* as Rotha puts it, " on a shoestring . . . ; it humbly brought to the screen the labour of the North Sea herring catch from such an approach that the ordinary person was made to realise, probably for the first time, that a herring on his plate was no mere accepted thing but the result of other men's physical toil and possibly courage. It ' brought alive ' (an E.M.B. phrase) not just the routine of the catch but the whole drama of emotional values that underlay the task, interpreting in its stride the unconscious beauty of physical labour in the face of work done for a livelihood. Moreover, there were brought to the conception all the poetic qualities of ships, sea and weather. In other words, Grierson took a simple theme (there for the taking), took actually existing material (there for the shooting), and built a dramatised film by interpreting the relationships of his theme and material in the sphere of daily existence.

" Leaving style and technique apart, *Drifters* laid the foundation for documentary in this country. Maybe it lacked a full expression of social purpose. Powers of production limited that. But it was inspired by a greater aim than mere description or superficial observation. It was inspired by a sincere understanding of the labour of man and the poetry of the sea. Beyond that, it served, and served well, a purpose beyond itself."

Certain documentaries from *Drifters* to *World of Plenty* have always stood out for their æsthetic and technical brilliance. Among those made pre-war films like *Song of Ceylon, Contact, Shipyard, Night Mail* and *Coalface* were outstanding.

SONG OF CEYLON: (Production, Ceylon Tea
British, 1934.   Propaganda Board.
                                    Director, Basil Wright,
                               assisted by John Taylor)

Song of Ceylon, the closest British documentary has
come to creating a film-poem of great lyrical beauty, is
divided into four parts, *The Buddha, The Virgin Island, Voices
of Commerce* and *Apparel of the God*.[1] Throughout the film
the director-cameraman (Basil Wright was his own photographer) worked in close co-operation with the composer, the
late Walter Leigh, who directed its recording. A troupe of
Sinhalese dancers and drummers came over from Ceylon to
assist in the work of post-synchronisation. The commentary
has an other-worldly dignity as delivered by Lionel Wendt
from descriptions of life in Ceylon written in the seventeenth
century by Robert Knox.

The structure of the film is imagistic; its theme of the religious and artistic tradition and mysterious beauty of the island
as they appear to Western eyes is conveyed, not by direct
statement, but by the accumulation of images, words and
music gathered for their emotional values by the poet-film-
maker. In the first part, which shows the pilgrimage to
Adam's Peak, occurs the beautiful image of the bells and the
bird, which I have described elsewhere as follows: "A procession is seen climbing a mountain-path to take part in a

---

[1] A correspondent from Ceylon points out that the film implies that
the Buddha is a god, whilst he was in fact an inspired teacher founding
a religion. Another point of criticism is also made of the nature of the
singing in the first part of the film: this section of the letter is interesting for its description of the pilgrimage which forms the main subject of
this part called *The Buddha*: " Another point is the singing on the top
of Adam's Peak. Buddha was supposed to leave his footmark on the
top of the mountain, and there is a flat slab with a footmark scratched
on by artificial means. I was amazed when I heard the tunes that were
sung by the people in the film as they walked round the shrine at the
top. In the first place, that is not done. People do not go round singing. In fact, there is no singing at all on top. The only sound is the
shout of ' Sadhu, Sadhu,' as the sun's rays strike over the horizon and
cast the peak's shadow in a purple cone on the western sky.

" Climbing up the Peak is a stiff business, and people sing about the
merit they will get for making the pilgrimage. A leader usually has
verses on a paper which he sings first and the followers take it up after
him. The tunes consist of three or four notes only. They sing to ask
Saman Devi, the goddess of the mountain, to help them to climb."

Buddhistic ritual. The sense of growing anticipation is intensified by the voices of the climbers, by the atmospheric music, by the sight of the older people resting on the way while a reader prepares them for worship, and the voice we hear recites in English the beautiful words of praise of the Buddha. When dawn comes we are high up in the mountain, and the people are singing. The singing strengthens in feeling, and the impression of a rising excitement increases. The great image of the Buddha is constantly seen, and a series of bell-notes begins to echo down the mountain-side with rising intensity. The bells combine into a varied music of their own, and a bird is startled into flight over the water, the camera following it until the images of the bird, the Buddha, the mountain-side, the water and the trees are combined together, and the resonance of the rising bell-notes sounded at intervals culminates in a feeling of ecstasy and worship " (" Experiment in the Film," p. 46).

In the last part there is to be found a beautifully handled sequence of a peasant's presentation of rice to the huge reclining Buddha, and it ends with the ringing climax of a masked dance to cymbal and drum.

In a different manner Paul Rotha was learning by means of experiment the difficult technical craft of the new sound film. By training a painter and designer, it was natural that the visual qualities of the silent film, which as a very young critic he had so eloquently praised in the first edition of his book "The Film till Now," should absorb his attention when he started on his career as a creative artist with films like *Contact*, *Rising Tide*, *Shipyard* and *The Face of Britain*. The photography of these films was outstanding: they were carefully cut (often to excess) in order to achieve the maximum possible effects in mobile composition. *Contact* was made for Imperial Airways, and in " Cinema Quarterly " (Spring, 1933) Rotha describes the vivid experiences, almost entirely visual, which excited him while making this film on the African and Indian air routes. *Rising Tide* was concerned with the construction of a dock at Southampton and its effect on the economic life of the country, which at that period was oppressed by the problems of unemployment. In it Rotha showed his desire to put theory into practice and relate his film to the social problems of his time. Grierson, in a critique of the film, complains that this social theme is not firmly resolved, and also that it is still dominated technically by treatment in which the advantages of sound are insufficiently appreciated. *Shipyard* was probably the finest of Rotha's early films: it records the construction of the "Orion" at Barrow-in-Furness, with a magnificent use of natural sound and a firmer relationship between the purely constructional side of ship-building and the life and outlook of the men who worked in what was then a precarious trade.

Two films made by the G.P.O. Film Unit, *Coalface* and *Night Mail*, were also experiments in the use of sound. *Night Mail* is still an important film, with its build-up to the delivery of the postal bags in the trap-net tense with drama, its wonderful dawn shots a final confirmation that trains moving at a distance are definitely part of the beauty of the countryside. But its sound, devised and recorded under the supervision of Cavalcanti, was considered its main feature. Trains make a comforting range of noises, and have their own rhythms, from the crescendo of buffers in shunting to the hypnotic rhythms of wheels on metals at speed. The casual remarks of sorters and railwaymen were used as natural sound. The poet W. H. Auden (experimenter in word-rhythm) contributed a letter-poem which ta-ta-ta-taad in time with the wheels of the train.

> " *Past cotton grass and moorland boulder,*
> *Shovelling white steam over her shoulder,*
> *Snorting noisily as she passes*
> *Silent miles of windswept grasses,*
> *Birds turn their heads as she approaches,*
> *Stare from the bushes at her blankfaced coaches.*
> *Sheepdogs cannot turn her course,*
> *They slumber on with paws across.*
> *In the farm she passes no one wakes*
> *But a jug in the bedroom gently shakes.*"

The whole thing was excitement and romance, with glimpses of men working in the sorting cars, shunting boxes and stations on the way.

Coalface (directed by Cavalcanti) was an oratorio of mining, and oratorios are not popular with film-goers. The visuals were good, but not exceptional. What mattered was the sound, which with Grierson as producer was recorded under the supervision of Cavalcanti by William Coldstream, Stuart Legg and Benjamin Britten. The usual method of speaking commentary to a background of music was avoided; both commentary and music were composed together. The effect was to incorporate commentary more clearly in the body of the film. To this foreground of sound were added a recitative chorus of male voices and a choir of male and female voices. The recitative chorus was used to fill out, by suggestion, the direct statement of the commentary. The choir was used to create atmosphere. This poem, sung by the female voices on the return of the miners to the surface, was written for the film by W. H. Auden:

> " *O lurcher-loving collier black as night,*
> *Follow your love across the smokeless hill,*
> *Your lamp is out and all your cages still.*
> *Course for her heart and do not miss*
> *And Kate fly not so fast,*
> *For Sunday soon is past,*
> *And Monday comes when none may kiss.*
> *Be marble to his soot and to his black be white."*

An important branch of pre-war documentary was the group of films sponsored by the British Commercial Gas Association, which became the most liberal of commercial producers in the range of social problems that were discussed in its films such as *Housing Problems, Children at School, The Smoke Menace* and *Enough to Eat* (the latter sponsored by the London Gas, Light and Coke Company). *Housing Problems* took the camera and microphone to Stepney and recorded the slum-dwellers' views on the slums: spot interviews, unrehearsed and unscripted, are the feature of the first part of the film, supplemented by remarkably revealing shots of slum property for comfortably housed citizens to contemplate on the screen. *Children at School* was very blunt about the bad schools of Britain: it showed teachers doing their job in the most appalling of conditions. Both films made a pointed contrast between what had been and what could be done to better the bad conditions they exposed. *The Smoke Menace* showed what was happening to our cities under the pall of smoke cloud thrown up by the chimneys. *Enough to Eat* analysed the diet of the nation and revealed the lack of public knowledge on elementary points of food values and the malnutrition due to mis-spending or being unable to spend on food: it is the prelude to Rotha's later film *The World of Plenty*, and like it made liberal use of animated diagrams and interviews with expert and public alike. These films did not aim at being beautiful: experiment lay in the realistic treatment of new subjects for the screen and the technique with which their importance could be emphasised to the audience. For this reason they were of greater long-term importance than the more beautiful and impressionistic films made alongside them which had their own, though different, place in the full range of British documentary achievement.

Earlier Documentary Theory.—The documentary directors were and are always ready to talk and write about their films. Their job has made them mix with everybody on equal terms, intellectuals, workers and business executives. It is a relief to find people in films who are not so terrified of discussion and criticism that they jump into legal proceedings to defend their films from critical evaluation.

The forum of discussion was first " Cinema Quarterly " (edited in Edinburgh by Forsyth Hardy and Norman Wilson, 1932–35), second " World Film News " which became " See," and is now to be found in " Documentary News." The chief writers among documentary film-makers are Paul Rotha (who is a distinguished film historian as well as an important director and producer), John Grierson, and latterly Basil Wright and Edgar Anstey. Their writings include some of the best film journalism of the thirties and early forties. Their work made them at once alive to what was going on in the world and keen to analyse it in film terms. This was good training for journalism. Because they made films they wrote only when they wanted to and because they had something to say to a critical and knowledgeable minority.

Grierson announced his initial principles in 1932 in " Cinema Quarterly " (Winter 1932):

" First principles. (1) We believe that the cinema's capacity for getting around, for observing and selecting from life itself, can be exploited in a new and vital art form. The studio films largely ignore this possibility of opening up the screen on the real world. They photograph acted stories against artificial backgrounds. Documentary would photograph the living scene and the living story. (2) We believe that the original (or native) actor, and the original (or native) scene, are better guides to a screen interpretation of the modern world. They give cinema a greater fund of material. They give it power over a million and one movements, and power over a million and one images. They give it power of interpretation over more complex and astonishing happenings in the real world than the studio mind can conjure up or the studio mechanician re-create. (3) We believe that the materials and the stories thus taken from the raw can be finer (more real in the philosophic sense) than the acted article. Spontaneous gesture has a special value on the screen. Cinema has a sensational capacity for enhancing the movement which tradition has formed or time worn smooth. Its arbitrary rectangle specially reveals movement; it gives it maximum pattern in space and time. Add to this that documentary can achieve an intimacy of knowledge and effect impossible to the shimsham mechanics of the studio, and the lily-fingered interpretations of the metropolitan actor " (p. 69).

Whilst admiring the symphonics of Ruttman in *Berlin* and the romantic feeling for traditional craftsmanship and custom in Flaherty, Grierson knew that he needed to use the documentary film essentially for social and educational purposes. He speaks of the beliefs of his colleagues which he shared and largely inspired:

" They believe that beauty will come in good time to inhabit the statement which is honest and lucid and deeply felt and which fulfils the best ends of citizenship. They are sensible enough to conceive of art as the by-product (the over-tone) of a job of work done. The opposite attempt to capture the by-product first (the self-conscious pursuit of beauty, the pursuit of art for art's sake to the exclusion of jobs of work and other pedestrian beginnings), was always a reflection of selfish wealth, selfish leisure and æsthetic decadence." ("Cinema Quarterly," Spring 1933, p. 137.)

Two years later he underlines the analytical tendencies of these young directors:

" Many of us, brought up in the post-impressionist revolt, have made structure our god. ' Observe and analyse,' ' Know and build,' ' Out of research poetry comes,' were the slogans we set before us. They suited the academic and the radical in our minds. They brought us more readily to the new material of our times.

" I have watched with some closeness the working of these influences in the films of Wright, Elton and Legg. All are painstakingly and rather proudly academic. When they shoot a factory, say, they learn how to ask the right questions. Elton, for example, knows more than a little about railways and mechanics; Wright has mastered the history of every subject he has touched; and I will swear that Legg knows more about the organisation of the B.B.C. than any outsider decently should.

" The only point at which art is concerned with information is the point at which ' the flame shoots up and the light kindles and it enters into the soul and feeds itself there.' Flash-point there must be. Information indeed can be a dangerous business if the kindling process is not there. Most professors are a dreary warning of what happens when the informationist fails to become a poet." (" Cinema Quarterly," Summer 1935, p. 195.)

Paul Rotha pursued a different line from Grierson. In those earlier days up to 1935 it might be fair to say that Grierson's directors were interested more in the demonstration of industrial processes than in their social problems, whereas Rotha was becoming increasingly interested in the propaganda potentialities of the film. He writes in 1935 in " Documentary Film ":

" In brief there exists to-day, on the one hand, an urgent need for the stimulation of wide interest among the public in matters of national and international significance, and, on the other, a gradual ripening of social consciousness among a small but increasing minority. There is no question, however, that if the future development of civilisation is to proceed with any prospect of security and social progress, a great deal must be done to spread knowledge about the simple workings of government and the essential facts of our economic and social ways and means " (pp. 38–9).

He was becoming interested in the social system underlying the working of the processes Grierson was presenting with such artistic vigour. He resented the way the film industry avoided subjects of social importance and chose to present life in the false colours of romance at a period of intense upheaval and change in political values. For it must not be forgotten that documentary was beginning when Hitler knuckledusted his way into the Chancellery of Germany.

The film must teach while there is time to learn; it must line up with the propaganda of healthy social progress:

> " Now it is very obvious that, by reason of virtues inherent in its form, cinema is one of the most powerful channels of expression for persuasion and public illumination. Its peculiar suitabilities as an instrument of propaganda are almost too patent to specify. In brief, it possesses:

> " (1) An introduction to the public shared only by the radio, with a resultant power of mass suggestion.

> " (2) Simple powers of explanation and capacities for making statements which, if presented with a craftsmanship that takes full advantage of artistic values, are capable of persuasive qualities without equal, and

> " (3) Virtues of mechanised repeated performance to a million persons, not once but countless times a day, tomorrow and, if the quality is good enough, ten years hence " (p. 49).

The artist, instead of being sunk in the expression of his own selfish æstheticism, can, through the film, come out into the sun where life lies around him. False individualism must end:

> " In this way the practice of the arts has become a matter of personal activity, detached from all social life, admirably suiting the cultural ideals set up by bourgeois æstheticism. The artist has become a man apart from other men, a human being with privileges denied the common mob, expressing and satisfying the whims of a small cultivated portion of society. Painting has become a tough symbolism and all-in wrestling with the subconscious mind unintelligible to the majority. Poetry has become a private experience far removed from most reasonable understanding. A great deal of literature is concerned purely with

the personal struggles and experience of unimportant individuals, seeking satisfaction in an imaginary world devoid of human relationships on a significant scale. And where cinema has pretended to be an art in itself, with no other ends than its æsthetic virtues, it has slobbered and expired in a sepulchre of symbolism or, still worse, mysticism " (p. 61).

The film must be prepared to deal with social problems:

" The big films of cinema, few as they are, have all served a special purpose and have not come into being primarily as the result of mere artistic endeavour or the desire to make profit. They are significant because of the sincerity of their creators in the part they were intended to play in social and political enlightenment. *Kameradschaft* and *Potemkin* are the two favourite examples. They were both propagandist.

" Without this aim of special service, I cannot see that cinema has any real significance beyond that of providing a temporary emotional refuge for the community, making profit or loss for its moneyed speculators and preserving a record for future historical reference which will give a partly erroneous picture of our age " (p. 65).

This new cinema must cease to be the tool of entertainment, even of a highbrow minority in Film Societies. It must serve the people as a teacher:

" Real and creative thought must be about real things. Let cinema explore outside the limits of what we are told constitutes entertainment. Let cinema attempt the dramatisation of the living scene and the living theme, springing from the living present instead of from the synthetic fabrication of the studio. Let cinema attempt film interpretations of modern problems and events, of things as they really are today, and by so doing perform a definite function. Let cinema recognise the existence of real men and women, real things and real issues, and by so doing offer to State, Industry, Commerce, to public and private organisations of all kinds, a method of communication and propaganda to project not just personal opinions but arguments for a world of common interests " (pp. 66–7).

This vigorous appeal had its effect, but only because it was an expression of what was already in the minds of the documentarians themselves.

With the titles already listed among the chief documentaries of the period no one can grumble that Rotha's admonitions were not carried out. Credit should go to the G.P.O. for its wide interpretation of its public relations, in spite of which Grierson resigned in 1937 and went on an Empire tour which ended with a Government appointment in Canada as Film Commissioner in 1939. Credit should go to the public spirit of the British Commercial Gas Association and the oil industry for sponsoring important films on social problems and technical processes. Len Lye alone developed film for film's sake in colour with his remarkable experiments, ostensibly to help post-office propaganda but really to please himself. The tolerance of the G.P.O. must have been remarkable, but he gave great pleasure to those whom he did not send home colour-blind.

Documentary in Wartime.—Then came the War. The G.P.O. Unit stepped in quickly and with quiet effect in *The First Days*. After a hesitant start and the beautiful G.P.O. film *Squadron* 992, the newly formed Ministry of Information decided to adopt documentary for the duration. By the end of 1940 it had started its dual distribution policy of persuading the exhibitors to show a five-minute film (which grew to seven or eight minutes) in their programmes, and more boldly by placing an initial fifty mobile film vans on the roads of Britain with full-length programmes of documentary to be shown freely to audiences in town or village. This began to solve the distribution problem for documentary, which, what with one thing and another, had been the main problem for the past ten years.

But for odd moments of relaxation, the Trade had hitherto told documentary where to put itself. Classed at the worst as highbrow and educational, at the best as " travelogue " or " interest," during which an audience could change its seats and buy its chocolate, documentary got little headway as a whole in commercial programmes. The growing number of News Theatres found it useful, but these did not exist widely outside

London and a few provincial houses, where its titles were buried under raucous publicity for bad imitations of Disney. The Film Societies showed the films religiously, but the biggest distribution was on the whole non-theatrical, as it was called. Non-theatrical means normally substandard and private showing on 16 mm. projectors owned by private persons or organisations, clubs, schools, institutes and colleges. As the film supply grew, the number of types of good talkie 16 mm. projectors placed on the non-theatrical market increased. A demand sprang up, necessarily largely from schools, but by no means entirely so. Film Libraries for documentary grew to promote and meet the demand. As an outcome of the Report of the Commission on Educational and Cultural Films, financed chiefly by the Carnegie Trustees (1929–32), the British Film Institute was set up in 1933 to foster the use of the film for educational purposes, and to preserve the cultural heritage (such as it is) of commercial film in the vaults of the National Film Library. Organisations like E.M.B., G.P.O., Shell-Mex and the British Commercial Gas Association had their own lending libraries from which films could be borrowed for the price of the postage stamp to be stuck on the returning parcel.

By this means a large, and measurable, non-theatrical audience was being fostered, and children were being taught to distinguish films from orange peel.

The Ministry of Information took over the G.P.O. and Empire Film Library, set up its own Regional distribution executive and played to five million people from factory to remotest countryside in the first year of its Film Division's existence. So successful was this plan, that within two and a half years it had trebled its initial operating staff and hit the twenty-million mark of people who see a programme of documentary on substandard film in a year. It revolutionised the documentary output, having commissioned, acquired and stuck together out of library material nearly a thousand films during the War. It suffered heavily from lack of enough good directors to respond to its needs, but in spite of so prodigious an output, the standards fell very seldom below the mediocre and in many instances rose above pre-war power.

Here at last was a great experiment in civic education through the film, and the hard work of documentary became recognised by its promotion into a major information service throughout the country. Nearly 1,500 shows a week of programmes lasting thirty to ninety minutes played before audiences of factory workers or villagers, Civil Defence personnel or school-children, social workers or doctors, specialists or general public made documentary known as never before, and, when it was well made, liked as education seldom is in this country. It demonstrated that the innate popularity of a visual presentation of subject-matter could overcome British sales-resistance to education. People learned not merely about the War but about the rest of the world and themselves merely by going to the pictures. The films were discussed long afterwards by audiences that had a regular social life of their own, like Women's Institutes. The Units themselves, turning out as many films as they could against the demands of the Ministry's Films Division, the hazards of air bombardment, labour and raw-material shortage, learned how to serve their new large public.

The G.P.O. Unit was taken over by the Ministry of Information and given the title of Crown Film Unit. It specialised in larger-scale documentary, following up its pre-war high-spot *North Sea* with *Men of the Lightship* and *Merchant Seamen*. Then it hit the Trade skywise with *Target for Tonight*. Exhibitors paid this film the supreme compliment of criticising the distribution agreement between the Ministry and the Exhibitors' Association. Here at last was a documentary they and the public asked to see because it had the star value of showing the R.A.F. at work. It revealed how a raid over German territory was actually carried out, at a time when explanation of this kind was both novel and thrilling. It did this by presenting R.A.F. personnel as human beings and not as Service automata: it allowed the audience to develop a personal interest in the crew of the bomber. It used dialogue, silence and music well; a beautiful sequence showed the bomber sailing over the clouds to Leighton Lucas's fine score. But it was Harry Watt's flair for choosing the right kind of non-professional actors which made this film a wonderful demonstration of bringing people together sympathetically by means of the screen.

Crown followed up with feature-length films like *Coastal Command, Fires were Started, Close Quarters* and *Western*

Approaches (in colour). All these films were widely shown in the cinemas and were of the dramatised type with Servicemen playing themselves under the superb direction of the Crown tradition, with no self-consciousness, no pose. All these films were brilliantly directed. They did not, of course, deal with social problems like the documentary of the pre-war period. They dealt with the typical life and typical duties of the Services concerned, and they illustrated their stories by the selection of men who by personality and photogenic quality epitomised the personnel who were fighting the War.

The smaller films were made largely for non-theatrical showing, though they were sometimes used in the cinemas. They more nearly carried forward the type of documentary of which Grierson and Rotha had written. These films were made to help the community get through the War, know something about it, and be as useful as possible. The analysis of production which follows errs on the conservative side in numbers of films made up to the end of the War.

Agricultural Subjects (instructional and documentary)	40 films.
War Record films, Air Force, Army and Navy	60 films.
Civil Defence (instructional and information)	25 films.
Education and Citizenship	50 films.
Food, Diet and Cookery	25 films.
Health, Hygiene and Medicine (technical and general)	40 films.
Labour and Industry	50 films.
Private Allotment Work (instructional films)	15 films.
Salvage (propaganda)	10 films.

Most of these films did not exceed one or two reels. They used little dialogue. A commentator helped the audience to grasp the significance of the film, sometimes through the flowing strains of unnecessary music. The sound-track had to be easy to hear, for the films would be shown on hard-worn 16 mm. projectors in halls with bad acoustics or in factory canteens where the clatter of dishes would rival voices or sound effects. Crown contributed some important films to these short subjects, such as *Health in War, Britain at Bay* (September 1940, after the fall of France), *Britain can take it* (with Quentin Reynolds, the American journalist, as commentator), *The Heart of Britain* (on the fighting spirit of Britain during the bombing) and *The Eighty Days* (the story of the V1 raids). The bulk of the Crown Film Unit's work was concerned with Britain in action. Occasionally, however, Humphrey Jennings made an experiment in film æsthetics, like *Listen to Britain, Lili Marlene* or even the unusual picture *The Silent Village* made in a Welsh mining village in memory of the massacre of the Czech Lidice. *Listen to Britain* (1941) revealed the life and spirit of Britain at war in terms of the sounds made by transport and industry, by men singing in a troop train or entertainers singing in a factory canteen, by Myra Hess playing in the National Gallery: it was a film of great beauty. *Lili Marlene* (1944) told the story, with the famous German song as theme, of the capture of the tune in North Africa. In *The Silent Village* (1943) the miners and their wives speak their native Welsh to match the Czech language, and act with simplicity and restraint as they reconstruct the story which might have been their own.

Another outstanding Unit was that under the supervision of Paul Rotha. His great film *The World of Plenty* (1943) dealt with problems of food production and distribution before, during and after the War. It was a film of argument, with many voices on the sound-track, from the expert to the man who doubts everything the commentator says. It was the most advanced documentary yet produced in the true tradition of the film of social problems: it is equalled only by Rotha's post-war film on food, *The World is Rich* (1947). The Unit made other notable films, *Our School* (directed by Donald Alexander, 1941, a study of an experimental school in Devon to which London school-children were evacuated), *Power for the Highlands* (directed by Jack Chambers, 1943, on the hydro-electrification of the Scottish Highlands), and *Children of the City* (directed by Budge Cooper, 1944, a study of the treatment of juvenile delinquency). Rotha has developed in ten years into one of the boldest and yet most analytical of producers in Britain today. His imagination is cinematic and he has not given up the old ideal of experiment in the wider use of film technique. His films are discussion pictures: they must therefore promote discussion in the audience. This *The World of Plenty* and *The World is Rich* were well calculated to do.

Of the other Units (Shell, Strand, Merton Park, Spectator, Realist, Verity, Greenpark and many more) none did so well as those which filmed the towns and countryside of Britain (*Winter, Spring* and *Summer on the Farm, Crown of the Year, The Crofters, Cornish Valley, West Riding,* etc.) and her industries (*Transfer of Skill, Airscrew* or *Steel* in colour for the British Council). Some of the films on health were quite outstanding (*Defeat Diphtheria, Defeat Tuberculosis, Blood Transfusion, Scabies, Surgery in Chest Disease, Malaria*). Nor should the many fine films made for civilian showing by the Service film units be omitted (*The Siege of Tobruk, Wavell's 30,000, Street Fighting, Naples is a Battlefield, A Date with a Tank,* etc.). To these should be added especially the film on which Len Lye worked, *Kill or be Killed,* for its interesting sound-track: it was produced by Realist. Like the Crown Film Unit's work, some of the Service films have been of feature-length for use in the cinemas: *Desert Victory, Tunisian Victory, Burma Victory* and above all *The True Glory* (the latter edited by Garson Kanin of Hollywood and Carol Reed of Britain) all were assembled with imagination and rose from the level of mere record into the creative presentation of these great campaigns so that their human significance could be appreciated. The sound-track of *The True Glory* was remarkable: the voices of men of many accents from America, Britain and the Allied countries gave personal comments on their experiences in the campaign that illuminated the impressive but impersonal shots on the screen.

Documentary in wartime was a great achievement in public service, an achievement in production and exhibition, a success in the public estimation. The figures for the period 1943–44 show that the mobile units gave over 64,000 shows to over 11 million people. In addition audiences assessed at over 7 million saw programmes of documentary and kindred films at special shows given in cinemas or on private owned projectors. The Ministry's films were also constantly shown as features or supporting pictures in the public cinemas, whose weekly audience reached the peak figure of 30 million.

The successor to the wartime Ministry of Information is the

present Central Office of Information, which has maintained the mobile-unit film service and is sponsoring a large annual production programme of documentaries. Recent documentary in this country is discusse(in a later section. It is sufficient to point out here that a system of film sponsorship unique in the world has survived the War as a permanent part of the educational system and the public information services of this country.

Documentary Theory in Wartime.—" Documentary News Letter," [1] product of the documentary consultants Film Centre, went on reiterating impatiently the need for stronger and better documentary propaganda than, in its opinion, the Ministry of Information had seen fit to allow. The main line of attack is stated bluntly in these two paragraphs from the leading article for March 1942:

> " Our propaganda has not failed merely for mechanical reasons. It has failed because it is bankrupt of ideas and bankrupt of policy.
>
> " It will continue to fail just as long as our propagandists continue to shut their eyes to the fact that we are living in the middle of a world revolution, and that therefore revolutionary tactics are not merely expedient but also absolutely vital." (Column 1.)

The Government reply was to stick pretty rigidly to war issues and leave the controversial future to evolve its own policy. It could hardly do anything else with so many colours sticking pins in each other on the political map. But that does not prove the D.N.L. policy to be wrong from documentary's point of view. Grierson, then Director of Canada's Film Board, contributed an occasional trenchant article, and Wright made an interesting criticism of Cavalcanti's film survey of documentary *Film and Reality,* in the course of which he writes as follows:

> " When the war began documentary was no longer in its experimental stage. Realist traditions had by then been firmly established, and the results of the experiments of the previous ten years had been crystallised into several different styles. Nevertheless that static stage, which in any movement is the prelude to complete necrosis, had in

[1] Later changed to *Documentary Film News*

no sense been reached. On the contrary, in the years immediately preceding World War II the realist movement was beginning to concern itself firstly with larger and broader treatments of subject-matter, and secondly with an increased use of dramatic incident and dialogue (cf. *The Londoners* and *North Sea,* to give but two examples)." (" Documentary News Letter," March 1942, p. 41.)

The war, he goes on, has placed limitations on the documentary workers and a discipline not altogether harmful. But he urges them to go beyond the demands of official sponsors, since it is their job, as pioneers, to blaze the trail of future social policy.

" I believe absolutely that the revolutionary technique is now the only technique. Whether you like it or not, we are undergoing a world social revolution here and now, and it is a revolution which must continue after the war, and continue with increasing strength. For that is the only thing the people of Britain are fighting for.

" It is today the job of documentary to integrate the immediate war-effort with the facts and implications of radical social and economic changes which are part and parcel of it.

" Only from this standpoint can we get into our films the dynamic impulse which will strengthen their propaganda value to this nation and its allies.

" The realist tradition is rich in the abilities for the job. The whole trend of the 'thirties was towards this dynamic concept (we said we were trying to make Peace as exciting as War), and the films which were made tended more and more to sacrifice purely æsthetic considerations to the need for pungent comment and the imaginative presentation of facts and problems.

" Today the intensification of effort which is so urgently needed depends on an equal intensification of morale-propaganda; and if we don't pull our punches any longer we have a vital contribution to make.

" I believe that the future of the realist film (if one can spare a moment to look ahead in such parochial terms) lies in the attitude and action which I have outlined. Our films must be the shock troops of propaganda. It is no longer policy to compromise with timidity—either among ourselves or in others. The documentary movement is part of a continuous process and a continuous progress towards a new deal in life for the peoples of the world. And the only slogan worth having today is 'Speed it up!'" (" Documentary News Letter," March 1942, p. 42.)

In a later letter he praises Grierson in a tribute which should not be omitted from this book. He writes:

" I am sure that I am expressing the feelings of documentary workers as a whole. I must point out that Grierson has always been and still is a remarkable technician, a magnificent teacher, and in short, a great producer. . . . Grierson is not merely the founder of the documentary movement. Since its inception it has been his own understanding of film technique, his encouragement of experimentation and . . . his uncanny grasp and knowledge of æsthetics as regards art in general and film art in particular, which have been the driving force and inspiration of the progress of documentary.

" These qualities . . . I have put first, but I must now add Grierson's political grasp and foresight, his incredible energy and organisational drive, and, above all, his unswerving loyalty not merely to the idea of documentary but also to all those working with him." (" Documentary News Letter," April 1942, p. 58.)

This is a statement which cannot be ignored, and which is important coming from a man who is himself a distinguished artist.

Grierson takes the long-term view in a striking statement on propaganda in " Documentary News Letter " for May 1941. A year later his views on " The Documentary Idea, 1942 " appear in the issue for June of that year.

The following are extracts which will do good if they lead the reader to the original, which is one of the great statements about the future produced by the War. It gives the documentary directors the lead they are accustomed to expect from the founder of their movement:

" The penalty of realism is that it is about reality and has to bother for ever not about being ' beautiful ' but about being right."

" What confuses the history is that we had always

the good sense to use the æsthetes. We did so because we like them and because we needed them. It was, paradoxically, with the first-rate æsthetic help of people like Flaherty and Cavalcanti that we mastered the techniques necessary for our quite unæsthetic purpose. That purpose was plain and was written about often enough. Rotha spent a lot of time on it. We were concerned not with the category of ' purposiveness without purpose ' but with that other category beyond, which used to be called teleological. We were reformers open and avowed: concerned —to use the old jargon—with ' bringing alive the new materials of citizenship,' ' crystallising sentiments' and creating those ' new loyalties from which a progressive civic will might derive.' Take that away and I'd be hard put to it to say what I have been working for these past fifteen years. What, of course, made documentary successful as a movement was that in a decade of spiritual weariness it reached out, almost alone among the media, toward the future. Obviously it was the public purpose within it which commanded government and other backing, the progressive social intention within it which secured the regard of the newspapers and people of goodwill everywhere, and the sense of a public cause to be served which kept its own people together. These facts should have made it clear that the documentary idea was not basically a film idea at all, and the film treatment it inspired only an incidental aspect of it. The medium happened to be the most convenient and most exciting available to us. The idea itself, on the other hand, was a new idea for public education: its underlying concept that the world was in a phase of drastic change affecting every manner of thought and practice, and the public comprehension of the nature of that change vital. There it is, exploratory, experimental and stumbling, in the films themselves: from the dramatisation of the workman and his daily drag to the dramatisation of modern organisation and the new corporate elements in society and to the dramatisation of social problems: each a step in the attempt to understand the stubborn raw material of our modern citizenship and wake the heart and the will to their mastery. Where we stopped short was that, with equal deliberation, we refused to specify what political agency should carry out that will or associate ourselves with any one of them. Our job specifically was to wake the heart and the will: it was for the political parties to make before the people their own case for leadership. I would not restate these principles merely out of historical interest. The important point is that they have not changed at all and they are not going to change, nor be changed. The materials of citizenship today are different and the perspectives wider and more difficult; but we have, as ever, the duty of exploring them and of waking the heart and will in regard to them. (Documentary is at once a critique of propaganda and a practice of it.) That duty is what documentary is about. It is, moreover, documentary's primary service to the State to be persisted in, whatever deviation may be urged upon it, or whatever confusion of thought, or easiness of mind, success may bring."

"No war aims, I am told, becomes 'no policy' for documentary. Yet those who insist on 'no policy' are correctly reflecting a phase which dares not go right and dares not go left and has no easy solution to offer except first winning the war. It would be wise to see the 'no policy' business for what it is, a present political necessity for governments which, for many reasons—some schizophrenic, some more realistically involving allies—may not speak their minds; and explore what can be done none the less and in spite of it."

"Once consider that England is only important as it is related to other nations, and its problems and developments only important as they are recognised as part of wider problems and developments, and many subjects will reach out into healthier and more exciting perspectives of description than are presently being utilised."

"A lot has to be done and done quickly if the public mind is to be tuned in time to what, amid these swift-moving changes of public organisation, is required of it. It is not the technical perfection of the film that matters, nor even the vanity of its maker, but what happens to that public mind. Never before has there been such a call for the creation of new loyalties or bringing people to new kinds of sticking points. Times press and so must production; and with it must go a harder and more direct style."

" In its basic meaning, culture is surely the giving of law to what is without it. That hard but truer way of culture will not go by default if we search out the design in the seeming chaos of present events and, out of today's experiments in total effort, create the co-operative and more profoundly ' democratic ' ways of the future. The verbs are active. To go back once again to Tallents' Mill quotation, the pattern of the artist in this relationship will indicate the living principle of action."

" So the long windy openings are out, and so are the carthartic finishes in which a good brave tearful self-congratulatory and useless time has been had by all. The box-office—pander to what is lazy, weak, reactionary, vicarious, sentimental and essentially defeatist in all of us —will, of course, instinctively howl for them. It will want to make ' relaxation,' if you please, even out of war. But don't, for God's sake, give it. Deep down the people want to be fired to tougher ways of thought and feeling and to have their present braveries extended to the very roots of their social existence. In that habit they will win more than a war."

Documentary Elsewhere.—The early story of documentary outside this country and Russia is the story of isolated titles. In France documentary was linked with *avant-garde* and produced Cavalcanti who made *Rien que les heures,* a film built on a structural pattern which traced the occupations of given individuals against the background of a day in Paris, and preceded the famous *Berlin* of Ruttmann, which was symphonic in treatment and influenced by Russian montage. Cavalcanti joined Grierson in Britain in 1934. Holland produced Joris Ivens who, after making some interesting Dutch documentaries, went to Russia to direct *Komsomol,* a film on the Russian League of Youth. Ivens later did notable work in Spain in *Spanish Earth* with Ernest Hemingway. In Spain, too, the remarkable film *Land without Bread* was made by the

Spaniard Bunuel in 1932. It was a devastating study of the Hurdanos who, living only a comparatively few miles from Burgos, existed and may still exist in a state of backwardness and misery behind a thin veneer of semi-civilisation. The camera dwelt at unrelenting length on disease and mental deficiency. Germany produced a long line of travelogues, often well made, to attract the visitor and his money to the land of Adolf Hitler.

The documentary mind in America showed itself in the distinguished work of Pare Lorentz, who made *The Plow that broke the Plains* in 1936 for the Resettlement Administration of the Roosevelt government. The film precedes *The Grapes of Wrath* in dealing with the Dustbowl. Rhetorical-poetic in presentation, it has undoubted power. The commentary was also a feature in *The River,* released in 1938 and made by Lorentz for the Farm Security Administration. It is an important film, one of the most important documentaries America has so far produced.

THE RIVER: (1938. Produced for the Farm Security
   American.   Administration, United States Department
                  of Agriculture.   Director, Pare Lorentz.)
   Theme.—A hundred years of the history of the Mississippi, its spoliation by successive pioneers in cotton, timber and corn-lands, the ruination of land and population by poverty and flood. The New Deal under the Roosevelt Administration starts new work to conserve and develop the devastated areas.

   Technique.—Sound: musical background of Mississippi folk-tune themes, a commentary skilfully ranging from the poetic (with emphatic use of lovely place-names like the rivers Kaskashkea and Monongahela) to the factual. General atmosphere and presentation has been called impressionist: the atmosphere of the Mississippi region is considered more important than an exact statement of statistics. The sense of greed and ruthless exploitation, which is the major theme of the film, is powerfully expressed; impressionism wins over statistics in the emotional reaction set up in the audience: this must stop: this must never happen again. It is good propaganda for the New Deal since, when the audience is most revolted by this exhibition of greed and human suffering, the solution follows simply in the plans to dam the waters in the Tennessee valley and rehabilitate both land and peoples.

In 1935 America produced the first issue of *March of Time,* as part of the Luce enterprises. It runs to this day, though from the point of view of the enterprises it has never been a money-spinner. Its fame and influence far outdo its profits; its style has had its effect upon the Canadian *Canada Carries On* and *World in Action* series; it has produced an effective rival in the British series *This Modern Age.*

Released once a month, it has covered a world front with its cameramen. Some of its issues included three items, some only one. Its range and journalistic flair can be seen from some of the subjects it has recorded or reconstructed, and it has often been courageous and outspoken in its criticism of dictatorship and fascism, when people who should have known better were praising Hitler's architecture and Mussolini's trains. Here are some of its subjects, the earlier dates significant.

1936. Japanese Imperial Policy in Manchuria.
Geneva (Italy; Mediterranean; Abyssinia).
The French Peasants and the Government.

1937. The Far East and Chang Kai-shek.
Bootlegging.
British Black Areas.
U.S.A. Child Labour.
The Dust Bowl.

1938. Inside Nazi Germany.
Nazi Conquest of Austria.
Czechoslovakia.

1939. The Refugees.
Mediterranean, Background for War.
Japan, Master of the Orient.
Britain, Peace and Propaganda.

1941. America Speaks her Mind.
China Fights Back.
Men of Norway.
Peace—by Adolf Hitler.

Its technique depends on lively camera-work, on the command of its high-powered sure-hit commentary and the rhetorical speed of its cutting. English audiences found the non-stop crescendo of the *March of Time* voice difficult to absorb. Statistics and social comment alike were delivered with a rich, harsh impersonality impervious to English susceptibilities for the sweet and facetious. But it was respected and sought out.

Other interesting documentaries made before the War include the work of Jean Epstein, Jean Lods and Robert Alexandre in France, where Painlevé is now the leader of the factual film movement. Painlevé's beautiful films of marine life are famous and were widely shown by British film societies. In Belgium Henri Storck made *Les Maisons de la Misère* in 1938 on slums and rehousing. From America, Paul Strand went to Mexico to make *The Wave* (1935) on the life of the fishermen of the Gulf of Vera Cruz and their commercial exploitation. Ralph Steiner and Willard van Dyke made *The City* in 1939, an interesting and amusing film on city life and the needs of replanning for the development of social amenities. Van Dyke also made *Children must Learn* (1941) and the remarkable documentary with musical recitative and song *Valley Town*, for which Marc Blitzstein was composer: it is a tragic study of a Pennsylvanian steel community hit by economic depression. The War stimulated documentary production in America, and many films like *Tanks* (with Orson Welles), *Henry Browne, Farmer, The Town* (Madison, Indiana), *Cowboy* and *T.V.A.* show the beginnings of a movement in the States which may lead to a permanent documentary tradition with a style of its own. The great film *The Forgotten Village* (a documentary feature) is discussed later. Mention should also be made of America's war-record films (*The Fighting Lady, Report from the Aleutians, Memphis Belle*, etc.) and the distinguished Pacific campaign action pictures, many in colour and taken in the heat of battle on 16 mm. Frank Capra produced a brilliant series of films edited from newsreel and other material called *Why we Fight*. They were intended originally to explain the War to the American serviceman. They were played also in British cinemas and their technical brilliance made them famous (*Divide and Conquer, The Nazis Strike, The Battle of Britain, The Battle of Russia*, etc.). Russia also sent her war-record pictures to the cinemas of her Allies: these included *Defeat of the Germans near Moscow, One Day of War, Story of Stalin-*

grad, The Partisans, The Drive to the West and *Justice is Coming.* Among the films of the War none was more exciting than the French resistance film *Le Journal de la Résistance*: other clandestinely made films are important for the permanent history of the War when once they become more widely known.

In Canada John Grierson became executive head of the Government's National Film Board as Film Commissioner in 1939. Here he was joined by Ivens, Stuart Legg and Raymond Spottiswoode. In 1944 the annual output of films was about 250 and the Board had 120 mobile cinema vans on the road, a scheme started in 1942 on the British model. It produced two series of films inspired by *The March of Time, Canada Carries on* (playing monthly in 800 Canadian theatres) and *World in Action* (playing monthly in 6,000 cinemas in America and Britain). Legg was in charge of the latter series. Most important are the citizens' forums which have grown out of discussion following the mobile-unit programmes, and the Trades Union Circuit which uses a " discussion-trailer " to start the audience talking after film shows covering 40,000 trade unionists a month. In the non-theatrical programmes the serious films are interspersed with lighter items and sing-songs. The animated films made by Norman McLaren like *Chants Populaires* (containing also sequences from the French *avant-garde* animator Alexieff of *Night on the Bare Mountain*) and his coloured propaganda shorts, are especially attractive among these lighter films.

The documentary film is now established in many other countries, in Scandinavia, Czechoslovakia, Poland and Italy, for example. It is the most practical and useful way in which smaller countries can enter production and make an individual contribution to world cinema. The film is an international medium, and where feature films are often impossible to produce, documentary, state-aided or privately sponsored, can introduce a country to an established world audience. More recent documentary production abroad is discussed in a later section.

9. *Social Realism in the Fiction Film*

In the novel it has become quite a commonplace to bring realism to the pitch that fiction merges into fact; for instance, Ralph Bates' " Lean Men," Steinbeck's " Grapes of Wrath,"

Koestler's " Thieves in the Night " or Alan Paton's " Cry the Beloved Country." Who is to say where these books cease to be novels in any traditional sense of the term and become a projection of actuality fitted with personnel and dialogue? It is better to forget theory and call such work – peculiarly twentieth century, though Thomas Deloney wrote in this manner in Elizabeth's time – the documentary novel. Its peculiar property is that the writer re-creates in the literary form the phases of life and the personalities of people he has experienced and met. It is unlikely that a satisfactory documentary novel will be produced except by a man who has lived under the conditions he describes either as partner or, like Flaherty, as intrusive observer.

The film presents the same dovetail. Where does fiction begin in the dialogue and acting of *North Sea, Men of the Lightship, Merchant Seamen* and *Target for Tonight*? Where does documentary begin in *The Foreman went to France* (with Cavalcanti as associate producer), *The Grapes of Wrath,* and, farther back, *The Covered Wagon,* D. W. Griffith's three-hour epics and Pudovkin's stories of the Revolution? The documentaries tell a story, or at least a continuous action; they excite sympathy for personalities who are none the less dramatised although played by themselves. The features tell a story with the more elaborate help of action, but the story is as much concerned with actuality, the stuff of documentary, as documentary itself. Once more, it may be better to forget theory and call the latter group documentary dramas, and the former documentary features. The success and importance of both groups spell permanence and development. But neither will oust the more traditional documentary or fiction films from their established approaches.

Two films of the documentary feature class, *Western Approaches* and *The Forgotten Village,* will be taken as examples:

WESTERN APPROACHES :   (Crown Film Unit.
   British, 1944.   Directed by Pat Jackson.
Photographed in Technicolor
by Jack Cardiff.)

Theme.—The strength and character of the British merchant seaman.

Story.—A number of shipwrecked merchant seamen in desperate need after days afloat on the Atlantic realise as the rescue ship " Leander " approaches that they are being used as a decoy by a submerged German U-boat. They warn her in time, but not soon enough to avoid her being struck by one torpedo. The master of the " Leander " tricks the U-boat into surfacing and then sinks her.

Treatment.—Endless time was spent perfecting this picture, the greater part of which was shot in an actual lifeboat out in the Atlantic, and not in a studio. · The merchant seamen were, of course, real servicemen, and were so skilfully handled by director and cameraman that their experiences and their words never seem reconstructed before the camera. The illusion is that of complete actuality, due possibly to the fact that no man remains long enough on the screen in any one shot to give away his lack of acting technique. Only rarely do we see change of emotion in a continuous shot, for it is here that the amateur begins to baulk. There is, however, one such extraordinarily expressive shot, when the look-out in the life-boat first sights the " Leander." His weary face sinks against the mast, and he counts with his fingers before looking again : this is a fine combination of direction and acting. The colour, as in many British coloured films, is most intelligently used, emphasising the dark greens and grey-blues of the all-surrounding Atlantic.

THE FORGOTTEN VILLAGE : (Directed and Produced by
   American, 1944. Herbert Kline in associa-
    tion with John Steinbeck.
    Music by Hans Eisler.)

Theme.—The struggle in the life of the little Mexican village community of Santiago between traditional ignorance and superstition and the new ways of science.

Story.—A young peasant Juan Diego and the village schoolmaster endeavour to save their village from colitis due to a poisoned well. The villagers under the influence of Trini, the Wise Woman, place every obstacle in the way of the visiting medical unit fetched to the village from Mexico City by Juan. Driven out by his father, Juan goes back with the unit to study medicine. " I must be a doctor and help save the lives of my people," he says.

Treatment and Technique.—" The working method was very simple, and yet required great patience. A very elastic story was written. Then the crew moved into the village, made friends, talked and listened. The story was simple: too many children die—why is that and what is done about it, both by the villagers and by the government? The story actually was a question. What we found was dramatic—the clash of a medicine and magic that was old when the Aztecs invaded the plateau with a modern medicine that is as young as a living man. To tell this story we had only to have people re-enact what had happened to them. Our ' curandera ' was a real ' wise woman,' one who had practised herbology and magic in the village; our teacher was a real teacher in the government school; our doctors real doctors; our mother a real mother who had lost a number of children. If they moved through scenes with sureness and authority it was because they had been through them many times before when no cameras were there. Such a method required, above all else, patience, tact and genuine liking for the people. . . . Such were the methods employed in making *The Forgotten Village*. A curious and true and dramatic film has been the result." (John Steinbeck.)

The film is a minor masterpiece. The visual story is enhanced by the quiet unobtrusive narrative (not commentary) spoken by Burgess Meredith, and by Hans Eisler's fine music. The photography is bright with the harsh sunlight and the contrasting shadows of black foregrounds of cacti and village walls. In the narrow home with its gaunt and bleeding crucifix the mother works and waits in her pregnancy. The men and older children work in the hot fields. When the small children grow sick from the infected well Juan, shy but purposeful, picks his way to Mexico City to appeal to a doctor to come to the village. The film is full of beautiful and expressive close-ups: the mother who smiles with her shawled head tilted, the friendly simplicity of the father, joyful at the birth of more children, as he wipes the sweat and the flies from his face. When his son dies an unforgettable shot turns from the villagers dancing before the funeral to the still face of the mother, resigned in fatalistic sadness. In the final moments of the delivery of her child the mother is suspended in the attitude of crucifixion with her husband supporting her heaving body and whispering encouragement in her ear. Behind them hangs the gaunt crucifix, its symbolic presence in curious contrast to that of the Wise Woman performing her rites of primitive midwifery.

In the style of *Western Approaches* the British Government Crown Film Unit working for the Ministry of Information made a notable series of short and full-length feature films. The chief of these were:

Merchant Seamen (Director Jack Holmes, 1941).
Target for Tonight (Director Harry Watt, 1941).
Ferry Pilot (Director Pat Jackson, 1941).
Coastal Command (Director Jack Holmes, 1942).
Close Quarters (Director Jack Lee, 1943).
The Fires were Started (Director Humphrey Jennings, 1943).

All these films expanded the original more generalised documentary approach by stressing the characters of the individuals in the story, and by using dialogue and script treatment after the manner of feature film narrative, employing commentary only for bridging purposes. The results have been remarkable, and have created a new field for documentary. These films have proved very popular with the public, who found in them the elements of characterisation and story already familiar from most of their cinema entertainment. Documentaries like these are, however, very expensive to make and depend therefore on reimbursement through box-office receipts like commercial feature films. This has tended to limit their production now the War is over.

A good deal of discussion has been raised about the use of the professional or non-professional actor in films which deal intimately with actuality. No one quarrels with the use of the professional in films where the occupational interest is not a definite part of the film's presentation: you need not put a salesman in a studio hat-store. On the other hand, where the interest of the story turns more on the man as a worker in a genuine environment, the case for using a carefully selected person who is by occupation one of the workers shown becomes much greater. A number of films illustrate this, from *Man of Aran* to *Children on Trial* and *Germany, Year Zero*. Directors like Rossellini use professional or amateur skill according to the nature and demands of the individual characters in the story, eliminating the unnaturalness of the amateur by skilful and sympathetic direction.

By a similar skill in direction, the Crown Film Unit reduced its merchant seamen and R.A.F. personnel to the dead level of inconsequent realism until the mystified audiences exclaimed "What! Weren't they really actors after all?" and hero-worship the R.A.F. and the merchant seamen all the more. How can the imperturbable sang-froid, the careless self-confidence, the cross-your-fingers-and-have-a-beer-old-man spirit survive the Crown Film Unit with its lights and cameras and microphones? The answer lies in the careful choice of the men to be used, the comparatively little they have to say at any one time, and the British sang-froid, which probably is as much I-am-bored-with-the-whole-bloody-business-anyway as a self-controlled piece of acting before camera and microphone. And there is Pudovkin and his Mongols, which is a good story:

> "For example, in the film *The Heir to Jenghiz Khan,* I wanted to have a crowd of Mongols looking with rapture on a precious fox-fur. I engaged a Chinese conjurer and photographed the faces of the Mongols watching him. When I joined this piece to a piece of the shot of fur held in the hands of the seller I got the result required." (PUDOVKIN, "Film Technique," p. 142.)

It would be pleasant to think that Harry Watt used this technique with the R.A.F.

Russia soon learned, however, to break good resolutions and have some actors who knew their job around the set. For, as soon as it comes to acting which requires emotion continuously and carefully developed, the theory of the actor as plastic material in the hands of the director breaks down. The theory of sticking together the same faces with the same expression but with a different cutting tempo, and calling the result a cine-study of hunger or sorrow or mother-love, ends where the emotion begins to develop, where the face itself has to move with feeling and mean it.

Documentary has got some remarkable acting results out of amateurs doing their jobs according to plan. It has been sensible enough not to ask them to do more. If a woman has just been through an air-raid she will probably look like it, but

I. THE FILM CAMERA: THE VARIETY OF THE CINEMA EYE

(i) RANGE OF MOTION PICTURE CAMERA

1 Boundless Universe (*UFA*)

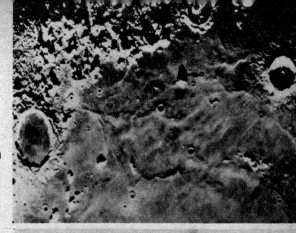

2
Stagecoach

(*John Ford : United Artists*, 1939)

3-4
Close-ups by Griffith in Intolerance, 1916

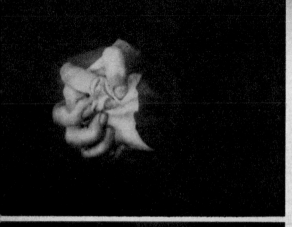

4

Intolerance

5

Libellen

(*UFA*)

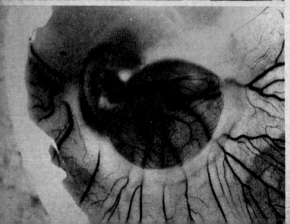

6

Embryo in
Egg of
Runner Duck,
showing head
and eye

(Secrets of
Life, *G.B.I.*)

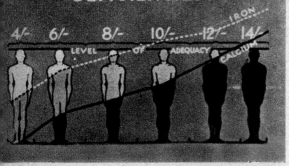

10

Enough to Eat: The Nutrition Film

(*Edgar Anstey: Gas Industry*, 1936)

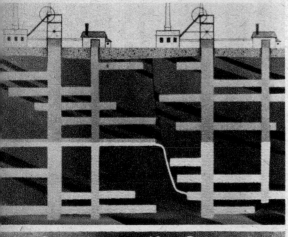

11

Coal

(*G.B.I.*, 1938)

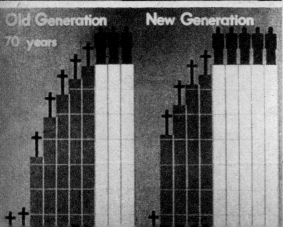

12

The World of Plenty

(*Rotha Productions*, 1943)

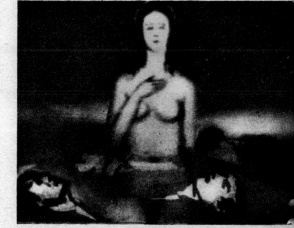

13-14
L'Idée
(Berthold
Bartosch,
1934)

15
Fantasia
(Walt Disney),
1941

16

The Cabinet of Dr. Caligari

(*Robert Wiene*, 1920)

17

The Fall of the House of Usher

(*Jean Epstein*, 1927)

18

A Matter of Life and Death

(*Michael Powell*: *Archers Productions*, 1945)

19
Siegfried

(*Fritz Lang :
UFA, 1924*)

20
The Student
of Prague

(*Henrik
Galeen, 1926*)

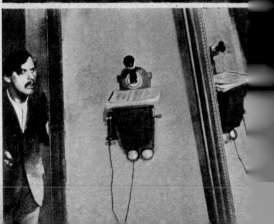

21
The Love of
Jeanne Ney

(*G. W. Pabst :
UFA, 1927*)

22
Waxworks
*(Paul Leni :
Viking, 1924)*

23
Metropolis
*(Fritz Lang :
UFA, 1927)*

24
Pandora's
Box
*(G. W. Pabst :
Nerofilm,
1929)*

25

Variety

(*E. A. Dupont:*
UFA, 1925)

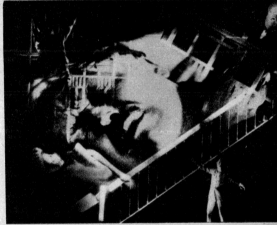

26

Secrets of
the Soul

(*G. W. Pabst:*
UFA, 1926)

27

Cinderella

(*Ludwig*
Berger,
1923)

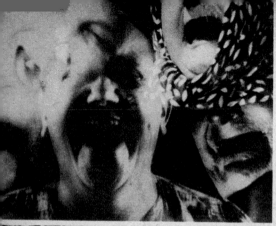

28
The Last
Laugh
(F. W. Murnau
and Carl Mayer :
UFA, 1924)

29
The Blue
Angel
(von
Sternberg :
UFA, 1930)

30
The
Threepenny
Opera
(G. W. Pabst :
Nerofilm,
1931)

31
M.
(Fritz Lang :
Nerofilm, 1931)

32
Westfront
1918
(G. W. Pabst :
Nerofilm,
1930)

33
Kamerad-
schaft
(G. W. Pabst :
Nerofilm,
1931)

II. THE
ODESSA
STEPS
SEQUENCE
FROM *THE
BATTLESHIP
POTEMKIN*

(S. M.
Eisenstein :
Soviet Russia,
1925)

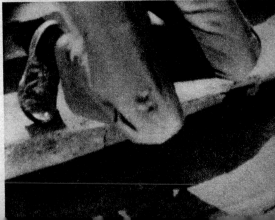

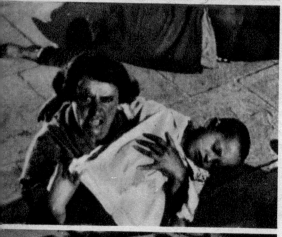

46

The End of
St. Petersburg

(V. I. Pudov-
kin :
Mezhrabpom-
Russ, 1927)

47

October

(S. M. Eisenstein:
Sovkino, 1928)

48

Earth

(A. Dovzhenko :
Vufku,
1930)

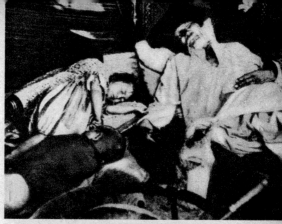

49

Turksib

(*V. Turin :
Vostokfilm,*
1928)

50

The General
Line

(*S. M. Eistenstein
and G.
Alexandrov :
Sovkino,*
1929)

51

The Ghost
that Never
Returns

(*Alexander
Room :
Sovkino,*
1929)

52

The Three Songs of Lenin

(Dziga-Vertov : Mezhrabpom-film, 1934)

53

Deserter

(V. I. Pudov-kin : Mezhrabpom-film, 1933)

54

Chapayev

(G. & S. Vassiliev: Lenfilm, 1934)

55

The
Childhood of
Maxim Gorki

(*Mark
Donskoi*,
1938)

56

Shors

(*A. Dovzhenko*,
1939)

57

Lenin in
October

(*Mikhail Romm :
Mosfilm*,
1937)

58

Storm

(V. Petrov : Mezhrabpom-
film, 1934)

59

Professor
Mamlock

(Minkin and
Rappoport :
Lenfilm, 1938)

60

The
Rainbow

(Donskoi and
Perelstein ;
Kiev Studios,
1944)

61

The Jazz
Comedy

(G. Alexandrov

Sovkino,

1934)

62

The Magic
Seed

(S. M. Eisenstein,

Artistic

Supervisor,

1941)

63

Land of Toys

(S. Obratsov,

1940)

64

Alexander
Nevsky

(S. M. Eisenstein :
Mosfilm,
1938)

65-66

Peter the
Great

(V. Petrov:
Lenfilm, 1939)

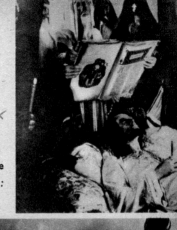

67-69

Ivan the Terrible

*(S. M. Eisenstein :
Alma-Ata
Studios, 1944)*

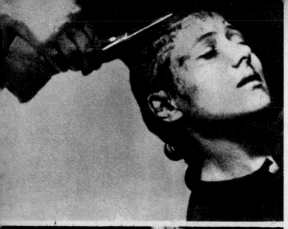

V. THE
FRENCH
CINEMA

70

La Passion
de Jeanne
d'Arc

(*Karl Dreyer.*
1928)

71

Rien que les
Heures

(*Cavalcanti,*
1926)

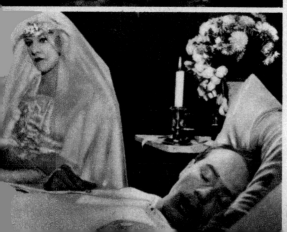

72

Thérèse
Raquin

(*Jacques
Feyder,* 1927)

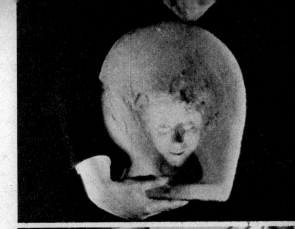

73

The Seashell
and the
Clergyman

(*Germaine
Dulac*, 1927)

74

Un Chien
Andalou

(*Luis Bunuel*,
1928)

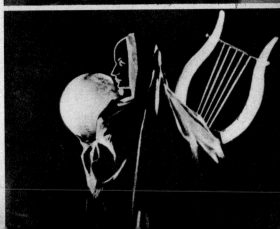

75

Le Sang d'un
Poète

(*Jean Cocteau*,
1931)

76

A Nous la
Liberté

(René Clair :
Tobis, 1931)

77

Zéro de
Conduite

(Jean Vigo :
Franco Film
Aubert, 1933)

78

L'Atalante

(Jean Vigo :
Franco Film
Aubert,
1934)

79

Un Carnet de Bal

(Julien Duvivier : Paris Export, 1937)

80

La Belle Equipe

(Julien Duvivier : Cine Arys Production, 1938)

81

La Kermesse Héroïque

(Jacques Feyder : Films Sonores Tobis, 1935)

82

La Grande
Illusion

*(Jean Renoir :
Réalisation
d'Art Cinéma-
tographique,
1937)*

83

La
Marseillaise

*(Jean Renoir,
1938)*

84

The Golem

*(Julien
Duvivier :
Produced in
Czecho-
slovakia,
1937)*

85

La Mort du Cygne

(Jean Benoit-Lévy and Marie Epstein, 1937)

86

Quai des Brumes

(Marcel Carné : Films Victoria, 1937)

87

Le Jour se Lève

(Marcel Carné, 1939)

88

Les Visiteurs
du Soir

(*Marcel Carné,*
1942)

89-90

Les Enfants
du Paradis

(*Marcel Carné,*
1944)

91

Intolerance

(D. W.
Griffith, 1916)

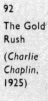

92

The Gold
Rush

(Charlie
Chaplin,
1925)

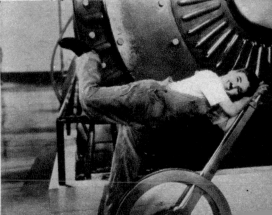

93

Modern
Times

(Charlie
Chaplin :
United Artists ,
1936)

94
The Marriage
Circle
(*Ernst
Lubitsch,*
1924)

95
Greed
(*Erich von
Stroheim,*
1923)

96
The Wedding
March
(*Erich von
Stroheim,*
1927)

97

The Crowd

(King Vidor, 1928)

98

Hallelujah

(King Vidor, 1929)

99

The Front Page

(Lewis Milestone, 1931)

100
Winterset
(*Alfred Santell:
R.K.O. Radio,
1936*)

101
The
Plainsman
(*Cecil B. de
Mille:
Paramount,
1937*)

102
Union
Pacific
(*Cecil B. de
Mille:
Paramount,
1939*)

103
Fury
(*Fritz Lang :*
M.G.M., 1936)

104
You Only
Live Once
(*Fritz Lang :*
United Artists,
1937)

105
The Long
Voyage
Home
(*John Ford :*
United Artists,
1940)

106

The Grapes
of Wrath

*(John Ford :
20th Century-
Fox, 1940)*

107

Emile Zola

*(William
Dieterle :
Warners,
1937)*

108

Dr. Erhlich's
Magic Bullet

*(William
Dieterle:
Warners,
1940)*

109
Skeleton
Dance
(*Walt Disney,*
1929)

110
Top Hat
(*Mark
Sandrich :
R.K.O. Radio,*
1935)

111
Room
Service
(*Marx
Brothers :
R.K.O. Radio,*
1938)

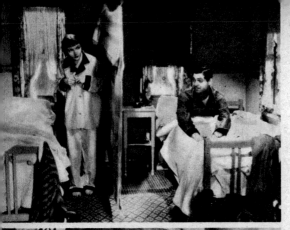

112

It Happened
One Night

(*Frank Capra :
Columbia,*
1934)

113

Mr. Deeds
Goes to
Town

(*Frank Capra :
Columbia,*
1936)

114

You Can't
Take It With
You

(*Frank Capra :
Columbia,*
1938)

115
The Good
Earth
(*Sidney*
Franklin :
M.G.M., 1937)

116
Dead End
(*William*
Wyler :
United
Artists, 1937)

117
Citizen Kane
(*Orson Welles :*
R.K.O. Radio,
1941)

118

The Magnificent Ambersons

(Orson Welles : R.K.O. Radio, 1942)

119

Christmas in July

(Preston Sturges : Paramount, 1941)

120

Hail the Conquering Hero

(Preston Sturges : Paramount, 1945)

121

**The Little
Foxes**

*(William
Wyler :
R.K.O. Radio,
1941)*

122

**The Ox-bow
Incident**

*(William
Wellman :
20th Century-
Fox, 1943)*

123

**The Lost
Weekend**

*(Billy Wilder :
Paramount,
1945)*

124
Wilson
(*Henry King* :
20th Century-
Fox, 1944)

125
The Story of
G.I. Joe
(*William
Wellman* :
United Artists,
1945)

126
The
Southerner
(*Jean Renoir* :
United Artists,
1945)

127

Nanook of
the North

(*Robert
Flaherty :
Reveillon
Frères*, 1922)

128

Moana

(*Robert
Flaherty*, 1926)

129

The Plow
that Broke
the Plains

(*Pare Lorentz :
Resettlement
Administra-
tion, U.S.
Govt.*, 1936)

130
The River
(Pare Lorentz :
Resettlement
Administra-
tion, U.S.
Govt., 1938)

131
Spanish
Earth
(Joris Ivens :
Contemp.
Historians
Inc., N.Y.,
1937)

132
Philippines
(The March of
Time, 6th Year,
Issue 2)

133
The Fighting
Lady
*(U. S. Navy: 20th
Century-Fox,
1945)*

134-135
The
Forgotten
Village

*(Herbert
Kline:
Grand
National,
1944)*

**136
Drifters**

*(John
Grierson :
E.M.B. 1929)*

137

**Head of a
Water Flea**

*(J. V. Durden :
G.B.I.,
Secrets of
Life)*

138

**Industrial
Britain**

*(Robert
Flaherty and
John
Grierson :
G.P.O. Film
Unit, 1931-2)*

139
Song of
Ceylon

*(Basil
Wright:
Ceylon Tea
Board, 1934)*

140
Man of Aran

*(Robert
Flaherty:
Gaumont-
British, 1934)*

141
Nightmail

*(Basil
Wright and
Harry Watt:
G.P.O. Film
Unit, 1935)*

142

Shipyard

*(Paul Rotha :
G.B.I., 1935)*

143

The Face of
Britain

*(Paul Rotha :
G.B.I., 1935)*

144

Housing
Problems

*(Edgar Anstey
and Arthur
Elton : British
Commercial
Gas Associa-
tion, 1935)*

145
Coalface
(*Cavalcanti :*
Empo, 1936)

146
North Sea
(*Harry Watt :*
G.P.O. Film
Unit, 1939)

147
Line to the
Tschierva Hut
(*Cavalcanti :*
G.P.O., 1937)

148

Britain Can
Take It

*(Harry Watt :
Crown, 1940)*

149

Merchant
Seamen

*(J. B. Holmes :
Crown, 1941)*

150

Target for
Tonight

*(Harry Watt :
Crown, 1941)*

151

Western
Approaches

(*Pat Jackson :
Crown Film
Unit*, 1944)

152

Naples is a
Battlefield

(*R.A.F. and
Army Film
Units*, 1944)

153

Children of
the City

(*Budge
Cooper :
Rotha Produc-
tions*, 1944)

154

Our Country

(John Eldridge
& Donald
Taylor :
Strand, 1945)

155

The Harvest
Shall Come

(Max
Anderson :
Realist, 1942)

156

Steel

(Ronald Riley :
Technique
Films, 1945)

157
Spring on the
Farm

*(Ralph Keene :
Green Park
Productions,
1942)*

158
The Crofters

*(Ralph Keene :
Green Park,
1944)*

159

West Riding

*(Ken Annakin :
Green Park,
1945)*

VIII. THE BRITISH FEATURE FILM

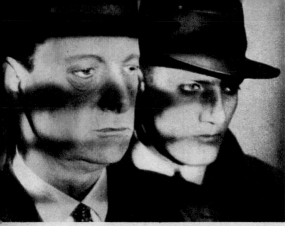

160
Blackmail
(*Alfred Hitchcock : B.I.P., 1929*)

161
Tell England
(*Anthony Asquith : B.I.P., 1930*)

162
The Man who Knew too Much
(*Alfred Hitchcock : G.B., 1934*)

163

Things to
Come

(W. C. Men-
zies : London
Films, 1935)

164

Rembrandt

(Alexander
Korda :
London Films,
1936)

165

Pygmalion

(Anthony
Asquith, Leslie
Howard and
Gabriel
Pascal, 1938)

166

The Edge of
the World

(*Michael
Powell :
Rock Studios.
1937*)

167

The Stars
Look Down

(*Carol Reed :
Grafton Films.
1939*)

168

The Proud
Valley

(*Pen
Tennyson :
Ealing, 1940*)

169
Gaslight
(Thorold Dickinson : British National. 1940)

170
Thunder Rock
(John and Roy Boulting : Charter Films, 1942)

171
The Common Touch
(John Baxter : British National, 1941)

172
49th Parallel
(*Michael*
Powell :
Ortus Films,
1941)

173
The Foreman
Went to
France
(*Charles*
Frend :
Ealing, 1942)

174
Next of Kin
(*Thorold*
Dickinson :
Ealing, 1942

175

One of Our
Aircraft is
Missing

*(Michael
Powell :
British
National,
1942)*

176

In Which We
Serve

*(Noel Coward
and David
Lean : British
Lion, 1942)*

177

We Dive at
Dawn

*(Anthony
Asquith :
Gainsborough,
1943)*

178
San Demetrio,
London

(*Charles
Frend : Ealing,
1943*)

179
The Gentle
Sex

(*Leslie
Howard : Two
Cities, 1943*)

180
Millions Like
Us

(*Frank
Launder and
Sydney Gilliat :
Gainsborough,
1943*)

181
Nine Men
(*Harry Watt :
Ealing, 1943*)

182
The Life and
Death of
Col. Blimp
(*Michael
Powell and
Emeric
Pressburger :
Archers, 1943*)

183
Fanny by
Gaslight
(*Anthony
Asquith :
Gainsborough,
1944*)

184

The Way
Ahead

(Carol Reed:
Two Cities,
1944)

185

Waterloo
Road

(Sydney
Gilliat:
Gainsborough,
1945)

186

The Way to
the Stars

(Anthony
Asquith: Two
Cities, 1945)

187

Henry V

(Laurence Olivier : Two Cities, 1944)

188

Johnny Frenchman

(Charles Frend : Ealing, 1945)

189

Dead of Night

(Cavalcanti and Others : Ealing, 1945)

190

I Know Where I'm Going

(Michael Powell and Emeric Pressburger : Archers, 1945)

191

Brief Encounter

(Noel Coward and David Lean : Cineguild, 1945)

192

Caesar and Cleopatra

(Gabriel Pascal, 1945)

193
Admiral
Nakhimov

(V. I. Pudov-
kin, 1946)

194
The Vow

(M. Chiaureli,
1946)

195
Unconquered

(Mark
Donskoi,
1945)

196
Robinson
Crusoe
(A. Andriev-
sky : Stereo-
scopic film,
1946)

(ii) CZECHO-
SLOVAKIA

197
Stolen
Frontiers
(Jiri Weiss
1947)

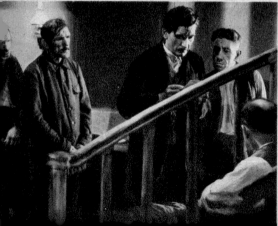

198
Strike
(Karel
Stekly: 1947)

199

Day of
Wrath

(*Karl
Dreyer*, 1943)

200

Ditte
Menneske-
barn

(*Bjarne Hen-
ning-Jensen,
Nordisk,
Film*, 1947)

(iv) SWEDEN

201

Frenzy

(*Alf Sjöberg,
Svensk Film-
industri*, 1944)

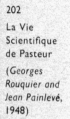

202

La Vie
Scientifique
de Pasteur

(*Georges
Rouquier and
Jean Painlevé*,
1948)

203

Farrebique

(*Georges
Rouquier :
Distribution,
R.K.O.*, 1947)

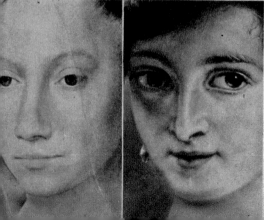

204

Rubens

(*Paul
Haesaerts and
Henri Storck*,
1948)

205

Les Portes de
la Nuit

*(Marcel
Carné : Pathé
Cinéma, 1946)*

206

Quai des
Orfèvres

*(Henri-
Georges
Clouzot :
Wipf, 1947)*

207

La Belle et
la Bête

*(Jean
Cocteau:
Production
Paulve, 1947)*

208

Monsieur
Vincent

(*Maurice
Cloche*, 1947)

209

Le Diable
au Corps

(*Claude
Autant-Lara* :
Trans-
continental,
1947)

(vi) MEXICO

210

Maria
Candelaria

(*Emilio
Fernandez* :
Mandiales and
M.G.M., 1946)

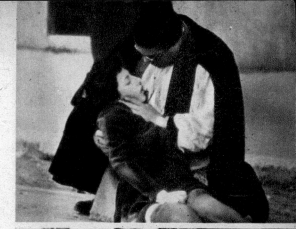

211
Roma, Città
Aperta
(Open City)
(*Roberto
Rossellini*,
1945)

212
Paisa
(*Roberto
Rossellini*,
1946)

213
Sciuscia
(*Vittorio
de Sica*, 1945)

✗

214
Vivere in Pace
*(Luigi Zampa :
Lux Pao,
1945)*

215
Proibito
Rubare
*(Luigi
Comencini :
Lux, 1948)*

216
La Terra
Trema
*(Luchino
Visconti :
Universalia,
1948)*

217

The
Murderers
Are Amongst
Us

(*Wolfgang
Staudte* :
DEFA, 1946)

218

Marriage in
the Shadow

(*Hans
Maetzig* :
DEFA, 1947)

(ix) AUSTRIA

219

The Trial

(*G. W. Pabst* :
Star Film,
Vienna, 1948)

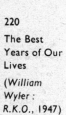

220

The Best Years of Our Lives

(*William Wyler : R.K.O., 1947*)

221

Crossfire

(*Edward Dmytryk : R.K.O., 1947*)

222

The Naked City

(*Mark Hellinger and Jules Dassin : Univ. Int 1948*)

223

Monsieur
Verdoux

(*Charles
Chaplin :
United Artists,*
1948)

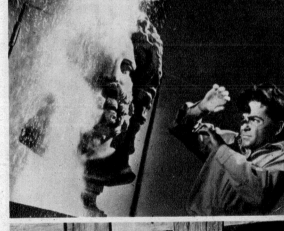

224

Dreams that
Money Can
Buy

(*Hans Richter
and others,*
1948)

225

The Treasure
of Sierra
Madre

(*John Huston :
Warners,*
1948)

226

Ceylon, the New Dominion

(*Clifford Hornby : This Modern Age*, 1947)

227

Children on Trial

(*Jack Lee : Crown*, 1946)

228

Atomic Physics

(*Frank Wells, J. V. Durden and Derek Mayne : G.B. Instructional*, 1947)

229

The World is Rich

(Paul Rotha : C.O.I. for Min. of Food, 1948)

230

Three Dawns to Sydney

(John Eldridge : Greenpark for B.O.A.C., 1948)

231

New Town

(Halas-Batchelor Cartoon : C.O.I., 1948)

232

Circus Boy

(*Cecil Musk :
Merton Park
for G.B.
Children's
Films*, 1947)

233

Odd Man Out

(*Carol Reed :
Two Cities*,
1947)

234

The Over-
landers

(*Harry Watt :
Ealing*, 1946)

235
Great
Expectations
(*David Lean:
Cinéguild*,
1946)

236
Hamlet
(*Sir Laurence
Olivier:
Two Cities*,
1948)

237
The Elusive
Pimpernel
(*Michael
Powell
and Emeric
Pressburger:
Archers*, 1949)

238
The
Fallen Idol
(*Carol Reed :
London Films,*
1948)

239
The Queen
of Spades
(*Thorold
Dickinson,*
1949)

240
Scott of the
Antarctic
(*Charles
Frend : Ealing
Studios,* 1948)

that is not acting. But if you want her to reconstruct the raid, to go through the processes instead of merely the results of emotion, then the imaginative forbearance and technical control of the actress will be required unless both the director and his film are to grow grey. For the larger canvases of *The Grapes of Wrath*, where personal situations are the means by which the theme itself is developed, only the actors and actresses will see the film through the box-office. And quite right, too, or what's the good of paying professionals the salaries we do?

Hollywood has produced thousands of feature films since Griffith made *Birth of a Nation* and the far greater *Intolerance*. Very few qualify to stand beside *Intolerance* with its courageous treatment of social evils shown in the story set in modern times. Although this story is told with a nineteenth-century dash of sentiment and melodrama characteristic of Griffith, its theme is rooted in the social problems of unemployment, poverty and crime. It does not balk at the issues involved, and its direct descendant is *The Grapes of Wrath*. In both the full form of fiction is used: actors impersonate fictitious characters. But the experiences upon which the films are based derive from actuality, from the observation of conditions existing in American society. The film, like the novel, is a medium well adapted to show these conditions vividly as the environment in which the fictitious characters move. *The Grapes of Wrath* becomes therefore a documentary dramatic film concerned with the true reflection of human beings and of society rather than with telling a story for casual entertainment.

THE GRAPES OF WRATH: (Twentieth Century Fox, 1939.
   American.   Director, John Ford)
Theme.—The Dust Bowl; the emigration to the Californian fruit-fields; man's inhumanity to man; the exploitation of poverty; and the crushing of the attempt of labour to unionise.
Story.—The Joad family pass through the valley of despair in a broken-down Ford: their adventures from Dust Bowl to California; young Tom Joad sees his future as a Union organiser.
Treatment.—One of the most courageous social films Hollywood has ever produced, even though it is a somewhat emasculated version of Steinbeck's great novel. Fonda, Jane

Darwell and John Carradine contribute very moving performances. The early sequences are Russian in style with their
sense of the roads and the earth, the long nostalgia of Tom
Joad's return home from a jail-break in another State and the
meeting with Casy, a preacher by the wayside crazy with anti-
religion. The homestead, the return, the mother's emotion, the
grandfather's madness, the sister-in-law's pregnancy and her
husband's empty ambition and final desertion. The land bought
up: the eviction: the tractor crushing the shack: the earlier
wonderfully lit shots whilst Mrs. Joad burns her letters and her
memories with the fire flashing over her face stricken with
emotion. The journey: its rigours: its difficulties: the death
of the grandmother: the deserts: the labour camps: the sense
of social security and social duty in the Government camp
contrasted with the pity and terror of life in the commercial
labour camp with its starvation and exploitation: the children
frightened by a lavatory which flushes in the well-run Government camp: Joad's manslaughter of a police deputy on the
journey and fear of arrest after escape: the wages racket and
undercutting through excess of labour: the fruit-fields electri-
cally barred and wired: the racketeers' police: the union meeting in the dark by the stream: the raid on the meeting and the
death of Casy, preacher-turned-labour-organiser. Joad's last
great scene with his mother whose maternal sense would hold
him back from the future she is proud to feel he will adopt.
His mission of succour to the exploited and of organisation to
conquer conscienceless privilege.

Other films in the history of American cinema have reflected
similar social problems. James Cruze's *Covered Wagon*,
although over-concerned with a purely melodramatic story,
contains some fine actuality material of the life of the early
pioneers and because of this maintains a reputation which
overshadows his earlier film *Beggar-on-Horseback* (1923). This
satirised the *nouveaux riches* and employed an expressionist
technique rare in American cinema. King Vidor also made a
series of important films seriously concerned with social issues
during the silent period. *The Big Parade* (1925), a film of the
War, was the outstanding success of its year, but in *The
Crowd* (1928) he depicted with far greater depth and truth the

problems of unemployment and of the individual struggling against submergence into the crowd. Needless to say, Vidor had to make two pot-boilers to retrieve the ground lost by the unpopularity of this remarkable film, the technique of which was as advanced as the theme. With the coming of sound Vidor made *Hallelujah* with an all-Negro cast which was less important socially than it was technically. Then he personally financed his second important picture *Our Daily Bread* (1934), which again was concerned with unemployment and tried to show that it could be solved by a return to the land. His next important picture he made in England, based on Cronin's novel *The Citadel*. This concerned the struggle of a young doctor in his efforts to deal with occupational disease in the teeth of the opposition of the industry which causes it and even of the men who suffer from it.

Most of the important American social films were made after the coming of sound, though the implications of a virulent social criticism in the early work of Lubitsch, von Stroheim and the later work of Charlie Chaplin should not be forgotten. In 1930 Lewis Milestone filmed *All Quiet on the Western Front*. 1931 was the year of Milestone's *The Front Page*, Mervyn Le Roy's *Little Cæsar*, Roland Brown's *Quick Millions* and William Wellman's *The Public Enemy*. In 1932 appeared *I am a Fugitive from a Chain Gang* (Le Roy) and *Cabin in the Cotton* (Michael Curtiz); in 1933 Capra's effective career began with *Lady for a Day*, William Wyler's with *Counsellor-at-Law* and William Dieterle consolidated his with *Fog over 'Frisco*. Roland Brown followed *Quick Millions* with another study of the gangster in *Blood Money*; Gregory la Cava produced his fantasy of dictatorship *Gabriel over the White House*. 1933 was an important year in American cinema.

Other films followed such as John Ford's *Informer* (1935), Michael Curtiz's *Black Fury* (1935) and *Angels with Dirty Faces* (1939), Fritz Lang's *Fury* (1936) and *You only live once* (1937), Mervyn Le Roy's *They Won't Forget* (1937), William Wyler's *Dead End* (1937) and William Wellman's *Nothing Sacred* (1937). Although Sidney Franklin's *The Good Earth* (1937) was a story set in China, it achieved a universality in the social issues involved. William Dieterle's important series of biographical films began in 1936: his films on Pasteur, Zola,

Juarez, Ehrlich and Reuter were made between 1936 and 1941. In 1938 he directed *Blockade*, the only serious film made by Hollywood on the Spanish war; it was sufficient for the powerful Catholic organisation called the Legion of Decency to attempt to get it banned and to exert boycott pressures against the exhibition of the film, presumably on behalf of Franco. In 1936 Capra's famous indictment of capitalist society *Mr. Deeds Goes to Town* proved him to be an important and original mind in cinema, as well as the wit of *It Happened One Night*, made two years earlier.

The War years brought other films of social importance, Ford's *The Grapes of Wrath*, Michael Curtiz's *Mission to Moscow* (1943), Dieterle's important fantasy *All that Money can Buy* (1941) based on Stephen Vincent Benet's novel " The Devil and Daniel Webster," William Wellman's devastating film of lawless lynching *The Ox-bow Incident*, which was released in Britain as *Strange Incident* and refused exhibition by the major circuits, and his fine film of the American infantryman *The Story of G.I. Joe*, Orson Welles' satirical portrait of the American tycoon *Citizen Kane* and Billy Wilder's study of dipsomania in *The Lost Weekend*. The vastly expensive film *Wilson*, although apparently guilty of considerable inaccuracy[1] and over-idealisation of Wilson, was a remarkable picture of American political life. Preston Sturges's films, especially *Sullivan's Travels* (1942) and *Hail the Conquering Hero* (1945), contain much social satire and great originality in presentation. Jean Renoir, one of the most distinguished of French directors, produced *The Southerner* in 1945, and made in it a companion picture to *The Grapes of Wrath*, as well as one of the finest films to come from an American studio.

This twenty-year record from America alone is sufficient to

---

[1] See the leading article in " The News Chronicle " of Thursday, January 4th, 1945, which records a discussion between the film critic Richard Winnington and the American E. P. Montgomery, the newspaper's Diplomatic Correspondent. Montgomery claims that many important facts have been left out of the film, so giving it a false emphasis in order to build up the idealistic character of Wilson. It omits the very important fact that Wilson threatened to make a separate peace with Germany if the Allies would not accept the policy of his Fourteen Points. The Allied leaders themselves are also under-played in the film as " tricky little political dummies."

prove the outstanding importance of the film as a medium for the serious presentation of social problems. The danger is always that, because social problems lead to personal conflicts, these conflicts will take possession of the film at the expense of the social problems themselves. But in films like *The Southerner, Mr. Deeds goes to Town* and *The Informer,* all very different in their approach to life, personal issues are never divorced from issues of state. It is impossible in the Dieterle biographies to forget the vital service of the individual to the community, mostly in the teeth of the community's opposition. These films atone in some measure for the thousands of pictures made as " pure entertainment " but which carry social implications which are only too often anti-social.

10. *The British Feature Film 1940–1945*

Everyone recognises now that there was an extraordinary renaissance in British feature-film production after about 1940. The story of British cinema, apart from documentary, has been a tragic one of opportunities squandered and pioneers unrecognised. In the earliest days of cinema, artists of the calibre of Cecil Hepworth, R. W. Paul, George Pearson and Will Barker were making films which pointed out the true technique of filmcraft before Griffith shook the world with his two masterpieces. Britain was in the forefront of the film-producing world and British films were shown everywhere. With the industry crippled by the First World War and by the rapid ascendancy of the Hollywood product at a time when we were prohibited from developing at a similar rate, Britain did not, like France, Germany and the Soviet Union, create a national cinema during the twenties. Production continued, but at no pace to match the demand of cinema-goers. In 1927 the Government introduced the famous Quota Act to protect the industry. Exhibitors had to show a gradually increasing proportion of British-made pictures, which by 1939 was only 15 per cent. The rest of the product shown was of American origin. This legal obligation unfortunately encouraged entrepreneur producers to finance films which were worthless and ill-made, and as often as not played as second-features to the American product. All that mattered to these producers was to make quick money. The dozen or so good films made each year in British studios by producers of repute[1] were insufficient to stem public reaction against almost all films bearing British credits, of which an average of 100 to 150 were made each year before the War with a peak production of 225 in 1937.

When War was declared in 1939 it did not seem likely that an industry for the most part so mismanaged and so riddled with unemployment could survive. But the Quota obligation was maintained, and survived the War years on the basis of about 15 per cent of the total films shown.

The studios were faced with immediate difficulties. The call-up left them with a bare third of their personnel. The Government requisitioned studio-space for storage. In 1939 there were 65 sound stages at the disposal of 22 studios. In 1942 there were only 30 sound stages in use by 9 studios. The raw materials for costumes and sets went into short supply. Film stock became rationed more and more severely. Production figures sank from 222 feature films in 1936 and 116 in 1938 to 56 in 1940 and 60 in 1942.

But a new spirit entered the studios. It was the new spirit of Britain challenged at last to undertake a war which she had been uncomfortably avoiding for too long. By the winter of 1940 British audiences were not as satisfied as formerly with the trivial product which formed the major import from Hollywood. Rest, relaxation and escape from worry were necessary, but shallow emotionalism was not enough. The first British war films were astonishingly successful, though the time they took to make pushed their release dates on into 1941–42. In other themes than those deriving from the War production standards were also rising; Carol Reed's *The Stars look Down* (made before but released during the War) and Pen

---

[1] Interesting films made in Britain during the ten years before the War include *Cottage on Dartmoor* (1928); *Blackmail* (1929); *Tell England* (1930); *The Private Life of Henry VIII* (1933); *Man of Aran* (1934); *Things to Come* and *The Ghost goes West* (1935); *Rembrandt, Secret Agent, Men of Yesterday, The Song of Freedom* and *the Robber Symphony* (1936); *The Edge of the World, Victoria the Great, The Great Barrier, Young and Innocent* and *Fire over England* (1937); *Pygmalion, The Lady Vanishes, South Riding, Bank Holiday, The Citadel* and *Vessel of Wrath* (1938); *French without Tears, Jamaica Inn, Goodbye Mr. Chips, Poison Pen, On the Night of the Fire* and *The Stars Look Down* (1939).

Tennyson's *The Proud Valley* both dealt with mining conditions without avoiding the major social issues of this unhappy industry. Roy Boulting directed *Pastor Hall,* adapted from Ernst Toller's play based on Pastor Niemoeller's arrest and confinement in a concentration camp. Thorold Dickinson directed the melodrama *Gaslight* in such a way that the artistry of the production made it a serious contribution to the new development of British cinema.

These were the films of 1940, together with *Convoy,* Ealing Studios' first war film, directed by Pen Tennyson. Their characteristic was an understanding of emotional values and a faithfulness to the environment in which the story was set. The use of the word ' realistic ' to describe this new British cinema was not enough. There is always a poetic quality about the emotional treatment in these films. Accuracy in the presentation of events and situations is not enough: there must also be understanding and humanity. Though, like the Americans, we rarely achieve the subtlety of characterisation found in the best French cinema, we have achieved in a large number of films this humanity and truthfulness to the requirements of situation. These qualities became characteristic of the work of our best directors, and placed it in the forefront of progressive cinema.

There was an influx of new names among the chief credits of these films, following a rapid series of promotions within the studios of men well known to their colleagues as editors, scriptwriters or lighting-cameramen, but whose names were unknown to the public. A few names were, of course, long-established, like the late Leslie Howard, Michael Balcon, Anthony Asquith and Cavalcanti. But most of the directors well known today had made few films of importance before the War, if they had made any at all. Michael Powell had already made *The Edge of the World* and Carol Reed *Bank Holiday* and *The Stars look Down,* but their more important work was to come. The first group of outstanding new directors included Thorold Dickinson, David Lean, John Baxter, the Boulting Brothers, Charles Frend, Frank Launder and Sidney Gilliat, all long-established in film work. Harry Watt and Cavalcanti left sponsored documentary to work for Michael Balcon at Ealing Studios. These directors were followed by a second more junior group of film-makers who gained their promotion to directorship towards the end of the war years, men like Charles Crichton, Basil Dearden and Robert Hamer.

These men all brought to the British screen a new vitality and individuality which was a direct product of the war years. They were consciously reacting against the streamlined showmanship of Hollywood. The work of these directors was greatly influenced by pre-war and wartime documentary. It was bound to the national life of Britain, to our people, our cities and our rich and varied countryside. It produced a new generation of actors and actresses then unspoiled by star values and as interested in their art as the directors themselves. It was to the credit of J. Arthur Rank that he realised the future of British films lay with such artists, because they alone, with those that eventually joined them, could produce the unique film out of the wartime period. It was also to the credit of the Service Departments, who continuously gave facilities to producers and released essential technical and acting personnel to make the films.

Their wartime record was inspiring. Here are some of their films:

1. *Films on War themes made from* 1941 *to* 1945:

49th Parallel (Michael Powell for Ortus Films, 1941).

In which we Serve (Noel Coward and David Lean for Two Cities, 1942).

One of our Aircraft is Missing (Michael Powell for British National, 1942).

The First of the Few (Leslie Howard for British Aviation Pictures, 1942).

The Foreman went to France (Charles Frend for Ealing Studios, 1942).

Next of Kin (Thorold Dickinson for Ealing Studios, 1942).

The Gentle Sex (Leslie Howard for Two Cities and Concanen, 1943).

The Lamp still Burns (Maurice Elvey for Two Cities, 1943).

San Demetrio, London (Charles Frend for Ealing Studios, 1943).

Nine Men (Harry Watt for Ealing Studios, 1943).

We Dive at Dawn (Anthony Asquith for Gainsborough Studios, 1943).

Millions like Us (Frank Launder and Sidney Gilliat for Gainsborough Studios, 1943).

The Way Ahead (Carol Reed for Two Cities, 1944).

The Way to the Stars (Anthony Asquith for Two Cities, 1945).

Journey Together (John Boulting for the R.A.F., 1945).

2. *Films not directly concerned with the War, made from 1941 to 1945.*

Kipps (Carol Reed for Twentieth Century Fox British, 1941).

The Prime Minister (Thorold Dickinson for Warners British, 1941).

Love on the Dole (John Baxter for British National, 1941).

The Common Touch (John Baxter for British National, 1941).

Thunder Rock (Roy Boulting for Charter Films, 1942).

The Life and Death of Colonel Blimp (Michael Powell for Archers Films, 1943).

Thursday's Child (Rodney Ackland for A.B.P.C., 1943).

Fanny by Gaslight (Anthony Asquith for Gainsborough, 1944).

This Happy Breed (Noel Coward and David Lean for Two Cities, 1944).

Waterloo Road (Sidney Gilliat for Gainsborough, 1945).

Johnny Frenchman (Charles Frend for Ealing Studios, 1945).

Dead of Night (Cavalcanti, Charles Crichton, Basil Dearden and Robert Hamer for Ealing, 1945).

Brief Encounter (Noel Coward and David Lean for Cineguild, 1945).

The Rake's Progress (Frank Launder and Sidney Gilliat for Individual Pictures, 1945).

Other films of importance were made during this period, but they mostly did not belong to this young and vigorous tradition.

Although the war films are now no longer shown, they were the true starting-point for the expression of this new art. Many of the less responsible producers left off making films. The War itself, with its tense situations and emotional complexities, offered a unique cinematic opportunity to the more imaginative British producers, an opportunity which Hollywood, through the accident of remoteness from the War and a late start, could not realise in her own films until the example had been well established. A sound reputation for British pictures with British audiences was established and is now generally accepted by exhibitors and public alike.

The problem of British stars was more complicated. For the most part they had to be created and achieve a quick maturity based more on emotional and artistic sincerity than on a thorough understanding of technique. Some, like the late Leslie Howard, Laurence Olivier, Robert Donat, Flora Robson and David Niven, had a considerable reputation before the War. But for many others it was their work during the War period that made the reputations they now have. It is essential that we retain their services as well as add new names to the acting strength. The expansion of the British market overseas will help considerably to keep them from going to Hollywood in the pre-war manner, often never to return. Many will probably stay in our studios if they can recognise a progressive spirit there which it would be difficult to find anywhere else.

The faults of British pictures are easy to find. Many are over-written, and lack the terse economy of the better American films. Words are wasted on inessentials and the action is held up. The treatment is often too polite. Acting technique is too frequently influenced by the needs of the stage, so that emotions realised by small-part players are too precise and emphatic for the enlargement and detail of cinema. There is an adolescent air about British films which has yet to be outgrown. It is on occasion triumphantly left behind when, as in films like *The Way to the Stars* and *Brief Encounter,* the emotional treatment is as mature as that in *La Grande Illusion* or in *Le Jour se lève,* which for characterisation and feeling are at the top of French cinema. This emotional maturity is the peculiar gift of the films of the Old World: it is common to the best of French, Italian, Scandinavian and the new British cinema. Hollywood has produced many remarkable films and occasional masterpieces: the story technique is superb in pictures like *All that Money can Buy, Double Indemnity, The Lost Weekend,* or *The Ox-bow Incident (Strange Incident).* But the emotional atmosphere is nearly always " dressed " with a too-obvious showmanship. It makes immensely effective cinema, but it seldom lives in the knowledge of the close and personal heart. It turns too easily to sentimentality, to sexual or social heroics. The maturity of American cinema is a technical one: it is immensely at ease with itself because of its huge and assured market, its top-line stars, its effective small-part players, its ace directors and its efficient and opulent studios. But it lacks the emotional purgation caused by struggle and stricture.

The artistic future of British cinema is in the balance. A large number of small studios are producing a widely varied product. Expansion is essential, and a wider market at home and overseas. The problems are economic, for without expanding distribution production will be forced to wither. And the economic problems are far from solved.

What matters is that British pictures should retain their national integrity. We alone can make films as closely related to our life as French pictures are to French life and Russian pictures to Russian life. We must not allow our nearly common language to lead us to repeat the disastrous pre-War policy of trying to copy Hollywood without the temperament or the resources to do so. We must not allow economic bargains to take place that will reduce our studios, or even part of our studios, to the status of a Hollywood annexe. We must respect our own integrity and the unique ability of our own directors and actors. To stage a post-war sell-out under the guise of some reciprocal deal which in the end gave Hollywood the whip-hand in our production policy, would be a national and cultural disaster in so important an entertainment medium as the cinema has now become for the British people.

INTERVAL

An Open Questionnaire and Manifesto from the Author and Reader to the Cinema-going Public

INTELLIGENCE TEST: GROUP ONE

How many films do you see every year?

How many have you seen in your life?

How old were you when you first went regularly to the cinema?

How many more films do you intend to see?

Do you go to the cinema every week, every month, every year?

Do you go to the cinema once, twice, three times or more a week?

Do you select the films you want to see each week?

Do you go regularly to see films with certain stars only?

Do you go to see only certain types of films: musicals, thrillers, romantic dramas?

Do you go because your friends recommend you to go to certain films they have liked?

Do you take your films as they happen to come to your favourite cinema?

Do you go to the cinema without even knowing what is on?

Do you read any film criticism in the press or listen to it on the radio?

Do you read film news or film gossip in the papers or the film magazines?

Do you recognise the difference between reading a genuine critical appreciation and just publicity blurb?

Why do you go to the cinema? Do you prefer it to reading, dancing, watching sport, gambling, drinking, staying at home or making love?

Do you remember the films you see? Do you remember them by their titles, their stars, or the emotional effect they have on you? By their music, their thrilling moments, their sets or their costumes? Do you remember them for their striking pictorial or visual way of telling their story; by close-ups, curious shots from long distance, high up, low down, by the speed or slowness of the way the shots follow each other, by the excitement of watching the way the film is told by pictures and sound?

INTELLIGENCE TEST: GROUP TWO

How many pictures have you thought worth seeing twice?

Would you go a long way at personal inconvenience to see a film again, or to see a film you missed on its first release?

Have you ever noted down the title of a film as one to go and see in the future?

Have you ever made a mental note in a cinema about any shots or parts of the film which have impressed you?

Have you ever made a written note in the darkness of the cinema or on return home about the shots or parts of the film which have impressed you?

Have you ever hated a film so much you would have liked to complain about it to the cinema manager? If so, did you do it?

Have you ever wanted to see a film that never came to any cinema within reach?

Have you ever seen a foreign film other than American?

Have you ever written or phoned a cinema manager asking him if he is going to show a certain film? If so, what was the nationality of the film?

How often are you prepared to see titled films in a foreign language?

But perhaps all this is too much like work anyway. The cinema is a place to slip into with a girl-friend, in which to have a good time and be damned to the world outside. And one film is as good as another, provided it has a kick to it of some sort.

Provided it has—that is the beginning of selection, of criticism, in the end of better films and keener enjoyment. Which is better than paying like a mug to keep the producers lazy.

So look through the lists of titles and directors starting on page 264. They are not complete. They are the records of some good cinema, but not of all good cinema. Can you add to them? How many of these films have added to your pleasure in the past?

By your selection and declared choice of what you pay to see your pleasure can be increased in the future.

Part Two

THE INFLUENCE OF THE FILM ON PRESENT-DAY SOCIETY

1. *The Place of Art in the Experience of Living*

THE civilisation of man might be measured by the manner in which he sets about planning and interpreting the flow of sense experiences which constitutes physical life. This planning and interpretation follow the bent of his philosophy—his common sense, or his temperamental make-up—combined with the habits of mind he has acquired from the society in which he lives, and the channels along which custom permits his instinctive energies to flow. Office routine is at once an act of temperament and a social business convention. The act of creation and of participation in the arts is also an act of temperament combined with social convention.

Most people participate in the arts in herds. They form part of an audience at theatre or cinema; they share the same emotion provided by the artistic stimulus. Where they do not congregate for their art, they buy it on the group system and hang it in reproduction on their walls or stand it in their living-rooms. Sometimes if their temperament bends that way they leave the major groups for the minor and hang pictures on their walls which the major group, whose temperament would break if it bent too far, calls highbrow. This pleases the minor group and confirms them in the superiority of their group choice. But it remains a group choice all the same.

Art in its widest aspect is a part of the instinct to order and interpret life, to isolate into some form of permanent and reliable experience the abominable flux of the universe. This aspect of civilisation the so-called primitive man shares with his so-called civilised brother, who is often only a dressed-up savage with the appurtenances of physical comfort and none of the true savage's dexterity and strength. That is why white men are always a little ashamed before the vigour of the native, and assume a superior air when talking in white ducks about their burden.   Genuinely civilised whites give the coloured races their due, and share their experience in bringing order to the mysterious chaos of living.   Variety is useful for the toughest job in the world.

People who never use the word ' art ' in their vocabulary take part in it for a variety of reasons which might be listed as follows:

It is recreative: you feel better for seeing a good film or play. Your enjoyment revitalises the spirit, and the flesh is renewed.

It is communal: you feel better for sharing a civilising experience with your fellow creatures. The gregarious urge is fulfilled, and not with those chill people with whom you work so unnaturally all day.

It is æsthetically satisfying: there has been a sense of order in it—a beginning, middle and an end. Whether the end is tragic or comic matters little provided it is æsthetically right. This is another aspect of enjoyment and civilised recreation.

Art must satisfy these principles to be popular: it must be communal, it must be complete and ordered, it must be a recreation. And most often it is quite unselfconsciously all these things without being thought " art " at all.

Art with the capital A begins when the minority set out to philosophise over their recreation, and when the creator becomes selfconscious about his work. Comparisons creep in and different levels of enjoyment assert their varying merits. People with the leisure to develop their temperaments and foster their susceptibilities begin to demand, not different satisfactions, but more complex forms of satisfactions than will be assimilable by the majority.   Trouble begins when the more complex satisfaction looks down on the simpler satisfaction and asserts that its form of enjoyment is vulgar and insensitive and no art at all; whilst the simpler satisfaction looks down rather than up at the complex satisfaction with a raspberry and a what's-art-anyway attitude.

The difference is purely in degrees of satisfaction, and, in the creation of a major artist like Shakespeare or Chaplin, it manages somehow to satisfy the whole range of demand.

In the long view, therefore, no good will be served by quarrels between highbrow and lowbrow, with the medium-brow keeping a foot in both camps by thinking Shakespeare and musical comedy just wizard. No good will be served by being rude to Hollywood because its productions have box-office pull. It is far better to try to understand why Hollywood has box-office pull, and whether its productions are really recreative, communal and æsthetically satisfying, box-office pull or no.

Art, whether unselfconsciously popular like ballads, folk-dancing, ballroom dancing, community singing, or developed to a degree which recreates the more highly civilised human beings in their more highly civilised moments, must fulfil its fundamental laws. Whether its philosophy be contemporary common sense or in line with the most advanced thought of the time, if the quality of recreation is not present the audience departs glum and thwarted. It is when I sense this glumness in a cinema audience that I am far more inclined to criticise the film than if the audience leaves in a mood of gaiety or quiet elation. For good art at all levels is a stimulant which does not demand lime juice in the morning; only more good art.

The manner, or technique, of art is as important as the matter. A comparatively little matter, provided it is grounded on contemporary common sense, will see a well-made film through. The recreative instinct is fulfilled provided the technique does not seem to be wasted on worthless people. It was good to see Astaire and Rogers enjoy themselves dancing because they were nice people and could dance supremely well. The fact that they are nice people, as it were, is sufficient justification for the attention paid to them in the first place, and then their dancing comes as a glorious technical surprise which is an æsthetic joy to watch in a crowded house enjoying the dancing too. The highbrows relax and have their fun, though the next night they will get a more developed, because more complex, elation at a smaller theatre reviving *The Grapes of Wrath*. They will leave the theatre invigorated by the beauty of it all, by the complex satisfaction that in a world which is a chaos of cruelties and muddle, the human spirit can and does rise with energy and tolerance to prepare an order with less cruelty and less muddle and less defeat of human goodness. And this is recreation indeed.

2. *What the Audience gets*

It is an obvious fact that the average audience does not enjoy the average film to the extent of such recreation. Why, therefore, they go so assiduously will be examined later. It is sufficient for the moment to examine the material provided. In a normal year just before the war England and America released in this country some seven hundred feature-length films. All of these films were made by large staffs, and a deal of money was invested in each picture. Some are classed at the outset as main features: others, with less money assigned and mostly without top-line stars, are condemned at the outset to be second (or inferior) 'supporting' pictures. This usually gives them an inferiority complex for a start.

The script departments are always on the look-out for new stories. These stories may come about in a variety of ways. One of the boys may just think one up for himself—it is then called an original screen story. Or maybe a famous play or novel will prove the groundwork for a film, and the conference gets to work to make a treatment and choose a star. Or maybe the stars are on contract anyhow with overhead salaries flowing out unless vehicles are found to exploit their talents for the period the contracts run. Or maybe the stars themselves find the script and choose the supporting players. Sometimes a famous author is contracted to go into conference with the scenario boys or wait unsummoned in the bungalows and script-offices of Hollywood so that his name can appear as collaborator on the credits when the film is finished. Or maybe all this is libel.

The ways of Hollywood are paved with good intentions. The executives have an honest regard for the millions who pay to see their works. So by their works shall you know them.

But wait a moment for the story of Luce, the American publisher and promoter of *March of Time,* who thought he ought to learn more about pictures, and so joined the Board of Directors of Paramount. From a thumbnail biography in " The New Yorker " we learn that:

> " For a time, Luce was on Board of Directors of Paramount Pictures. Hoped to learn something of cinema, heard nothing discussed but banking, resigned sadly." (" New Yorker," Nov. 28, 1936.)

Why is it we always get back to money? Why is it that the best continuous cinematic tradition has been made where the background money counted for least in the directors' minds—in German silent cinema, in French independent productions, in early Russian cinema, in British documentary? Why is it that if Hollywood has produced tens of thousands of feature films it would be difficult to pick out 500 memorable titles in any category of first-class entertainment?

The answer lies in production policy. It is absurd to say that with all the elaboration of the production executive Hollywood does not watch its public. On the other hand, the weekly audiences are so huge (the equivalent of 60–70 per cent. of the population in America and Great Britain) that the public is extremely difficult to watch. None the less, fluctuations do occur in cinema attendance, not in the aggregate for the week, but as between the various 'attractions' at the various houses. The golden rule has, therefore, become the box-office rule: what will they pay to see in sufficient numbers?

Now for reasons which we will consider later, rather than see nothing at all many people are content to see anything, a factor of importance, and point number one against the box-office rule. For reasons of a similar kind, the cinema with the most comfort or luxury to offer will act as a draw; people will pay to sit in it whatever it may show: point number two. Point number three is that a film will sell on its star, and judgment be warped by the degree of attraction a sellable personality and appearance can exercise on the public.

Production policy, however, has to satisfy the Board of Directors. For the Board the profit motive is the only motive which counts. Prestige may occasionally outweigh expediency, and some seemingly worthwhile production (Shakespeare for instance) be given a try-out. Art with a capital A has its due, and sometimes the box-office endorses the choice. Often when the choice was ill-made it does not. But the Board is interested primarily in investments, and, for the social themes of its films, in the status quo. It will seldom promote controversial discussion.

Production policy is normally conservative and inelastic. Trouble seems to be taken in only a minority of films to make them audience-worthy and recreative. Anything passes for entertainment, and audiences seem to care little enough for progress. So production policy, rigid to the last, forbids progress in the name of box-office.

To sell the films, elaborate publicity blurbs are prepared for the trade itself, and for the public in the picture magazines and screen trailers. Bombarded by adjectives and flashes of stars in laughter and panic, the audience is sold bad films and good with equal bombast. High-spot hooey sells every film on the same level of hysteria to a stolid house. An atmosphere of romantic scandal is allowed to surround the lives of the glamour-stars, until the moralists induce a purity campaign, when the quietude of their luxurious domestic lives is surrounded with lilies.

Small wonder, therefore, that the films are usually hectic rather than recreative, and that entertainment is mostly thought of in terms of more or less stupid adventures derived from successful novels and novelettes and acted by the sexier sort of stars. Entertainment is, therefore, largely made up of:

(*a*) Handsome men getting their girls (without or with sophistication).

(*b*) Handsome girls getting their men (with or without sophistication).

(*c*) Handsome clothes and handsome surroundings (luxury).

(*d*) Absence of clothes from women, and to a lesser degree from men (sex).

(*e*) Ambiguous situations involving sex issues.

(*f*) Excitement deriving from crime (gangsters) and cruelty (sadism).

(*g*) Excitement deriving from the detection of crime.

(*h*) Excitement deriving from extreme physical danger.

(*i*) Excitement deriving from crude supernaturalism.

(*j*) Belly-laughs deriving from domestic incompatibilities.

(*k*) Belly-laughs deriving from naughty children.

(*l*) Belly-laughs deriving from ham silliness (knock-about comedy).

(*m*) Belly-laughs deriving from the flouting of authority (sergeants, policemen, magistrates, mothers-in-law).

(*n*) Sentimentality deriving from patriotism and private duty (service versus love).

(*o*) Sentimentality deriving from children and babies and animals.

(*p*) Sentimentality deriving from mother-love and betrayed faithfulness.

(*q*) Curiosity about foreign people with fake customs and accents (Chinatown, natives, etc.).

(*r*) Curiosity about strange ways and strange glamorous institutions (Foreign Legion, Convents, etc.).

(*s*) Curiosity about fake science and art (personalities, not ideas).

(*t*) Awe at religious beings and fake-mysticism (Lamas preferred to parsons).

(*u*) Awe at the divinity of the love of beautiful women (well lit).

(*v*) Awe at anything other-worldly and glamorously unspoken but oh so true.

I submit that without finishing the alphabet this covers the bulk of Hollywood's endeavour. I do not say that the results are not often entertaining. What I submit is that the greater bulk of all this leaves you nowise different from when you went in, except perhaps a bit glummer the morning after. It is stimulant without recreation: entertainment without relish. And it is made by people who hold down good money for making it, and would often gladly make better if only they dared. And when occasionally they do, they are so surprised at their success that they copy and recopy themselves way back into the old gags and attitudes and thank God for experiment and daring. And if they take a sally at Art with a capital A and make hay of it, then they sink back secure in their box-office winners, because they knew it would be no good anyway before they started.

A letter written by Frank Capra to the " New York Times " (April 2nd, 1939) and quoted by Margaret Thorp in " America at the Movies " reveals the stranglehold the promoter-producer set-up has over the creative freedom of the director. Capra writes as President of the Directors' Guild, which was formed in 1936 to combat the middleman who controls the director's activities, as producer or associate producer. Capra says:

" There are only half a dozen directors in Hollywood

who are allowed to shoot as they please and who have any supervision over their editing.

"We all agree with you when you say that motion pictures are the director's medium. That is exactly what it is, or should be. We have tried for three years to establish a Directors' Guild, and the only demands we have made on the producers as a Guild were to have two weeks' preparation for ' A ' pictures, one week preparation time for ' B ' pictures, and to have supervision of just the first rough cut of the picture.

"You would think that in any medium that was the director's medium the director would naturally be conceded these two very minor points. We have only asked that the director be allowed to read the script he is going to do and to assemble the film in its first rough form for presentation to the head of the studio. It has taken three years of constant battling to achieve any part of this.

"We are now in the process of closing a deal between director and producer which allows us the minimum of preparation time but still does not give us the right to assemble our pictures in rough form, but merely to assemble our sequences as the picture goes along. This is to be done in our own time, meaning, of course, nights and Sundays, and no say whatever in the final process of editing.

" I would say that eighty per cent. of the directors today shoot scenes exactly as they are told to shoot them without any changes whatsoever, and that ninety per cent. of them have no voice in the story or in the editing. Truly a sad situation for a medium that is supposed to be the director's medium.

" All of us realise that situation and some of us are trying to do something about it by insisting upon producer-director set-ups, but we don't get any too much encouragement along this line. Our only hope is that the success of these producer-director set-ups will give others the guts to insist upon doing likewise." (Quoted in " America at the Movies," pp. 146–7.)

The fact that only directors of the calibre of Capra and Ford are allowed producer status led Capra to initiate a strike-threat

by the Guild in February 1939. This obtained for the lesser
directors some short leeway of preparation time with pay,
before shooting, but it has not yet given them the right to
handle their material from start to finish, from story-conception
to cutting-bench. The British industry maintains the producer
system, but our directors have far greater freedom of creative
treatment.

And then when you think you'll give it all up, a good film
comes along, a really good film, right in the teeth of the opposition. And it wasn't made by an independent scratching around
for finance. It was made by the big shots themselves—for
profit. And it has everything in it which makes recreation—
wit, charm, tolerance, gaiety, sensitive understanding of the
smaller human details, love and tenderness and human affec-
tion, kindliness and gracious living. How did it happen? A
producer, a director, a scenarist, a star? It does not matter;
one's confidence is restored; and one endures once more the
crashing of trumpets and braying of shawms until the next
miracle breaks.

3. *"It's the Larst Vord in Pitchers"*

Publicity for the Exhibitors' Trade itself knows no limits.
" It's the larst vord in pitchers," said a film salesman to me at
a Trade Preview. I have been looking for that famous " larst
vord " ever since in the elaborate spreads of the Trade Press,
of whose formulas these are typical examples:

" It's fun and frolic, it's music and romance in a frozen
paradise—but it's got sizzling pay-box temperature! "
(*Iceland.*)

" A story as lovable as *Mr. Deeds goes to Town,* as great
as only a Capra, a Cooper, a Barbara Stanwyck can make
it! While thousands sweep across the screen, drama
reaches new heights and Capra achieves his finest production with a direct hit straight to the hearts of the world's
leaderless legions of ' Little Men.' " (*Meet John Doe.*)

" It's a scorcher! It's a sizzler! It's punch-packed
with Melody! Comedy! Romance! " (*The Gay City.*)

" Paramount's up-to-the-minute Blitz romance—whirl-
ing from our bombed London to gay Lisbon! " (*One
Night in Lisbon.*)

" A boy with a sock—a girl with a heart—a picture with a punch! " (*Knockout.*)

"The first picture to lay bare a woman's mind! " (*Shining Victory.*)

" Where men asked no questions—women revealed no pasts—no mercy expected! " (*A Man's World.*)

" What every woman knows—and no man can understand! " (*Unfinished Business.*)

This type of salesmanship actually adds to the fun of life for the most part, and a whole social philosophy can be constructed out of its implications. The tragedy begins when films of first-class importance are sold in the same language, encouraging people to expect the same formulæ of romance and crime and disappointing them when the comfortable clichés they love are disregarded by a director who ruthlessly portrays life as it was (*The Ox-bow Incident*) or as it is (*The Southerner, Brief Encounter* and *Citizen Kane*) or as it can be for some people (*The Lost Weekend*). The publicity blurb presented the film *The Life and Death of Colonel Blimp* in America as " A Lusty Lifetime of Love and Adventure in Lavish Technicolor " and " The Lusty Lifetime of a Gentleman who was sometimes *Quite a Rogue!* "; for *The Lost Weekend* the blurb ran in America " What Powerful, Desperate Passion Lured Him from the Arms of Two Lovely Women in that Lost Weekend " and in Britain " From the best seller that was talked about in *whispers.*"

The central London audience with whom I saw this last remarkable tragic study of a dipsomaniac, in which Ray Milland gives the performance of his screen career under Billy Wilder's brilliant direction, thought the film was bound to be funny from the moment they saw the first bottle of whisky. The cliché treatment of alcohol on the screen is normally comic. It was not until the stage of delirium tremens was reached that they settled down to take the film as a sort of drama, and Billy Wilder conquered an audience educated to think any picture with Ray Milland and a bottle of whisky bound to be this week's funny story.

On the other hand the reviews, as distinct from the publicity in the Trade journals, are usually extremely accurate and alert to screen as well as box-office values. I would particularly like to apply this to the reviews in the British exhibitors' journal " Kinematograph Weekly " which are often more responsible than those that appear in many national newspapers. The reviews of the class B or secondary pictures in American trade journals employ their own devastating vocabulary. Here is one from the American " Independent," which writes with a deadly accuracy of *Arson Squad* as

" A nifty little secondary, this—with plenty of action, peppy pace and pert performances. Slanted for the nabe market, it should hit the hinterland jackpot and do yeoman service elsewhere on the lower shelf.

"An exposé of arson methods, the story includes standard measure of romance, rugged rough-stuff and righteousness triumphant.

" Lew Landers' direction is competent.

" SLICK SMALL-BUDGET STUFF."

" The larst vord in pitchers." I should ask when.

4. *The War of the Critics*

Against all this ballyhoo the major critics have maintained the war of standards. In their own particular way and style they have fought since silent days for good films, and have sat through thousands of press shows in search of the better things of cinema.

"Just often enough to keep a man from giving up religion, some small miracle will come along. A lot of us sourpuss commentators who are reputed to look on pictures through the jaundiced eye of intellect, and to pan everything on the principle of preserving superiority, are really soft soulers with an anxious love for cinema; we go along protesting that the tripe doesn't really count, and keeping alive that little flame of faith in the possibility of the movie as the art with the largest common denominator. And every once in a while a film quietly made, no drums of *Anthony Adverse,* no bugles of *Romeo and Juliet,* slips through the mill, and we see the thing and experience a slight sense of strangeness, and after a while we remember, rather than realise, that we've seen a picture that demonstrates that our own theories are quite possible, quite possible." (" Garbo and the Night-Watchmen," p. 119.)

This ray of hope comes from Meyer Levin, an American critic anthologised in Alistair Cooke's brilliant collection of Anglo-American film criticism, " Garbo and the Night-Watchmen." Through the hail of publicity and the shower of star glory—(" The furore which has accompanied the producing, promoting and exhibiting of *A Midsummer Night's Dream* could, if properly harnessed, have prevented the Ethiopian war," says Robert Forsythe, batting for America)—they have steadily publicised what they thought good and castigated, pulverised, debunked and derided what they thought evil or merely absurd. Sometimes they feel that judgment falters before the perpetual hypnosis of mediocrity. Writing in 1929 Mr. Robert Herring says:

> " Not a single one of these films is as good as it ought to be, yet there is something to be said for all of them. They are, in fact, distressing examples of the tendency of the whole cinema, which is evolving an alloy that it is still a little hard to reject entirely. In those old days which we are now hearing so much about, films were so bad that one could reject them, whilst seeing through to what they hinted at. Then came a few one could accept. There is now none among the average releases that one can either refuse or welcome. That is why, among other reasons, talkies are welcome. They set us back again to the days of out-and-out vulgarity and stupidity, sometimes avoiding both, and one still has hope that the next phase of efficient mediocrity may be leapt. But the general run of films shows them to be all so competent and so hopelessly un-worth-while, and that is a sign of loss of youth." (" Garbo and the Night-Watchmen," pp. 29–30.)

A steadily increasing number of film critics with a responsible attitude to their work has been writing now for some time. The national press of Britain, in spite of the drastic curtailment of its space, has increased its column allocation to film reviews since the War period. The critics as a body have not hesitated to resist all pressure to curtail their freedom of speech, whilst treating with a gay generosity many films which were little better than routine. They have supported every British film which has come from the new school of direction with a progressive style and treatment. They have supported the distinguished films which Hollywood has made over the past twenty-five years. The result of all this writing, this campaign for good films and more good films, is that a steady body of public opinion is gathering itself together which reads informed criticism before it selects its cinema. But its growing numbers are still small against the vast collective queues that stand in the rain to buy three hours of warmth, comfort and star-solace for lives spent in factories and counting-houses or shopping in dismal little streets.[1]

5. *What the Public wants: Symposium from All Sides*

This is open for everybody's opinion, yours, mine and the psychologist round the corner talking to a man who's been in "pitchers" since 1908. Miss Elizabeth Bowen, in Charles Davy's excellent " Footnotes to the Film ", provides a realistic answer.

" I go to the cinema for any number of different reasons —these I ought to sort out and range in order of their importance. At random, here are a few of them: I go to be distracted (or ' taken out of myself '); I go when I don't want to think; I go when I do want to think and need stimulus: I go to see pretty people; I go when I want to see life ginned up, charged with unlikely energy; I go to laugh; I go to be harrowed; I go when a day has been such a mess of detail that I am glad to see even the most arbitrary, the most preposterous, pattern emerge; I go because I like bright light, abrupt shadow, speed; I go to see America, France, Russia; I go because I like wisecracks and slick behaviour; I go because the screen is an oblong opening into the world of fantasy for me; I go because I like story, with its suspense; I go because I like sitting in a packed crowd in the dark, among hundreds riveted on the same thing; I go to have my most general feelings played on. These reasons, put down

[1] In a census of opinion published as a result of an investigation carried out by " Kinematograph Weekly " (December 20th, 1945), in answer to the question, " Do newspaper critics influence your choice of films? ", 14 per cent. admitted being influenced by the critics and 76 per cent. read the critics' columns for information, though they preferred to form their own judgment.

roughly, seem to fall under five headings: wish to escape, lassitude, sense of lack in my nature or my surroundings, loneliness (however passing) and natural frivolity." (" Footnotes to the Film," p. 205.)

Miss Bowen has had the courage to put herself in with the lowest common multiple.

Mr. Sidney Bernstein, from the enlightened exhibitors' side, tried the experiment of measuring public reception by questionnaire methods. He distinguishes in an article for " Footnotes to the Film " between the gaga and the film-fan. The gaga's

" . . . approach to the film is one of identification. For him the hero is the answer to his own day-dreams and the picture a world which causes the realities around him to dissolve for a while. The films are his release from the frustrations of a dull day." (" Footnotes to the Film," p. 225.)

The film-fan class, a small proportion of the audience, is increasing in number.

" His critical faculty is developing, he can distinguish between good and bad photography and knows something of the technique of film-making. Sometimes he can even differentiate between the good and bad acting of his favourite stars. He is acquiring some degree of articulateness in the correspondence columns of his fan magazines and is eager for pertinent information." (" Footnotes to the Film," p. 224.)

The gaga audience brings to the cinema an urgent bodily as well as psychological need which cannot be overlooked.

" As a social institution, the local cinema represents to a section of the population the peak of glamour. Warmth and colour are to be had there; there are pleasurable distractions; there are comfort, richness, variety. The cinema is so often the poor man's sole contact with luxury, the only place where he is made to feel a sense of self-importance. With his ninepence in his hand he is able to command something approximating to the attention and service which is part of the pattern of the rich man's everyday life. The West End picture-goer and the film critic should bear in mind that his own appreciation of the cinema is not typical or general. Not only the film programme, but the deep carpets, the bright lights, the attention 'fit for a king,' are the weekly delights of the majority of picture-goers." (" Footnotes to the Film," p. 230.)

The film-fan, on the other hand, picks and chooses with a growing sense of what he likes and dislikes. He works on the whole from stars, and sometimes directors, out to themes and stories. His taste in themes varies according to locality in some instances. Films which delight huge audiences in the large central cinemas of London and the big provincial cities are often completely beyond the range and taste of audiences in industrial areas on whom the social subtleties of Bette Davis or Greer Garson are lost. They prefer tough action and belly-laughs.

Mr. Bernstein points out an important fact about the box-office measurement of success.

" The fact that there is no general outcry against the standard of entertainment which is offered at the cinema is not a sure indication that the majority of films are up to the level of public taste. A more accurate deduction can be drawn from the fact that, of the five hundred films issued in any one year, only six or so are record-breakers at the box-office, whilst another twelve, perhaps, produce excellent receipts and another twenty good receipts." (" Footnotes to the Film," p. 223.)

From the critic's angle, Mr. Meyer Levin makes an important statement on what seems now to be an acknowledged part of cinema psychology—screen hypnosis.

" I rarely walk out on a picture, and never want to walk out on a simple programme picture. It is only the more pretentious cinema efforts, the ones that try to be something besides just another movie, that may stimulate me to walking out. Such pictures attain a kind of individuality, and if it happens to be the kind of individuality that rubs me the wrong way, the spell is broken and I want to walk out. But even in the most obnoxious picture, I can feel the basic, physical hypnosis of the medium. I want to sit and let the thing roll on and on, but there is the conflicting desire to get up and out of the room invaded by the personality of some actor, or by some idea I dislike.

"Now, I know I'm not alone in feeling this hypnotic, habit-forming need for the movie. Sociologists, through the activity of social service workers, have in the past few years secured a fairly wide acceptance of the idea that the motion picture is a necessity, rather than a luxury, to the population. It is no longer a shock when a relief client confesses that a quarter out of the minimum-standard-food-budget allowance for the week is devoted to the purchase of movie tickets.

"We are all familiar with the escape-mechanism theory as an explanation for this strange need. Perhaps it is the complete and the proper explanation. An escape once a week into the other-world of the films, and the heart is able to go on. I think there is something more involved than simple escape; I think the need for congregation is there, the need to feel one's self in a room with other folks, sharing a common experience; and also a kind of religious experience in confronting the unnatural together with other folks. Something primitive, like what makes a bunch of savages gather together and watch a witch-doctor.

"Too, there is the factor which those who have recently looked at Veblen will call conspicuous consumption. The need to show one's self spending money for something that is not as obviously necessary as food. This is a secondary factor, for it cannot be operative in the screening room, to which we are admitted free; so below this spending factor must be some really elemental, sensory effect of the moving picture.

"Maybe it is simple hypnotism. The hypnotist holds an object before the eye—some shining object, that flickers, reflecting light. The willing subject keeps his eye fixed in this single focus. And the hypnotist drones out something simple, something familiar. There is no element of surprise. The subject knows exactly what is coming next. The hypnotist is going to repeat the same phrase, over and over—go to sleep, sleep, sleep—or he is going to repeat it in established, progressive variation, as in counting. He is not going to skip any numbers.

"And presently, the subject is in a trance state, freed of responsibility, freed of himself, happily guided by an outside force. He is often disappointed when the spell is broken.

"Maybe that is why people want to sit in the theatre and see two pictures instead of one. Periodically, this craze for dual programmes returns to plague the theatre exhibitors. And as the dual-craze progresses, more and more pictures are made in the secondary category, fill-time pictures which exemplify the trance factor most perfectly. Pictures like *The Luckiest Girl in the World*, or *Adventure in Manhattan*, or *Without Orders*, or *the Isle of Fury*, or—what's that little picture I saw yesterday? They roll along, and you would be really shocked if they should roll out of the routine. It would be like a pulp story turning Faulkner." ("Garbo and the Night-Watchmen," pp. 124–6.)

Hypnosis breeds an uncritical tolerance, provided the girl and the seat are comfortable.

"The point I am making is one I have made often before: to wit, that familiarity with motion pictures breeds tolerance. Coming upon them after a long absence, one is likely to blink the eye and be amazed that such nonsense can be accepted peaceably by human beings. After a period of regular attendance, the spectator begins to make the comparisons which are fatal to his intellectual integrity. He begins to convince himself that while the particular movie before him is awful, it is not worse than something seen last week." ("Garbo and the Night-Watchmen," pp. pp. 124–6.)

In other words, the public has no formalised list of the things it wants, and, to a lesser degree, is fairly tolerant in the circumstances of being shown what it does not want. Mr. Graham Greene unconsciously takes up Mr. Bernstein's point about the fallibility of box-office measurement in a criticism of the private emotionalism of Bing Crosby.

"Bing Crosby mournfully croons. That is the common idea of popular entertainment, a mild self-pity, something soothing, something gently amusing. The film executive still thinks in terms of the 'popular' play and the 'popular' novel, of a limited middle-class audience, of the tired business man and the feminine reader. The public which rattles down from the North to Wembley with curious hats and favours, tipsy in charabancs, doesn't, apparently, ask to be soothed: it asks to be excited. It was for these that the Elizabethan stage provided action which could arouse as communal a response as bear-baiting. For a popular response is not the sum of private excitements, but mass feeling, mass excitement, the Wembley roar, and it is the weakness of the Goldwyn Girls that they are as private an enjoyment as the Art Photos a business man may turn over in the secrecy of his study; the weakness of Bing Crosby's sentiment, the romantic nostalgia of 'Empty saddles in the old corral,' that it is by its nature a private emotion." (" Garbo and the Night-Watchmen," pp. 222–3.)

What the public really wants is excitement.

" ' People want to be taken out of themselves,' the film executive retorts under the mistaken impression that the critic is demanding a kind of Zola-esque realism—as if Webster's plays were realistic. Of course he is right. People are taken out of themselves at Wembley. But I very much doubt if Bing Crosby does so much. 'They don't want to be depressed,' but an excited audience is never depressed: if you excite your audience first, you can put over what you will of horror, suffering, truth. But there is one question to which there is no answer. How dare we excite an audience, a producer may well ask, when Lord Tyrrell, the President of the Board of Censors, forbids us to show any controversial subject on the screen? " (" Garbo and the Night-Watchmen," p. 224.)

On excitement, in the form of Boris Karloff, Mr. Don Herold has the last succinct word.

" Nature must have placed within each of us a certain definite appetite for the horrible, otherwise there wouldn't be tabloid newspapers, and there wouldn't be such crowds around sick horses, and there wouldn't be so many terror movies.

" I can't quite figure why we should pay real money at a box-office to have somebody scare us half out of skins and wits or to put us on the verge of a nervous breakdown. Goodness sakes alive, I don't have to hire anybody to drag me to the verge of a nervous breakdown; I live there; but I suppose some people live miles back from one all the time and have an actual hunger for the jitters.

"An immense number of scream and screech pictures seem to have been batting around, this past month, and I guess I had better hand in a theme about them. I hope I get an 'A.'

"Personally, I would never (if I weren't a hired movie sitter) (this work is not at all unlike sitting as a decoy in a Coney Island bus at so much per hour) place two bits on a box-office window-sill to see one of these chillers. Yet millions of my fellow men pay dough to get in to see these spoovies. Lon Chaney was always surefire at the box-office, and Bela Lugosi and Boris Karloff are Clark Gable to a lot of people. (Clark Gable is usually Boris Karloff to me.) My own idea of fun is to see Fred Astaire or Charles Butterworth or W. C. Fields or even Stan Laurel, but maybe I'm just a scaredy-cat.

"I suppose that the satisfaction lots of people get in watching hair-raising movies is in seeing something going on in the world that is worse than their home life."
(" Garbo and the Night-Watchmen," pp. 68–9.)

Women still form the majority of the cinema's patrons—there are more genuinely tired working women and housewives than weary business men at the pictures. Women are interested in other women, clothes, houses and men. Cecilia Ager watches pictures from the first two angles and writes with acid in the ink. Here she is on Joan Crawford and screen clothes and manners:

"Now she quietly looks any actor, no matter how English, straight in the eye, confident of the mastered casualness of her own pronunciation. Nobody's coiffure is more cleanly swept-off-the-brow, more intent upon character and therefore disdainful of artificial coquetry, than hers; nobody's wardrobe more starkly simple—but only on the surface, mind. That calm and repose she's now achieved, that feeling of firm ground beneath her feet, must not be mistaken for just pure simplicity. Far from it. It wells from knowledge—from knowledge, at last, gained the hard way. No more do 'beans'—for 'beens'—jut out from her speech naked and terrified; no more do unresolved trimmings distract from the compact and self-contained silhouette of her clothes. Still self-conscious but with a new self-assurance that shows her self-consciousness is only an expression of her awarenes of her duty of high-class-example-setter to her public—instead of the mark of self-doubt it used to be—now Miss Crawford goes about doing right things, wearing right things, with deafening poise. Now her quality asserts itself from the inside out, instead of insisting on itself with externals; and the whole show is much more convincing, besides being a lot easier on everybody and cosier to watch." (" Garbo and the Night-Watchmen," pp. 301–3.)

A picture can set a hair-style or build a new costume-line. The market watches the cinema, and the cinema has been known to watch the market. *Things to Come* started a new craze in beach-wear ahead of its time—the penalty of forecast in dress design. Though the dresses and make-up and coiffeurs leave the girls pondering and their mothers muttering what will they leave off or put on next, there is no doubt that the fashion-demands shape themselves to the sweep of this star's hipline and the uplift of that star's bust.

And so there we are back where we started from; the audience is receptive, but, apart from the film-fans, generally uncritical and averse to using much intelligence from its own side of the screen. It expects to be excited, thrilled, amused and emotionally lit-up. If in the process of fulfilling these needs a director slips in an idea, it will not matter if the situation keeps up the tension. If the ideas are strong or continuous, as in *Citizen Kane* or *The Grapes of Wrath,* then the suburban or provincial audience begins to cast around for something to laugh at. So this makes the directors wary. King Vidor says about *The Wedding Night*:

" Artistry does not consist of making a film that only a limited group of people can understand. Rather, we must seek a great common denominator, a means of telling a story that is understandable to all classes of audiences—the poor, rich, old, young, European and American. One must hold to human emotions to achieve this goal, because emotions are universal and can be understood by every human being. . . . Emotions can be portrayed by a gesture, a facial expression, a step or two, a lifted eyebrow. The complexity of sophisticated people makes such simple expressions impossible. To explain their situations, one must go into long dialogue, movement must stop, each point of the story must be told by the characters in detail. Speed, movement, and reality vanish. In the picture I have just completed, *The Wedding Night,* I have followed the same formula." (" Garbo and the Night-Watchmen," pp. 102–3.)

Hitchcock says generally:

" I must say that in recent years I have come to make much less use of obvious camera devices. I have become more commercially-minded; afraid that anything at all subtle may be missed. I have learnt from experience how easily small touches are overlooked.

" In a film you keep your whole action flowing; you can have comedy and drama running together and weave them in and out. Audiences are much readier now than they used to be for sudden changes of mood; and this means more freedom for a director. The art of directing for the commercial market is to know just how far you can go. In many ways I am freer now to do what I want to do than I was a few years ago. I hope in time to have more freedom still—if audiences will give it to me." (" Footnotes to the Film," pp. 10 and 15.)

We had better wind the forum up with a quotation from one of the trade papers, " Kinematograph Weekly." This epitomises the Exhibitor's angle on the subject.

" When people stop to think they realise that the power of the screen is directly dependent upon the fact that about 25 million patrons every week pay for admission to our kinemas because they want to be amused. They are satisfied or they would cease to attend. . . .

" But what is the real desire of the kinema patron? If anybody takes the trouble to inquire he will find it is to get away from the whole nasty business for a couple of hours—to live in another world and build up resistance to the wearying anxieties of the day by enjoying a spell of make-believe.

" Call it ' escapism '—why not? What else is there in any form of mental relief from hard conditions outside? And so long as the world can get this relief, however temporary, so long is the kinema doing a good service. When it is necessary to inflame the public passions or fears, let us find some other medium than the kinema." (" Kinematograph Weekly," Thurs., Sept. 4th, 1941, Editorial, p. 4.)

6. *The Effect of the Cinema on Adults and Children*

Attendance statistics of the cinema in this country and America outclass any other available national attendance. In America it is calculated almost 100 million seats are sold in the cinemas weekly. In this country, with a substantial war increase, some 28 to 30 million seats a week are sold. In assessing these estimates one must allow for the small age-groups at either end of the scale—infancy and old age—which cannot be effective potential audience, and for the fact that many people attend the cinema more than once a week. Perhaps 50 per cent. of the available population of both countries are regular cinema-goers.

The weekly statistics of juvenile attendance in this country are about $4\frac{1}{2}$ millions; in America 11 millions. Many children go to the cinema two or even three times a week. In a normal school survey very few go once a month or never at all.

Many cinemas in this country, notably the Rank circuits, are organising regular children's matinées, usually on Saturday mornings. Here the staple make-up of the programme is the cartoon, the serial, the interest picture and the more-or-less suitable feature originally made for adults, though recently a number of special short films for children have been produced by the Rank organisation.

The Board of Censors, working along its own lines, awards films in this country three types of certificate, a U, an A and an H. Any child can see a Universal certificated film; any child can see an Adult certificated picture when accompanied by a *bona-fide* parent or guardian (the way the children pick up their *bona fides* on the cinema doorstep is notorious); no child under sixteen is allowed to see an H film.

On the whole this classification is sound, but the present practice of film-going leaves the child free to see films which were never intended for him, provided his parents assume the responsibility of taking him, which too many of them do quite thoughtlessly. On the other hand, although the melodramatic scenes of horror, brutality and sordiness in some films must affect children adversely, sex and romance normally interest them very little. Adult sexuality does not really enter the normal child's line of country until the approach of adolescence. Then the partially clothed woman stirs repressed interests in the awakening male, and the adolescent girl gets a pash for a film-star and a precocious taste for make-up and cinematic clothes.

Most of the sex situations and innuendoes of dialogue pass the child by as so much waste time. "The Film in National Life" quotes a Methodist minister: "I know that many good-well-meaning people—and associations as well—believe that the influence of the films is a bad one . . . ; even the sex film may do no harm, for the simple reason that a child does not understand half what is being said. Passionate kisses simply give them the giggles. What I do object to is coarseness—not the Rabelaisian coarseness, which does not seem to be particularly harmful—but the crude, sneaking coarseness which the children recognise at once."

Disney's *Snow White* was given an A certificate by the Board, which caused much controversy in the press and much certificate revision by local authorities. Disney, of course, has never set out to be a film-maker for children. It is the children who have adopted Disney, despite the horrific element, symbolic of evil, which is an essential part of the Disney folklore. In *Snow White* an A certificate was given as a warning to child and parent that an horrific element was to be expected: an H certificate would have kept the children away from what everybody persisted in thinking was a children's film.

The element of horror has the worst effect on children as far as the content of the screen is concerned. Children, who in moments of personal fantasy can be astonishingly brutal to other children and animals, do not like violence when it is directed at themselves. The horrific element in screen fiction is frequently so presented as to give the audience as great a shock as the victim in the drama. Richard Ford describes frightened children in the cinema : " ... there is usually a tense hush when children are frightened during a film, and they hold their breath, with small restrained squeaks, while they grip the edges or arm of the seat. The noise of healthy screaming during a chase scene is entirely different." But this type of fear is rare, and in a questionnaire to 142 managers responsible for the Odeon children's matinées, 83 per cent. stated that the children were never frightened by incidents in cartoons, and 61 per cent. that the children were never frightend by incidents in serials. The lists of the rather obvious things (spiders, horrific animal close-ups, grotesque faces, King Kong and clutching hands, extreme danger to screen favourites) provided by the minority of managers are probably justified in consideration of the more sensitive child, whether boy or girl.[1]

The dangers to the adult (and even more to the impressionable not-yet-worldly-wise adolescent) are far greater, though always to be seen in the light of the fundamental common sense of the people as a whole, who know the difference between a picture and real life, and, indeed, are rather affronted when in films like *The Lost Weekend* they are asked to look at actuality on a night off.

The psychology of advertising and propaganda includes the principle of repetition. If the cinema assumes in the majority of its products certain attitudes to character, customs, manners and institutions, these attitudes which in an individual picture

[1] At the request of the American Motion Picture Research Council the Payne Fund Committee of Educational Research initiated a series of twelve studies on the general subject of " Motion Pictures and Youth." These were summarised in a short volume of that title by W. W. Charters published by the Macmillan Company, New York, 1933. Henry James Forman published " Our Movie Made Children " in the same year, basing his argument on the Payne studies. Many striking facts are revealed connected, for instance, with the effect of exciting films on children's sleep: motility in bed for boys was increased by 26 per cent. after a night at the pictures. Young children are three times and adolescents twice as excitable as adults in the cinema. Sex films (in 1930 72 per cent. of the films released dealt with crime, sex and love) affected adolescents most. Fifty per cent. of high-school children investigated admitted ideas of sex-love came from the pictures. Films affect delinquent children more than non-delinquent. And so on. The actuality shots of children watching a horrific film in the Realist documentary *Children learning by Experience* are interesting in this consideration.

may be regarded as fictional and unreal may after a protracted period of cinema-going become absorbed as correct for decisions and behaviour in real life. Though I do not suggest that a girl when choosing her husband deliberately looks for someone like Van Johnson or Stewart Granger, I do suggest that the qualities of manhood accepted by her in the continuous contemplations of her ideal will colour her reactions to the men she has to meet in the real world. Certain patterns of behaviour in the attitude of men to women and women to men will seem acceptable to her, and she will be less adaptable to the exigencies of real male behaviour when she has to deal with it. Here the world of her own fantasy (coloured so real on the screen) will affect her behaviour for good or evil.

Similarly in the matter of her own behaviour and appearance. Few women can afford to dress like a film-star even if it were possible to do so in the broad light of day. But the personal appearance of many girls can be, and is, considerably modified by what they come to regard as their style, and whether this style is a direct copy from a film appearance or an amalgamation of film appearances, it is obvious that the cinema is the most consistent educational force in personal appearance and bearing offered to a woman today.

The position for men is similar. Young men, normally self-conscious with women, look around for attitudes and phrases with which to impress them. The cinema is a ready source of patterns of behaviour. With faltering taste, young men dress themselves and go out to kill. The cinema, as their favourite resort, guides them in the appropriate approaches to their women, and colours the tone of their cinematic phrasing.

None of this may be for the bad, provided one factor is observed, namely that the fantasies built up from consistent film-going do not unfit an adolescent for normal living, especially on the emotional plane. It is obvious that the cinema has done immense good. It is a communal activity. Its cheapness does not lead to the impoverishment of people who go continuously. In a world as yet unfitted for creative leisure, it provides a steady fill-up for otherwise empty hours. It must in the long run prevent much anti-social behaviour in drunkenness and individualised vice.

Where some of the harm lies is in the propaganda element,

which is insidious rather than obvious in the content of motion pictures financed by some of the hardest big-business combines in the world. It is obvious that the 'no controversy' ban by the British censors is matched by a 'no controversy' ban from the promoters themselves. In the broader issues of right and wrong, the cinema is on the side of the angels—gangsters are evil, detectives are good. But certain themes are implicit in most pictures (American and British alike, but more vividly in American) and might be listed as follows:

(a) Wealth in the abstract is a good thing.

(b) Luxury, especially associated with women, is normal.

(c) The full-time pursuit of women by unoccupied business men and rich young rulers is normal.

(d) The desks of high-power executives are always clear.

(e) Fathers spoil their daughters with money-gifts.

(f) Men are the source of money for women.

(g) The desirability of the night-club-with-cabaret life.

(h) A sock in the jaw is an honest man's answer.

(i) Men should appraise women by externals, with close-ups of essentials.

(j) Women should be judged satisfactory on the basis of desirability.

(k) Sex is probably the most important sensation in life.

(l) Women can be come-hither till you don't know where.

(m) Women may appraise men by externals and invite intimate attention at speed.

(n) Things of the spirit are either funny, eccentric, charlatan, or ever so wonderful. (Art is usually debunked as artiness, religion as mania, mysticism as a yearn in soft focus.)

(o) Reformers are either harmless saints or agitators. (No controversy, please—Promoter and Censor.)

(p) Brainless patriotism is preferable to national self-criticism.

(q) To be foreign is to be under suspicion. To be Eastern is to be horrific.

(r) Life is a lark if you have the facilities. Boy gets girl is the end of life's difficulties, divorce is as easy as knife, and riches are the reward of virtue.

A cynic will say that this is a picture of actuality anyhow, and since the screen is realistic, it is merely reproducing real life. But the answer lies in attitudes and emphases, in suggestions and comparisons, in the absence from the screen of a due sense of proportion in all these things. I do not think a working girl should take her standards from a socialite, since she cannot carry them out in practice—all she will be able to do is to copy the socialite's sexual attitudes without the money to pay for them.

The absence of any social sense from so many films is compensated for by personal, that is individual, glamour and charm. To be charming is enough, together, perhaps, with the exposure of some flagrant vice in the villain of the story. The emphasis on the personal satisfactions (for screen love is normally selfish love since the prizes are so desirable) induces a wrong political emphasis in a period when the world will survive only by collaboration between communities and nations.

To sum up, cinema at its worst reflects an impoverished hedonism, an appalling absence of cultural background or international understanding, and a dangerous escapism from the social problems which only an alert public opinion can lead to a satisfactory stage of solution. These problems are often misrepresented, sentimentalised, or treated, as in the gangster films, as a medium for a little vicarious sadism on our own behalf in passing. Gangsterism is only Fascism writ small, and little can be done to clear the larger evil while the smaller remains a favourite form of public excitement in the armchairs of the cinemas. The vicious circle of the box-office prevents the healthy development of documentary fiction, which the public would take in its stride if well directed; and where the box-office would open its chromium doors to fictionalised discussion, the censors step in with grandmotherly fervour to stop the children thinking for themselves.

Yet despite all this, the miracle happens, and certain problems of social importance have been worthily treated in successful box-office films.

7. Censorship. No Controversy, please: No Fires

The famous signature of T. P. O'Connor on a smudgy censor's certificate always preluded the feature film from the year

1916. His death did not, however, alleviate the censorship situation, which has, during the course of the years, developed into an anomalous position. Its history is complicated, and bound up with the Fire Regulations in the eyes of the Local Authority through which the cinemas obtain their licences like public houses. The stages in the history are these:

1. In 1912 The British Board of Film Censors was set up *by the trade itself,* and was financed by it, in order that the trade should gain respectability in the eyes of the community. Mr. T. P. O'Connor proved an enterprising President, and vastly developed the powers of the Board in the teeth of legal opposition after his appointment in 1916.

2. In 1921 the Middlesex County Council inserted *a clause in its cinema licences* that no films could be shown without the Board's certificate. This is universally accepted by Local Authorities, who can, however, over-rule the Board's category certificate, and who also retain the power, which they very rarely use, to license the showing of a film without a certificate. Most Local Authorities never question the Board's certificate. For the sake of their licences, neither do the exhibitors.

3. By the Cinematograph Act of 1909 no cinema without a licence issued by the Local Authority can exhibit inflammable films to a public or private audience. Thus a censorship regulation is linked with a fire regulation.

4. In 1922 the Home Office approved the following conditions, namely that the Local Authority could alter the Board's A certificate to a local U certificate, could grant permission for the exhibition of films uncertificated by the Board, and could restrict the entrance of children under sixteen to A films. The Home Office recommended all Local Authorities to carry out these so-called model conditions.

5. In 1924 the High Courts, questioned on the legality of the conditions, decided they could be enforced.

The position rests that most Local Authorities accept the Board's censorship rulings implicitly, and impose them on the exhibitors within their area of jurisdiction through the granting of cinema-opening licences based on a fire-clause. Public-spirited Local Authorities can, at the request of an alert public or exhibitor (such as a Film Society), grant permission for the showing of an uncertificated feature.

But the law of the box-office means in effect that no film will be made in Britain or America which will not pass the Censorship regulations and so automatically be barred from all but a tiny minority of cinemas.

Films made on the Continent under easier censorship conditions can be shown in this country only after being mutilated to suit the Board's regulations, or, if unsubmitted, by the tolerance and progressive outlook of the Local Authority. The Local Authority usually acts through its Watch Committee if ever requested to permit the exhibition of such a film. The answer usually goes without saying.

The Censorship staff's preoccupations when watching its hundreds of films a year can be briefly summarised under the following general prohibitions:

1. *Religious.*—The materialised figure of Christ (you remember the trouble over *Green Pastures*). The irreverent treatment of religious practices and rites. The irreverent treatment of the Bible and biblical allusion (*L'Idée* banned).

2. *Political.*—Anything calculated to wound foreign susceptibility (*Inside Nazi Germany* banned). Anything calculated to foment social unrest and discontent. (The universal release of Russian films in Britain came only since Russia's entry into the war.)

3. *Social.*—Nudity (except Negroid), swearing (beyond certain limits: the Hays Code is more particular than the Board: controversy over language in *Hamlet* and *In Which we Serve*), indecent orgy, contempt of State and King's uniform, lascivious behaviour (difficulties here!), lascivious dress, gross drunkenness, child-birth and its pains, venereal disease, sexual relations between white and coloured people (half-castes passed), incitements to crime, exhibitions of drug habits, prolonged scenes of brutality, hangings and executions, cruelty to children and animals, antagonistic scenes between Capital and Labour, seduction without restraint, marriage nights without restraint, illegal operations, prostitution, incest, realistic epilepsy.

There can be little doubt that the Board takes a wide view of what might be classed as the sexual headings above. Normally the humorous treatment of sex is more easily allowed than the serious, the romantic ' glamorous ' sex than the purely sensuous. Nevertheless, it is amazing what is allowed, and how near the intention of the regulations some scenes can be allowed to go. Also, with special fuss, and with alert Local Authorities putting in a ban of their own, clinical films on childbirth and venereal disease have been shown in this country.

The Censor's ban has in the past been stringent on political issues. Film Societies have on the whole been allowed to show themselves Russian films during the thirties when these were normally without certificate. Certain Local Authorities, notably the broadminded L.C.C., have permitted their public exhibition. But these films were made on foreign money, and one or two prints only sent to this country. The Censor's attitude to matters of political controversy normally prohibits the making of films on sociological problems, both here and in America, until they have reached that stage of solution when their portrayal can no longer appear to 'foment' public opinion.

Even for films under feature length the Censor's certificate must still be obtained. Only the newsreel is exempt. Controversial issues can, however, be introduced more easily into the short than into the expensive and prominent feature film. *The March of Time* has not always succeeded in gaining its certificate in this country, but it has with reasonable consistency taken up subjects which troubled the world's politics, as the list on page 121 shows.

Most countries have their censorship, but it largely takes a political rather than a moral umbrage. In France a more frank approach to sex is permitted, but the sight of a political issue raises a storm at once. French films, therefore, are normally either passionate or lighthearted. René Clair's *A Nous la Liberté* caused trouble despite its final dance between Capital and Labour. Malraux's *Espoir* was banned before the War. Clouzot's *Le Corbeau* was banned for a time after the War.

The story of American censorship is different from that of Great Britain. I am indebted to Margaret Thorp's " America at the Movies " for the facts. State censorship began in 1911. The industry set up its own self-sifter in 1922: this was the Motion Picture Producers and Distributors of America. Will H. Hays, campaign-manager to President Harding, Postmaster-

General to Harding's Cabinet, was appointed president with a salary of a hundred thousand dollars a year. When he retired in 1945 he was succeeded by Eric Johnston at a salary reported as $150,000, with $50,000 expense allowance.

The Hays Office is a bureau of reference for the industry: it will advise on pictures before they are made. In 1930 one of Hays' departments produced a " Code to govern the making of Talking, Synchronised and Silent Motion Pictures," a survey of social and sexual immoralities which must not appear on the screen.[1] Since this sort of thing is the same the whole world over, there is not much to choose between the American Code and British custom. All scripts are submitted to the Hays Office before they are shot, and all finished films must get a Code seal before general release. The seal makes no reference to release for children as distinct from adults.

The Hays Office also acts as liaison between trade and public. It is a goodwill agency. It seeks out what is honourable in the American public's intentions towards the cinema, and encourages what is best and cleanest. America is a land of clubs and societies. Among these are some six thousand Better Film Councils, the solid expression of we-want-good-films from the more on-coming of America's hundred-million-a-week moviegoers. These Councils organise support for what they are led to believe are the better films produced in America.

Finally there is the National Legion of Decency, organised by the Catholic Church, which is twenty million strong in the States. The Legion indexes all films in lists issued weekly. It classes films as A (Section I, unobjectionable for all; Section II, unobjectionable for adults), B (objectionable in parts), and C (condemned). Films likely to get a C grade on moral or political grounds are not made in America. *Things to Come* received a B; *La Kermesse Héroïque* a C. Walter Wanger's *Blockade*, because it appeared to attack Franco's side in the Spanish war, was not classified at all, and arrangements were made to boycott it.

Addressing the Trade in 1936, T. P. O'Connor's successor, Lord Tyrrell, expressed his pleasure that so far he had not licensed any film dealing with " current, burning political

---

[1] The Code is published in the Motion Picture Almanac each year. See also " Freedom of the Movies," by Ruth Inglis.

questions," and that he was prepared to put " some check " on those subjects which showed a sign of being the " thin end of the wedge." " Cinema needs continued repression of controversy in order to stave off disaster," he said. Russian films, films like *L'Idée*, and issues of *The March of Time* like *Inside Nazi Germany* received no certificate. The only solution here was for the showing to be given by the private group and the minority cinema, the work of which demands a section of its own.

The common-sense solution to the censorship problem is difficult to reach. To take the two extreme cases of divergent viewpoint, it is intolerable that intelligent people should be deprived of the right to see films on the most important sociological issues of the time, or films which deal with matters of sex or religion with critical integrity. On the other hand, films which deal with such subjects in a manner which can be tolerated for the intelligent and worldly-wise may well be harmful if exhibited to the uncritically receptive adolescent or oversensitive child. It is intolerable that all films for public exhibition should be measured by the standards of the culturally under-privileged, for by such standards, if applied to great literature, a large measure of the world's masterpieces would have to be bowdlerised or abandoned. The burning of the books would cover much Greek and Latin literature, the contes of the Middle Ages, some stories of Chaucer and plays of Shakespeare, the dialogue of Congreve and Wycherley, the coarse gaiety of the novels of the eighteenth century, the essential strength of Balzac, Flaubert, Zola, Proust, Dostoevsky, Tolstoy, Lawrence, Huxley, Joyce, dos Passos, Steinbeck and many modern novelists in America, France, Britain, Russia and elsewhere. Much of this literature which troubles the unbalanced adolescent is strength to the culture of the adult mind, which can bring a wider background of comparisons and moral standards to bear in the reading of these contributions to human self-discovery.

So far in this battle of divergences, the culturally under-privileged have received the protection of the Censor, which is a protection by half-measures only since so much of the material passed is harmful by standards other than those the Censor is called upon to watch.

The culturally privileged have had to found private societies to see unlicensed films either behind the closed doors of admittance by membership only or by means of the projection of the films on 16 mm. substandard stock which escapes the fire-prevention order and so the opening-licence which in turn operates the Censor's ban. Substandard, however, is not the best medium for seeing the more complicated type of film technique, and the only adequate solution to date has been the private society in the larger communities making use of standard-size sound machines either in the cinemas when not open to the public or in private buildings equipped for sound-film projection.

Either you must have a censorship, or not. There can be no half measures. Since it seems unlikely that there will be any time in the immediate future without censorship, the most sensible thing to do is to accept its existence as temporarily inevitable, and mitigate as far as possible its evil effects. The solution which most obviously presents itself is the issue of a further certificate—the ' S ' certificate—which should be given to any film not granted any of the other certificates and which is not a piece of mere pornography as such. The viewing of S films could be restricted to S audiences, namely Film Societies and other private bodies of the specialised type. The fact that a film carried an S certificate would mean that the Local Authorities would not, as now, regard it as uncertificated and therefore ' banned ' in the worst sense, but rather would class it with Shakespeare as something remote and possibly of cultural advantage to someone. It would be automatic that films bearing an S certificate would be allowed without question to Film Societies, and with very little question to those few minority cinemas specialising in film repertory and foreign films.

The S certificate is the way out of the worst effects of censorship as now practised, and the way in for the film with minority appeal. No damage would be done to public morals, and the phrase " banned by the Censor " would be confined to those products of a poverty-stricken mentality which are usually classed as commercial pornography.

8. The Economic Aspect of the Film Industry

(i) AMERICA AND BRITAIN

The production, distribution and exhibition branches of the world's film industries are on a considerable scale. Statistics are available from various sources, official and unofficial, but they are often contradictory, unreliable or not sufficiently co-ordinated to be easy to interpret. It is, however, possible to build up a fair picture of the workings of this complicated machine for the production and marketing of visual entertainment.

The world audience for cinema pre-war was estimated at 235,000,000 seats sold each week. The figure now is far too conservative when we bear in mind that during the War British seat-buying reached nearly 30 million a week, and American some 100 million. In Britain we are closely bound to the Hollywood wheel, and during the War we saw some 85 per cent. American pictures to 15 per cent. British. The quota regulations of 1948 have increased the percentage of British films which must be shown to 40. A tiny fraction only of our screen space in London is given to Continental and other productions: in the provinces their exhibition is in most cases limited to a few repertory cinemas and to Film Societies. These carry no weight in the big business of film marketing. Our British productions are now seeking an overseas market mostly through the Rank, Korda and A.B.P.C. groups. Hitherto British productions, like those of all other countries except America, have been limited for their exhibition largely to the cinemas of their own land.

Film production is, however, a world-wide activity. Here are some comparative figures of the number of feature films produced:

	1937–8	1946–7		1937–8	1946–7
Japan	575	30	Argentina	50	50
America	545	397	Italy	47	62
India	200	100	Czechoslovakia	41	25
Britain	162	70	China	33	100
Germany	137	15	Sweden	30	45
France	122	70	Hungary	26	2
Philippines	67	24	Poland	25	5
Mexico	60	60	Finland	20	15
Russia	51	30	Egypt	16	40
Norway	3	4	Spain	—	42

Apart from Russia, which still allows only limited entry to the foreign product, few of the above countries were producing enough films to meet their exhibition needs. Once a country becomes cinema-conscious its demand for continuous change of programme outpaces the production capacity of all but the most prolific industries. These have been limited so far to Japan, India, and America. Of these America has for long been the only recognised exporter of films on a world-scale dating from before the first World War, when Britain was forced to retire from competition.

America pre-war produced over 500 feature films a year, though the number gradually dropped during the War to 350 and is now about 400. She has a large number of cinemas to supply in her own territory, and an export market representing a third of her total receipts. Britain alone sent her in 1946 some £17 million in film rentals. The following figures, by no means complete, show the proportion of Hollywood feature films exhibited in representative countries overseas:

Country	Approximate No. of Cinemas with Sound	1946–1947		
		Total Films Imported	American Films Imported	British Films Imported
Argentina	1,600	520	375	29
Australia	1,700	342	293	36
Belgium	1,200	450	300	25
Brazil	1,540	497	427	—
Canada	1,560	797	638	24
Chile	270	323	248	—
China	300	—	75% [1]	3%
Czechoslovakia	2,200	167	79	23
Denmark	430	267	181	41
Ecuador	70	492	351	13
Finland	460	317	188	44
France	5,500	—	46%	8%
Germany	3,600	122	26	16
Holland	440	467	272	68
India	1,800	300	250	40
Italy	6,000	485	381	37
Japan	2,000	—	80	—

[1] Percentages indicate total proportion of films exhibited, not imported.

Country	Approximate No. of Cinemas with Sound	1946–1947		
		Total Films Imported	American Films Imported	British Films Imported
Mexico	1,430	392	261	33
New Zealand	400	345	293	44
Norway	360	398	50%	15%
Poland	520	125	—	10
Portugal	300	173	116	9
Sweden	2,500	264	183	33
Switzerland	380	460	188	22
Turkey	300	450	250	30
Uruguay	170	335	195	15
U.S.A.	17,700	—	—	46

These figures show the dominating position of Hollywood, which can afford enormous sums in financing its films, and has created a taste for lavish expenditure on costumes, sets and stars among audiences in countries which, like Britain, can ill afford to spend so much on window-dressing the home product. Any industry seeking to build up a world market for its pictures is faced with two initial disadvantages. The first is that world taste has for years been moulded to the Hollywood pattern. The second is the impossibility of being able to invest as much money in the larger type of production as Hollywood without an initial period of subsidising. These are the two problems the Rank organisation in Britain is trying to solve.

The organisation of Hollywood[1] is important, since its standards have become the popular measure of what is good or bad in pictures. First some figures, all pre-war:

In 1939 Hollywood spent $187 million making films, and supplied 65 per cent. of the films used throughout the world.

Hollywood employed pre-war a maximum of 33,683 persons a month in making films.

Of the 251 films made by six major studios 19 (7·6 per cent.) cost over a million dollars, 60 (23·9 per cent.) cost from half-a-million to a million dollars, 40 (15·9 per cent.) cost from a quarter to half-a-million dollars and 132

[1] The facts which follow are derived for the most part from Leo Calvin Rosten's important book "Hollywood." Harcourt Brace, 1941.

(52·6 per cent.) cost under a quarter-million dollars. Normally those costing under half-a-million dollars rank as secondary features only.

Hollywood paid its élite of some 250 persons $75,000 a year or more. (In 1947 Betty Grable earned over £50,000, Charles Laughton £70,833, Tyrone Power £57,756, Ray Milland £63,333: in 1945 Louis B. Mayer earned £227,000.) Normal pre-war earnings for sound engineers were $3,000 a year and for carpenters $1,000. In 1936 there were 20,000 extras wanting work: in 1940 6,500 only. In 1940 only 3·1 per cent. of those employed averaged $150 a month. Only 630 earned as much as $1,000–3,000 in the year.

In 1938 34 directors earned between $100,000 and $300,000, but the average for all directors was $16,500. 30·6 per cent. earned less than $10,000.

In 1938 over 54 actors received $100,000 or over.

In 1939 half of Hollywood's 1,753 registered actors (not extras, who are classed separately) earned $4,700 or less. The median in 1938 was $5,000 and in 1937 $6,000.

In 1938 of 159 producers, 33 per cent. earned over $75,000.
    of 235 directors, 20 per cent. earned over $75,000.
    of 1,250 actors (not extras), 6·4 per cent. earned over $75,000.
    of 800 writers, only 17 individuals earned over $75,000.

The structure of the studio-organisation is as follows:

   I. The Big Five:
        1. Paramount.
        2. Twentieth Century Fox.
        3. Metro-Goldwyn-Mayer (Loew's Inc.).
        4. Warners.
        5. R.K.O. (Radio-Keith-Orpheum).

  II. The Little Three:
        6. Universal.
        7. Columbia.
        8. United Artists.

III. THE INDEPENDENTS:

> 9. Selznick.
> 10. Roach.
> 11. Wanger.
> 12. Republic.
> 13. Monogram and
> 14. A number of other independents.

Of these in 1939: 1 to 4 took 95 per cent. of the net profits of the year, 1 to 3 85 per cent. and 2 and 3 together 71·6 per cent. These statistics exclude the unpublished figures of United Artists.

The structure within the Studios themselves approximates to the following:

1. The Executive Head. Deals with the financial level only.
2. The Executive-Producer. Supervises 40 to 60 features a year, plus shorts (e.g. Jack Warner of Warners, Louis B. Mayer of M.G.M. or Darryl F. Zanuck of Twentieth Century Fox).
3. Producers-in-Charge of " A " Pictures. Supervise 20 to 30 films costing half-a-million dollars each, or more. Receive their budget from above.
4. Producers-in-Charge of " B " Pictures. Supervise films costing under half-a-million dollars each.
5. Producers or Associate Producers. Supervise 1 to 6 pictures a year.
6. The Directors.

The exceptions to this system are

(a) The Independent Producers such as Chaplin, Goldwyn, Selznick, Wanger, Roach, etc., whose work is distributed through United Artists, or the other distributing companies.

(b) The Producer-Directors who work with full production authority. There are about 30 of these, including Capra, Ford, Gregory la Cava, Milestone, Ruggles, and producer-directors heading their own corporations, such as Cecil B. DeMille and Frank Lloyd.

To see that the world knows all about the work of Hollywood 400 newspapermen were assigned to Hollywood before the War, and over 15 style-reporting agencies in Los Angeles worked as style-scouts for the world's department stores.

Apart from the regular newspapers and journals, eight fan
magazines are published with an average circulation of from a
quarter- to half-a-million.

There is obviously no film-producing organisation in the
world which begins to rival Hollywood in influence and quan-
tity of showmanlike output. The numerous films of the Far
East are suitable for the most part only for limited regional
exhibition. Industries producing films of high quality like
France and Britain obviously want to export their productions
and so increase both their prestige and their profits. They are
faced with the firmly established distribution-exhibition tie-ups
of the Hollywood agents based overseas.

The position in France is explained in the next chapter.
That in Britain must occupy us now. First a few basic figures: [1]

There are about 4,750 cinemas in Britain selling between 25
and 30 million seats a week.

The bulk of the programmes shown consist of two feature
films. During the War only 15 per cent. of the films
shown were British in origin. The quota has now been
raised by the Government to 40 per cent.

Of the 4,750 cinemas, some 2,000 are key cinemas which have
control of the new product for first-run exhibition and
the highest box-office takings. Of these 2,000, about
half are controlled by the three big circuits in the
following approximate proportions:

Odeon, 310; Gaumont-British, 250; Associated British
Cinemas, 414.

The circuit houses represent about a third of the total seating
capacity of the country. The importance of the circuit
system in Britain can be assessed from the fact that *no
first-class British feature film can at present be produced
and regain its expenditure without circuit booking.* This
means that production policy is directly dependent upon
exhibition policy; it is no use making films which will
not be in line with the requirements of the circuits.

In 1941 both the Odeon and Gaumont-British circuits were
acquired by the Rank organisation, which has also
acquired before and during the War some 50 per cent.

[1] Derived mostly from the Monopoly Report, published by the Board
of Trade. Stationery Office, August 1944.

of the studio space of the country. A great deal of British production is therefore tied directly to the Rank organisation which finances and distributes it. London Films–British Lion (associated with Korda) has no circuit, but sponsors and distributes films. The company owning the Associated British Cinemas circuit, the Associated British Picture Corporation, is financially linked with Warner Brothers, and owns a further 20 per cent. of British studio space, the greater part of which is therefore under the direct control of the same organisations as the three circuits.

This is very different from the case of France, where exhibition is almost entirely independent of production, or even of America, where only about one-fifth of the cinemas (representing about a quarter of the seating capacity) is directly owned by the producers. The position in Britain has reached the stage where many people inside and outside the film industry fear the effects of the monopolistic control of film production so effectively tied to exhibition. On the other hand we have seen that many producers are for the present allowed a degree of freedom in the expression of their various styles of film-making within the production-distribution set-up of the big organisations.

The overseas market for British films is important.[1] Though their actual earnings may remain small, their so-called invisible export value can be high, ranging, for example, from the artistic prestige deriving from good films to the demonstration of British fashions by the stars. However much the output of British films may increase in the next few years, Britain will remain inevitably in a subsidiary position as far as America is concerned. We shall need her products much more than she can ever need ours. Once more it is necessary to realise that no good can come of adapting British pictures so that their intrinsic quality is modified to please potential audiences overseas. It is also extremely doubtful if good can come of over-financing super-productions like *Cæsar and Cleopatra* when the home market yields barely £200,000 for

[1] British films earned just over £1,000,000 overseas in 1945. Recent annual expenditure in Britain on American films was about £17,000,000, but is now reduced to £4,500,000.

the producer of a film. It is better to produce primarily for the home market and that of the English-speaking sections of the British Commonwealth, and to finance films accordingly. If they are good enough for us, with our highly critical standards, as appreciation of film technique goes in the world, they should also be good enough to spread our reputation as film producers in other countries, including America.

First-grade films in Britain now cost £100,000 to £250,000 to produce. These figures are about the same as those in America for all but her super-productions. These costs we can just meet in our own market, though our salary scales are markedly lower than those of Hollywood. With increased efficiency of studio organisation and more economic scripting we can reduce substantially the amount of time spent on production, which has been known to extend to a year and in exceptional cases lasts longer. In America films are put through the studios at much greater speed, though allowance must be made in Britain for weather variability which holds up production in the very pictures that tend to represent our studios at their best, those involving large-scale location work in the beautiful countryside of the British Isles. Every day saved in the studios means a cut in costs, and it is here that British films must in future learn to economise. There is every indication that this will happen, since new studios cannot be built extensively during the present long-term housing shortage, and the existing space must be used as economically as possible in order to increase the annual output of British films.

The problem of independent film production remains crucial in British films, and the various Government regulations and loan arrangements can scarcely be said to provide the answer. While production costs remain at an inordinately high level, it is virtually impossible for new blood to enter film production except the slow, hard way or by means of a dubious back door. The distributors' hand and taste lie heavy on any new-comer who has managed to get a financial sponsor or arrange for a loan. Experiment, the courage of a new art, is simply not wanted, because it is too dangerous at the box-office. Only the well-established producers dare gamble with public taste, and they are usually far too weather-wise to go more than a fraction of the way towards going too far.

A way out may be through the second feature film, which is budgeted on a low cost and does not therefore risk much money. Distributors are not likely to fuss so much about it. New blood can easily be tried out here with a reasonable measure of freedom. Perhaps the second feature and the films for children will provide the field for experiment which may modify our main production policy.

(ii) THE CINEMA IN FRANCE

The importance of French film production [1] in the development of world cinema was apparent before the war. The work of her great directors such as Jean Benoit-Lévy, Jean Renoir, Marcel Carné, René Clair, Julien Duvivier, Claude Autant-Lara, the late Jean Vigo, Jacques Feyder, Marcel Pagnol, André Malraux and Jean Grémillon became the most consistently sensitive and poetic realisation the history of the film had known. The skill of her artistes, such as the late Raimu, Louis Jouvet, Jean-Louis Barrault, Michel Simon, the late Harry Baur, Pierre Blanchar, Pierre Brasseur, Jean Gabin, Arletty, Michèle Morgan, Françoise Rosay, combines humanity with realism, and made France famous for what came to be known in America as her " characterisation." The structure of the French film industry is therefore a matter of importance to all students of the cinema, especially in relation to the problems which France is now facing economically and æsthetically in the period of her recovery and reconstruction.

This structure is very unlike that of the British industry, with its cinema circuits and close financial tie-up between production, distribution and exhibition. The ownership of the cinemas of France is almost entirely independent of the producers, and there are few circuits. There are 5,500 cinemas in France but only about 1,500 of these are of first importance; many only open spasmodically during the week. Some 300 of the more

[1] In the case of a number of European film industries, most useful statistics were compiled by the investigators who undertook for UNESCO research into conditions obtaining in a number of war-devastated countries. Their findings were published 1947–48 in two Reports from the Commission on Technical Needs in Press, Radio and Films. Statistics in this account of the French film industry are taken from this Report, but I am also indebted to the Cinémathèque Française and M. Georges Sadoul for information.

important cinemas are in the area of Paris alone, and there are large stretches of France with very few cinemas, such as Brittany, the Juras and the centre of France. There are, however, some 7,000 substandard mobile cinema-vans covering these and other areas with road-shows. Programmes in the cinemas are changed normally each week, but in Paris and important provincial towns such as Marseilles, Lyons, and Nice longer runs for important films are usual. Double-feature programmes are illegal in order to encourage as far as possible the development of documentary and short film production, in which Painlevé is an outstanding figure. During the Occupation French films were shown alternately with German pictures, the exhibition of which was compulsory. French film production was, however, encouraged by the Germans, because they held investments in it.

The French have long been jealous of their national cinema and have tried to protect it from the encroachments of Hollywood upon French screen-time. Before the War France had been making some 120 feature films a year, and provided some 40 per cent. of her programme needs. The rest was largely met by American importations. After the Liberation the French producers greatly resented the attempts of Hollywood to involve itself in French distribution and production; there are, for instance, financial links between Pathé and R.K.O. France does not want to import more than about 40 American films a year, and these of her own selection. Actually she has to take, through the Blum–Byrnes Agreement,[1] a greater number than this, to the detriment of French production, which now has greatly reduced playing-time. The French export market (mainly to Belgium, Switzerland, North Africa and Syria, but also on a lesser scale to Italy, Spain and Argentina) accounts for some 15 per cent. of her whole turn-over.

The French studios are situated in Paris (Rue Francourt and Buttes Chaumont), near Paris (Joinville and Billancourt) and at Nice. These studios made some 200 feature films during the Occupation, encouraged by Vichy and the Germans, who had

[1] By the Franco-American Film Agreement, 1947, revised 1948, French cinemas must show French films only five weeks each quarter. The Americans have also agreed not to import more than 124 films a year, provided all other imported films are reduced to 65; the British share of this is only 20.

invested money in French feature films.   There was little active collaboration with the Germans by film directors and artists: the results of the Occupation can be seen rather in the type of subjects filmed; escapist pictures, sentimentalities and historical romances, or detective stories kept production going with no reference to immediate political or social issues.   Only a spiritual *malaise* seems to be at the root of such important films as Marcel Carné made from Jacques Prévert's scripts (*Les Visiteurs du Soir* and *Les Enfants du Paradis*), a development of that *malaise* which was evident in much of the best French cinema before the War, a poetic feeling for emotional frustration, anticipating sorrow and desiring purgation.   It has much in common with Tchekov's sensitive adjustment to the *malaise* of the society in which he lived, and to the self-immolation of Dostoevsky's characters.

The costs of production as compared with pre-war have risen enormously.   The official figure given in the UNESCO Report shows an increase in costs of 10·7 times, whereas the price of cinema-seats has risen only 3·9 times.   The State taxation on the film industry is fantastically high, possibly because France has few industries to tax, and films are the second of her national trades.   There has been a rise in the price of seats in cinemas, as in Britain, but without a rise in wages to match it. Cinema attendance amounts to only some 480 million seats sold a year, as against the British figure of some 1,300 million. Yet taxation in France (December 1945) absorbs some 60 per cent. of the total receipts of all branches of the industry. This tax must be drastically reduced if French cinema is to survive its battle with Hollywood.

Distribution remains the key to the French film industry. The variety of independent producers receive their returns from the distributors.   The exhibitors obtain the product from them.   The whole work of the industry is, however, controlled by a Centre National de la Cinématographie, set up in October 1946, and directly responsible to the Government. Unlike Britain, production remains independent of America for both raw stock and equipment.   France is considerably short of both, and of good studio space.   It is part of her reconstruction plans to develop the industry as soon as the crippling incidence of taxation can be reduced to more reasonable proportions.

At present she is producing about 70 features a year. Some of these are financed by the distributors, some by Government loan and some from independent sources. In this way pictures of the highest quality can be made by artists of faith who are able to obtain the necessary financial support. Experimental production by men such as the late Jean Vigo becomes possible, especially when the actual expense of the films can be kept small.

Before the War the French studios employed some 50,000 workers. There are two State training schools for apprentices to various branches of work in the cinema. The first is the Ecole du Cinéma in Paris giving two years' training to cameramen and still photographers, with courses on montage and editing. The senior academy is the Institut des Hautes Etudes Cinématographiques with a three-year course for directors, set designers and sound engineers. Cameramen who have passed through the Ecole can have a shorter more advanced training at the Institut. This basis of training is important since it must obviously result in the beautiful finish to so much French camerawork. In Britain there is no adequate training for the complicated work of the studios: graduation is by trial and error as men and women climb from junior to senior grades in the actual process of making films.

France has made bad films, and many of them. But she is also the source of some of the most beautiful works of cinematic art of our time. The most compelling element in her great films is their *sensibilité,* that quality which reveals with sensitive tenderness and profound feeling the values of goodness and beauty in human beings. French acting matches the mastery of the dialogue in such films as the fatalistic works of Carné and Jacques Prévert (*Quai des Brumes* and *Le Jour se Lève* with Gabin and *Les Enfants du Paradis* with Jean-Louis Barrault, Pierre Brasseur and Arletty), or the realism touched with poetry of Renoir's *La Grande Illusion* (Gabin and von Stroheim) or Duvivier's *La Belle Equipe.*

These, with other actors and actresses, have made of French cinema a glass in which many people have come to recognise the poetry of the humanistic approach to life. Many films in which the mastery of their restrained performances appeared were decadent with a helpless fatalism, but that does not vitiate their greatness.

The present problems of French cinema are not therefore merely economic. The creative problem of combining the *sensibilité* of the past with a more purposeful reintegration of the spirit has now to be solved. There is the beginning of a spirit of a new time and place in France today. It must create its own expression in the life of a country with such an impeccable tradition of artistic feeling in its cultural history.

(iii) THE CINEMA IN THE U.S.S.R.

The organisation of the Soviet film industry is quite unlike that of any other country. In the successive Soviet Five-Year Plans, the development of the industry has always figured, and the fact that hopes have exceeded what has actually been done should not blind us to the extraordinary achievement of the Russian film-workers. The pressure put upon them in the Plans shows the high degree of importance attached by the Soviet authorities to the cinema, which is interpreted by them as part of the cultural and propaganda forces in the life of the Union. Although the stress on the cinema as an ordinary entertainment medium has increased considerably since the early thirties, Soviet film-makers never forget that the background to their films, whether they are historical, dramatic or even musical, should be the new life in contemporary Soviet Russia.

The growth of the industry can be seen from the figures given below, which are a conservative estimate of the rise of projector usage and film attendance over the past twenty years. It should be remembered that right up to the War silent projectors were almost as common as sound, and that silent film production continued late into the sound period, and also that twice as many projectors work the rural areas as the urban, many of them being mobile; the population of the Soviet Union is 193 million, and approximately two-thirds of the people work in the rural areas.

The approximate number of projectors in use has risen in the following proportions: 1917, 1,095; 1926, 3,000; 1936, 28,000; 1941, 31,000; 1944, 17,000 (after the destruction of the war period). Annual admissions have been: 1936, 650 million; 1941, 900 million; 1944, 600 million. The aim now is to in-

crease the number of projectors in use to 46,000, and to raise
feature-film production, which was about 60 films annually
before the war, to between 80 and 100 films a year. The
industry manufactures its own equipment and raw stock.

The Soviet Union, therefore, with four times the population
of Britain, registered in 1944 less than half the cinema attendances of this country. Urban cinemas in Russia are small,
seating only 300 to 700 people. The seats are wooden tip-ups,
the floors bare, the lighting sparse, the projection and sound
rough. The programmes are organised on a single-feature
basis, with supporting newsreels and short films. Richard
Ford, writing in January 1937, describes a typical Russian
cinema and its audience:

"Imagine a worker going to the cinema. He has heard
that the new film, showing in all the big cinemas, is worth
seeing, and he decides he can afford five roubles for himself
and his wife. He does not know the names of any film
stars (they scarcely exist in the U.S.S.R.), but a friend says
there is plenty of excitement in this film. He does not
like sophistication, but wants a strong story full of action,
with the triumph of right over wrong, and the heroine, if
possible, helping to shoot the wrongdoers.

"At the box-office he stands in a queue. He sees the
time of the performance—twenty-five minutes to wait—
buys the tickets (numbered for a specific row and seat) and
walks into the foyer, well-lit and furnished with seats and
benches. At the far end a jazz band is playing on a plat-
form, with a woman singer in a long silk dress. He stares
at them, nods his head to the rhythm, and goes to the food
counter to buy a cake for his wife. The previous show
ends. Still wearing his cap, he rushes into the cinema,
elbowing his way to find his seat number, in a hurry in
case the lights go down. Then the doors are shut, the
lights are out, and he fixes his eyes on the white screen.
There is no smoking or eating in the cinema. At the end
of the film the lights go up, he is told to hurry along,
and he goes out by a different door from the entrance. Prevented from seeing the jazz band again, he
goes into the street to queue in the cold for his tramcar
home.

" The average Moscow audience is similar to a child audience in England. It wants excitement and action. The faster the pursuit, the more the shouts of encouragement. Dirty deeds and wanton cruelty evoke groans of horror. Stirring acts of national patriotism with the appearance of the Red Flag, and a singing marching song, get plenty of cheers. Long-drawn love scenes give rise to imitated kisses amongst the audience. Only the heroic aspect of sex is tolerated.

" Going to the cinema is regarded more as a cultural experience than an evening's entertainment. The audience stares at the screen as if attending an important lecture. Its attention seldom wanders. There is, in fact, far less conversation during films than during plays in theatres. There is very little laughter except at clowning; dialogue seldom provokes laughter; but any joke at the expense of priests is always well received." (" Sight and Sound," No. 21, p. 11.)

None the less, the industry is placed on a sound footing for development, and has its place in the new Five-Year Plan. Again, because of its distinction from British and American commercialism, Ford's summary of the structure of the industry in 1937 is of great interest:

" The following brief summary of the structure of the industry may help to emphasise the importance placed upon this great propaganda industry.

" (a) The Film Industry is controlled by the Committee on Arts, one of the highest State authorities.

" (b) Studios: There are film production studios in each of the separate Republics. The Moscow Studio—the largest and most active—contains four main groups for the production of full-length features, for children's films, for newsreels, and for cartoons respectively. In Moscow there are also two units, called factories, for producing technical and educational films. In 1936 the Moscow Studios released 15 full-length sound films, compared with 4 in 1935 and 4 in 1934. About 3,000 people are employed in production in Moscow.

" (c) Apparatus: Five factories.

" (d) Institutes: In Moscow and Leningrad there are

Academic Institutes for the study of scientific and technical problems connected with the industry.

"(e) Schools: In Moscow there is one technical school for training specialists for the industry.

"(f) Chemical Trusts: Six chemical factories for making and distributing film stock.

"(g) Copy Factories: Eight factories for making copies of completed films.

"(h) Building Trust: This organisation is responsible for building and planning new cinemas. Its activities are limited by the vast amount of new buildings urgently needed for housing, factories, and offices. In Moscow, for example, the Trust has plans for a large new cinema in the main square, to seat 3,000 to 4,000 people; for there is at present only one large cinema in the centre of Moscow. But the difficulties of construction, and the slowness due to adverse winter weather, are shown in the fact that completion is not scheduled until 1940.

"(i) 'Russian Hollywood': A film production town is being planned in the Crimea. It is intended to concentrate there all the most expensive imported apparatus and to make the town a focal point for the widely scattered national studios. The equipment and personnel for 'dubbing' foreign films will also be concentrated there." ("Sight and Sound," No. 21, p. 9.)

Writing in "The Cine-Technician" (August 1937), after an official visit to the U.S.S.R. in May 1937, Thorold Dickinson and Alan Lawson, delegates of the Association of Cine-Technicians, give in their Report a very full description of conditions in the Soviet film industry before the War. Whilst the costs of film production were kept low (as far as costs can be compared they quote £30,000 for a fairly ambitious Russian feature film), directors were not forced to work against time on important films:

"For instance, the brothers Vassiliev began their research work for the film *Chapayev* early in 1932; after completing their researches, they spent six months on writing the scenario. They began shooting exteriors during the summer of 1933, made the interior scenes during the winter, returned to their exterior location during the following summer, edited the film by the first week in October, and presented the film publicly during the first week of November 1934, more than two and a half years after receiving the assignment. And the result, to anyone familiar with the Russian language, was a good film."

Sergei Eisenstein describes the expansion of film enthusiasm to the borders of the outermost Republics.

" The motion picture has become a prime cultural necessity to the Soviet citizen. The best films are distributed in thousands of copies and shown everywhere, not only in the big modern theatres in the cities and the cinemas in the countryside, but in clubs, the apartments of our Stakhanovites and other people of note. They are shown to collective farmers far out in the fields, to army and navy men and passengers on ships at sea.

" Then there are the itinerant cinemas employing a great army of operators equipped with portable projectors. They show films in the most remote corners of the country, the Siberian forests, the Alpine meadows of the Caucasus, the villages of Turkmenia and Tajikztan and the auls (native villages) of Kazakhstan.

" To the far northern districts new pictures are delivered by air. The operators there take them on their itineraries by dog or reindeer team. In Yakutia, for instance, one operator recently made an interesting tour by dog-team. In a few months he covered about fifteen hundred miles and demonstrated his films in all the wintering camps on his route. But this, of course, is an exception.

" Itinerant cinemas are generally installed in motor vehicles of the latest make. Among them are a fair number of the new outfits which show films out of doors in broad daylight. Considerable attention was paid to the question of motion pictures as an important department of cultural development during the discussion of the new Five-Year Plan at the recent eighteenth Congress of the Communist Party. Provisions were made for a sixfold increase in the number of sound picture installations by the end of the Third Five-Year Plan." (" Culture and Leisure," pp. 38–9.)

In the same way, the multi-lingual production of films was expanding before the war.

"The Five-Year Plans created a substantial technical base for the industry. The Soviet Union now produces its own film in large quantities. Several large plants have been built for the equipment of moving-picture theatres and studios.

" Fine studios have been built in Moscow, Kiev, Minsk, Tbilissi, Leningrad and elsewhere. The Soviet newsreel service has branches in all the main cities.

" Under Soviet rule the non-Russian republics, too, have developed film industries for the first time. The picture-goers of the Ukraine, Georgia, Byelorussia, Armenia, Azerbaijan, Turkmenia, Uzbekistan, and Tajikistan see films with the dialogue in their own languages. These films are made by their own nationals." (" Culture and Leisure," p. 41.)

The principle of distribution is described by Richard Ford as follows:

" Before a completed film is shown to the public it is first shown to a select Commission whose work it is to see that it does not transgress in any way the written Constitution of the U.S.S.R., and secondly, does not offend against public morality. It is also shown privately at the Kremlin to high officials of the Government, who can demand alterations. Finally, it is shown privately at the Film Club where all film workers can see it, and criticise it from a technical point of view.

" The film then passes to the Distribution Trusts, of which there is one for each of the Republic Areas that form the U.S.S.R., who control distribution and exhibition. When a Trust has viewed the film, it orders from the Copy Factory the number of copies which it considers sufficient for the cinemas under its control. In Moscow, for instance, the Trust usually gives a first order of 120 to 240 copies.

" Every cinema, excepting five special cinemas in Moscow, is directly controlled by its Distribution Trust. Each cinema has a house manager appointed by the Trust. The Trust decides all details for each cinema; what film to exhibit, when to take it off, times of showing, prices of admission, and so on. In Moscow the five largest cinemas, including the Children's Cinema, are responsible directly to the Committee on Arts, which controls the film industry. They appear to have some similarity to first run or pre-release cinemas; and from their box-office receipts some estimate can be formed of the popularity of films." (" Sight and Sound," No. 21, p. 9.)

Leading film-makers and artists are not paid extravagant sums to work in films. Thorold Dickinson and Alan Lawson describe the rates of pay in the studios in 1937:

"Skilled employment in a film studio brings a salary averaging from 500 to 1,100 roubles a month. A leading lighting cameraman (or woman) would receive up to 1,500 roubles a month. Leading players under contract, writers or directors, receive up to 2,000 roubles per month. The idea of the cameraman receiving five times the salary of his assistant is alien to the system. It is interesting to note that a crack railway engine-driver receives 1,250 roubles per month, based on the fact that while he is at work several hundred human lives are entirely in his charge. Wages of the production staff and of the controllers of studio finances run parallel with the other departments."

A producer was given a premium if he completed a film to schedule, and the director and script-writer shared $1\frac{1}{2}$ per cent. of the gross takings of their film.

Recruits to the industry are trained at the special institutes set up for the purpose.

"Producers, operators, scenario writers and studio artists are trained at the State Institute of Cinematography in Moscow. This Institute has specially equipped laboratories, demonstration halls, studios and a collection of practically all the films that have appeared on the screen anywhere. The influx of students is so great that a new extension is being made, equipped with the most up-to-date motion picture technique.[1]

"The doors of the Institute of Cinematography are wide

---

[1] An account of the course conducted at the Moscow Institute is given in Herbert Marshall's " Soviet Cinema," and by Thorold Dickinson in " The Cine-Technician " quoted above. In 1944 an experimental Film Actors' Theatre was founded in Moscow. This is described by Catherine de la Roche in " Sight and Sound " (Summer 1948).

open to talented youth. As in all colleges in the Soviet Union the Institute's training is free of charge and the students receive a regular allowance from the State. After graduating from this Institute they go to the studios where, after a trial period, they are given work to do on their own responsibility.

" Motion picture technicians are trained at another institute in Leningrad. A third institute, in Moscow, conducts research on the problems of stereoscopic films and the improvement of cameras, projectors and film." (" Culture and Leisure," pp. 42–3.)

The result of this completely different perspective cannot easily be imagined by an audience trained in the British and American commercial cinema. The Russian position is more nearly that of documentary turned feature, with the entertainment film as such developed as a side-line and welcomed in its due place. The conception of the film is idealised into a major cultural medium. " Cinema is the most important of all arts for us," said Lenin. " The cinema in the hands of the Soviet power represents a great force," says Stalin. And the directors echo this promise: " the great international art of cinematography," wrote Pudovkin, and Eisenstein stated ten years later: " We say that the screen is of all arts the most popular in the Soviet Union."

In 1946 the Cinema Committee which controlled the affairs of the Soviet Film Industry was promoted into the Ministry of Cinema of the U.S.S.R., with I. Bolshakov as the first Minister. The challenge offered to this Ministry was to reorganise the post-war film industry in accordance with the Five-Year Plan, 1946–50. This required the building of new studios and the expansion of production to as near a hundred feature films a year as possible. It put down 46,000 projectors as the goal on the side of exhibition.

The Soviet cinema has in thirty years established itself in the life of the U.S.S.R. It has experimented in different techniques, and made good films as well as bad. It has produced one rare genius, the late Sergei Eisenstein. Yet it has been too isolated from the rest of the world. In its present formative stages the cinema has everything to gain from sharing its ideas and experiments.

9. *The Instructional Film*

The documentary film could be described as the higher journalism of the screen. Its purpose is broadly to help the world understand the world. It is creative in so far as it analyses and interprets society from the viewpoint of an individual or a school of thought. It is, therefore, broadly educational. It is also popular, but its aim is allied more closely to propaganda than to simple instruction.

The instructional or teaching film, whether designed for child or adult, is in an entirely different class of cinema. It is shown where groups of people assemble, willingly or unwillingly, to be told how to do something, how something works, or what something is like. The film becomes a moving visual textbook.

All over the civilised world hundreds of thousands of teachers are left alone with groups of children, adolescents or adults, and are paid to instruct them. In hundreds of centres of research into the technique of instruction, thousands of more specialised teachers are studying the best methods of study. In a few key places the limited number of teachers of genius do what they can to lead the general trend of the theory of education along progressive lines. Only in recent times could the broader mass of the people gain any direct access to the enlightened few. They had to depend on books and reports, and on the specialised interpretation of educational theory by the research specialists.

Now we have radio and film. A vivid direct access to important teachers is provided, cheaply and easily by radio, more elaborately by the film. Schoolchildren during the day-time can hear the voices of the country's specialists; they can discuss with their own teachers the results of these talks. All this can be done for the price of a wireless set.

The film presents certain technical difficulties which in this country have not yet been adequately overcome. It is no use making instructional films if there is no consistent coverage of schools by projectors. It is no use buying projectors if there is no consistent policy of instructional film production. The former Board of Education had given no adequate lead in the matter of equipping all senior and secondary schools with sound projectors, and had merely given good advice to Local Authorities. We have the absurd position that large cities buy two or three sound projectors for general use by all their schools (probably 150 to 200 buildings), and train groups of teachers over the week-end as hesitant and unskilful projectionists.

The reason for inaction was reaction. Reaction to a new medium among the teachers themselves, the teachers who once thought their livelihood threatened by broadcasting, and were too indifferent and too lazy to adapt their repetitive annual curricula to include new material. Reaction among Local Education Authorities watching the extra fraction of a penny on the rates. Reaction in the Ministry of Education itself in not taking a firm financial stand and equipping all major schools with sound projectors.

For the cinema is pre-eminently suitable for instruction if money, time, thought and skill are given to the preparation of first-class films. It starts with the assured attention which the hypnosis of the bright moving picture in the dark room exercises on the child. It has the closest approach to actuality of any medium of reproduction as yet devised. It can, by its processes of slow and quick motion, its use of telephoto and photomicrographic shots and its innumerable technical advantages, reveal the processes of life with vivid accuracy. It can guide attention and concentrate interest. It can reproduce history in terms which can be understood by the child. It can visit foreign lands, and explore peoples and remote places. It can explain mechanical, mathematical and industrial processes. It can summarise vocations for the adolescent choice. There is nothing in the material world which seems barred to it. Its limitations are apparent only in the realm of philosophy or dogma: here it can teach only by objective example. But by the time such subjects are of interest to the human being, books are recognised as the proper medium for discussion of them.

For some time now various schemes for the production of educational and instructional films have been proposed. It should be recognised that the production of such highly specialised films is work for skilled technicians. Too many of the bad instructional films of the past have been the result of hasty assumptions by people with little or no educational knowledge: it was thought necessary merely to throw together so many feet of library shots from old commercial travel and nature films to promote a series of geographical or biological " interest " shorts to sell or rent to the schools. No scheme can work adequately unless the following points at least are kept in mind:

(1) Production should be in the hands of specialised film-makers who are prepared to study and experiment in educational film technique.

(2) Planning of films should be carried out not with a view to wide sales or private profit, but as a definite part of the nation's educational curricula. Many important advanced films (or for that matter the right sort of simple ones) can be made only under subsidy.

(3) Both planning and production should be intimately linked with the users' needs. The teacher knows little of the technique of film production. The technician knows little of curricula and classroom practice. Only by sympathetic collaboration between the two groups of specialists can the films be adequately made. The film producer should be as interested in the practical use of his finished product in the classroom as the teacher himself and should, as part of his researches, attend schools where his films are showing.

(4) The scheme must involve the provision of projectors on a generous scale in schools and colleges. It must involve the establishment of Regional Film Libraries, possibly assembled by the Local Authorities themselves either singly (in certain cases) or in groups so that prints of films required by teachers can be easily and systematically booked. The medium of the instructional film in the past has gained a bad reputation with potential users as much through the trouble it takes to get films at all, as through the badness of them when eventually they arrive. Films should become, like textbooks, apparatus in the hand of the teacher as and when he wants it, and of a guaranteed quality which ensures they are not an insult to his class.

(5) The scheme should involve the pooling of international resources, so that instructional films made abroad can be interchanged with those made in Britain to the mutual benefit of all film-making countries. International exchange of opinion will be of the greatest value in the development of new techniques.

For any scheme to operate which involves all these considerations State subsidy and promotion seem essential. The films should be made by the units which have already begun to study the technique of the instructional film. But only the State is in the position to originate a comprehensive scheme which, once it is launched, will become part of the normal educational provision of the community.

The only planned use of the film for instructional purposes on a wide scale is in the Services. This, of course, is financed from public money. The Army, Navy and Air Force have elaborate film training, at any rate in theory. The films exist, and in some measure the widespread need for projecting equipment has been met.

The use of films in colleges and universities is only spasmodic. The scarcity of good material, except on the scientific side, is still a deterrent from the wider recognition of the use of cinema in adult education. In the hands of a good teacher of the social sciences, the documentary film itself is an important promoter of interest and discussion, apart from its artistic and propaganda values.

No good teacher need fear the competition of the film. The good teacher is the chairman of his group's discussion. The film can promote that discussion. When prolonged explanation is necessary the teacher does not fear the competition of the textbook or the wireless talk. Well made and well projected, the film can give his class the stimulus to learn about life and society and to discuss all problems with him.

The bad teacher has everything to fear: the exposure of his ignorance, the absence of his humanity. If the film can help to rid the schools of his influence, education and society will have advanced a stage nearer world civilisation.

10. *The Minority Theatre*

In the course of discussion the minority theatre has frequently been mentioned. The minority theatre begins with the private group exhibiting films on a substandard projector and ends with the small specialised commercial cinema playing repertory (revivals of notable films) or short runs of films of minority appeal, such as documentary and foreign cinema appeared to be before the war. When the issue of an S certificate was discussed in connection with Censorship, it was this type of theatre which was in mind for the exhibition of S films.

All over Britain small groups have been formed for the exhibition of films which could not be found in the programmes of the commercial theatres. These groups may meet in large rooms, halls, institutes, colleges or public buildings of all types, or even, if membership and opportunities allow, in cinemas out of the hours of commercial showing time. Societies with specialised interests have developed, such as the Scientific Film Association.

At the time when the little *avant-garde* cinemas were beginning to open in Paris, the London Film Society initiated the film-society movement in Britain in 1925 with its season of programmes held at the New Gallery cinema. There were about forty British film societies in operation by 1939; now the number approaches two hundred. Meanwhile, the specialised cinemas, so much beloved in London during the thirties, are operating with increased audiences and long runs for popular Continental films. The provinces, however, have few cinemas that venture to show foreign-language films as a matter of routine; nevertheless, the general bookings for films in foreign languages have risen considerably since the War.

All this is to the good. But it has to be realised that the amount of money coming back to the producer, after import charges, titling or dubbing costs, distribution levies and local exhibition overheads have been accounted for, is very small indeed. The prestige value may be enormous, while the commercial value is two or three thousand pounds after two or three years. A foreign-language film, after a short season in London and a few bookings at other specialised cinemas, enters the film-society market, where a single print gradually tours round earning a few pounds a week.

This means that almost all film production (unless independently sponsored, for example by a Government not requiring box-office returns to equal costs, which in turn means paying for a film's production out of public money) has to pay its way in its own national cinemas. There is no equivalent yet to the Little Theatre movement as a forcing house for experimental films. There can be no such equivalent until there is an assured world market for the unusual film in the form of an international system of specialised cinemas whose aggregate takings are sufficient to pay normal productions costs, with the film societies and cine-clubs as an additional margin of revenue.

The lovers of calculation can get to work on this. It would take distribution in many countries to show a producer a guaranteed return of £30,000 over an interval of, say, three years. And £30,000 worth of mixed currency will not produce an elaborate film. But it could begin to put heart into film-makers of vision and courage. It is good to work for international audiences, and it is good to know your work is really wanted everywhere, if only by audiences attending the small specialised cinemas.

The more properly conducted international Film Festivals help to bring film-makers together from all over the world to see each other's work and to discuss new techniques and uses for films. The Edinburgh Festival has become a recognised event of this kind, its film section inspired by the enthusiasm of the Edinburgh Film Guild, the largest and best-organised film society in Britain.

The audiences of the specialised cinemas, film societies and cine-clubs everywhere are the vanguard of public film taste. No community is complete without one or the other. Often both a specialised cinema and a film society can function together. Their joint aim is gradually to increase the number of those people who love a good film and know something about what they love.

Part Three

THE FILM TODAY

1. *Soviet Russia*

EVEN though Russia is naturally very much alive to the powers of the cinema, since she is one of its artistic pioneers, she has not yet recorded cinema attendances which are greater than those of Britain. Nevertheless, all Russian films are widely discussed; critics pull them to pieces in the Press on their release. The importance of the cinema has been further recognised by the establishment in 1946 of a special Ministry to control its affairs, replacing the long-established Cinema Committee.

As we have seen earlier, the wide range of the Soviet cinema covers technical films, films for children, special production centres in most of the Republics of the Union, and the sponsorship of experimental techniques such as the third dimensional film. The scientific documentary film is highly developed; Dovzhenko has made a biographical film of the botanist Michurin, and Roshal a film about Pavlov. The use of colour has advanced considerably in Russia since the War, especially now that the German Agfacolor system has become available for use. The Russians have supplemented their own studio space with hired stages at the great Barrandov studios near Prague, where Ptushko, the director of the puppet film *The New Gulliver*, produced in 1946 a film of folklore and magic called *The Stone Flower*, very reminiscent of Lang's *Siegfried* and photographed in Agfacolor.

Another branch of film-making in Russia is the adaptation of nineteenth-century period plays, such as *Innocent though Guilty* (Ostrovsky) and *Marriage* (Tchekov). The plays of the great Russian dramatists are produced carefully for the film, with decor and costuming worthy of the country which created the Moscow Art Theatre. Some of them remain photographed plays, even though they are brilliantly acted; others are adapted more closely to the technique of the cinema. The quality of most period films produced in Russia is high, whether they are romantic (like *Glinka*) or realistic (like *Peter the Great, Kutusov* or the early sections of *The Village Teacher).*

Nevertheless, the key style of the modern Soviet film is to be found in important productions like Michael Chiaureli's *The Vow* (1946) and Friedrich Ermler's *The Turning Point* (1946). These are both official films in the full meaning of the term, the first celebrating the career of Stalin since his vow after the death of Lenin, the second celebrating the strategy which turned the War on the Eastern Front at Stalingrad. The style in which these films are made is as closely realistic as that of a documentary, while the characterisation continuously emphasises the human element. It is only to be expected that both these films glorify the Soviet social and political point of view, but not without humour or humanity.

The death of Sergei Eisenstein in February 1948 was a grave loss, not only to the Soviet film, but to the art of the world. Eisenstein was the most theoretical of the world's film-makers. He conceded little to his audiences or to the readers of his critical works. His scientific imagination was constantly formulating new concepts of film technique. He was greatly concerned with the implications of colour and the psychological factors governing its use. The Soviet newsreel record of his death and lying in state showed his body laid out in his apartments surrounded by books on art, philosophy, history and politics. His desk and chairs were covered with half-read books and unfinished manuscripts. He was half-way through an article on the third dimension at the time of his death.[1]

Russia is the first in the field with this latest development of the cinema, the projection of film images on to a special screen so as to give a stereoscopic effect. A special theatre in Moscow seating 220 people gives continuous public exhibitions of three-dimensional films. The process is described by the inventor Semyon Ivanov in *The Cine-Technician* (No. 67). The process is unique, because members of the audience do not have to wear spectacles: they have, however, to keep their heads steady in a given position or the illusion of spatial depth is lost. Joseph Macleod, after a visit to the cinema to

[1] Published in " Penguin Film Review," No. 8.

see *Robinson Crusoe,* describes the effect of this new experience as follows:

> " It was only when Crusoe in his shipwreck throws a rope to a drowning sailor that you get the first shock. The rope comes hurtling and curling right out of the screen into the darkness over your head. At you! You duck. We all did. After that we were ready for anything. . . . Sometimes the foreground itself comes alive. As Crusoe advances down a corridor of undergrowth, the camera tracks backwards in front of him. Out in the auditorium, about three rows in front of you, leaves and lianas materialise in the air, dangle and dance, and float away into Crusoe's face. Parakeets and small birds sit on them; or fly out at you from the screen and vanish over your head; or form themselves out of nothing into a cluster of wings in the darkness. Their musical chattering is also in the air all round you, and there is no need here, as in an ordinary cinema, to adjust this depth of sound to the flat conventions on the screen several yards away " (" Sight and Sound," No. 63, p. 118).

Serious thought on the æsthetic of the third dimension in moving pictures has scarcely begun. It is very typical of Eisenstein that he should have been working on this subject at the time of his death.

2. *Czechoslovakia*

We have already seen that the Czech film industry is completely nationalised like that of Russia. The Czechs have shown, however, that they do not want to remain isolated, but to link their production with the rest of the world. Since the War a number of Festivals and World Conferences have been held in Prague or elsewhere in Czechoslovakia, notably in connection with the World Federation of Documentary.

Such Czech films as I have been able to see have shown two main artistic trends valuable in the cinema, realism and gay fantasy. Films of the War like *Stolen Frontiers* (Jiri Weiss) and *Men without Wings* (F. Cap) were story documentaries in which dramatic effects are always based on the drama of real events. These films take their place alongside the best productions of other countries like Italy, Denmark and France which were concerned after their liberation with making films out of their wartime suffering. On the other hand, the Czechs are creating a lighter kind of film full of gaiety and song, such as *The Singing Bachelor*, and cartoon and puppet films of great vigour and charm. These short films, like Czech and Slovak documentaries, are shown in all cinema programmes, and their costs are recovered from the general takings of the nationalised cinemas.

An outstanding achievement in Czechoslovakia is the historical research work undertaken by Dr. Jindrich Brichta, of the Czech Film Institute. As well as being a documentary film-maker, Brichta is a student of the development of film apparatus, and has assembled one of the finest historical collections in the world for permanent public exhibition. The Institute also undertakes the training of film technicians before they enter the studios.

3. *India and Pakistan*

Few if any Indian fiction films have been shown in Britain, though many documentaries are in constant use in the Central Film Library. The Indian film industry, however, is over thirty years old and has an output of some 200 films a year. Within the limits of distribution and exhibition available, these films are very popular, and the industry is highly commercialised with an established star-system. The form of the Indian film is also established, with set conventions of length, slowness of technique and the introduction of songs spaced out over the story.

Writing in " Documentary Film News " (May 1948), Achmad Abbas, one of the outstanding progressive film-makers in India and director of an important film on Bengal, *Children of the Earth,* explains the favourite kinds of Indian film and their treatment. Audiences like tragic films, he says:

" We have an unhealthy desire to see, not only martyrdom, but even frustration sublimated on the screen. It is interesting to mention in this connection that, unlike the experiment of Hollywood, the Indian movie-producer generally finds films with tragic themes more paying at the box-office than flippant musicals or comedies. Besides films of religious appeal or those dealing with emotional frustration, social justice and the struggle for freedom and the realisation of democratic ideals provide some of the most popular themes to the Indian producers. Sentimental stories sympathetic to the poor, the dispossessed, the Untouchables and attacking the rich and the powerful are always popular."

The stories of the saints and historical subjects, always accompanied by songs, stand high in public taste. The realism of Abbas's own film *Children of the Earth,* with its study of the effects of the Bengal famines, is not typical of India's social films, which usually romanticise the problems they portray. On the other hand, the documentary film in India is being used to assist in the immense task of teaching health and other communal subjects to the peoples of India and Pakistan.

4. *Latin America*

In Latin America the bulk of the films shown come from the U.S.A., but the local industries, led by the Argentine and Mexico, which together provide Central and South America with over a quarter of the films required, are beginning to develop a larger output.

The Argentinian film has scarcely yet developed a high artistic standard, though the best work of Mario Soffici (such as *La Cabalgata de circo*) has a genuine indigenous quality. It is in Mexico that we find a more clearly established school of film-making in process of development, set in the beautiful, strongly sun-lit countryside familiar in such American-sponsored films as Kline's *The Forgotten Village* and Ford's *The Fugitive.* Already the name of the comedian Cantiflas is linked with those of the outstanding actors of American screen farce, while the work of the director Emilio Fernandez (director of *Flor Silvestre, Enamorada* and *Maria Candelaria*) is discussed at international film festivals. *Maria Candelaria* (when unimpeded by American dubbing) has the simple, direct passion of folk-drama, the cruelty and the beauty of primitive legend. The Mexican industry produces now about sixty films a year, though few have the individual national quality belonging to the work of Fernandez. Mexico is making some of her chief films in both Spanish and English.

Brazilian production is for the most part made up of short films, since this country shows more American feature films than the others. On the other hand, educational documentaries are well developed under the direction of Professor Roquete Pinto. Feature-film production has commenced in Cuba, Peru, Uruguay and Chile.

5. *Scandinavia*

Both Denmark and Sweden are old centres of production, their films dating back to the early years of the century. The Danish film industry preceded that of Germany itself. Its output of feature films is small, only about ten a year, although during the War the average was nearer twenty. Denmark has, in addition, recently become an important centre for the production of documentary films.

The outstanding Danish directors are Carl Th. Dreyer, whose *Day of Wrath*, though disliked in Denmark, created a sensation in London, Bjarne Henning-Jensen, whose sympathetic films of children and adolescents, *Ditte, Child of Man* and *Those Blasted Kids*, were first seen in England at the Edinburgh Festival of 1948, and Theodor Christiansen, director of the film record of the Danish resistance, *Your Freedom is at Stake*, and many documentaries. The Danish contribution to documentary will be discussed later.

Swedish films are better known in this country than Danish, and many Swedish artists have worked in Hollywood since the brief ascendancy of Swedish productions in the European silent cinema during the early twenties. Victor Sjöstrom, one of the pioneer directors of this period who went for a time to Hollywood, is still outstanding as an actor in the Swedish cinema. After the War it was the showing in London of Alf Sjöberg's *Hets* (*Frenzy*) which excited us all and drew attention to another source for the programmes of the specialised cinemas and the film societies. In spite of its hopeful ending, *Hets* was a grim tragedy of a neurotic schoolmaster's evil influence on the life of a sensitive boy, the schoolmaster being brilliantly played by Stig Järrel, himself a film director. The claustrophobic atmosphere of the school and the exposure of the meanness of education conducted under such tyranny made the film almost as much a satire as it was a psychological melodrama.

Sweden has always been famous for setting its films in superb natural scenery. Some of these open-air films show the Swedish farmers and peasants, or take the religious folklore of the people for their themes, like *Ordet* (*The World*) or Alf Sjöberg's other film *The Road to Heaven*, which is a kind of Swedish " Pilgrim's Progress." The simplicity of treatment in such films as these should, however, be contrasted with the mature psychological study of nymphomania found in Gustaf Molander's *Woman without a Face*. The outstanding Swedish director of documentary is Arne Sucksdorff, whose work will be mentioned later.

6. *France*

We have already seen that in the first years after the Liberation French film producers were faced with acute economic difficulties involving costs rising out of all proportion to box-office receipts, which amount to only a tenth part of those of British cinemas. The root problem, however, lay in the adverse economic agreement between France and America, which gave American films a greatly increased hold upon the French screen. Faced with receipts threatening gradually to sink below even the basic costs of the simplest production, it is small wonder that the number of feature films produced in France sank from 113 in 1938 to about 70 in 1947.

In these circumstances it is surprising that so many unusual and striking, if not always necessarily good, films have come from France in recent years, especially when directors like Clair, Renoir, Duvivier, who were absent from France during the Occupation, have produced only *Le Silence est d'Or* (Clair) and *Panique* (Duvivier) for their native industry since 1945. *Le Silence est d'Or* was a charming trifle given a certain comic strength by its setting in the old film studios of fifty years ago. *Panique* was a melodrama turning on unpleasant characters living in a slum district of Paris, in which a young murderer and his girl bring about the death of a sinister recluse (a part played for all it was worth by Michel Simon), only to find he has posthumously directed the attention of the police to them. Technically, this film was brilliantly handled with every trick of violent melodrama and macabre characterisation set off by the actuality of the Parisian environment and of the large cast of minor characters. Yet it was fundamentally a distasteful picture, belonging to the post-war group of violent films featuring the spivs and tarts of the London, Paris and Hollywood urban underworld.

Renoir has not yet made a post-war film in France, but his last production before leaving for America, *La Règle du Jeu* (1939), was one of his finest films, and reached London only in 1946 after being banned by the Vichy Government as an immoral subject. This study of a society without values or principles changes from satire to fantasy whenever the winds of Renoir's humanity blow too keenly for the bonds of realism to sustain his feeling. These crazy, rootless people who attend a house-party in the country live on the edge of civilisation, shooting birds and making love, until eventually one of them shoots another out of misplaced jealousy and intrigue. *La Règle du Jeu* will remain a masterpiece, not merely because it contains brilliant montage in the famous sequence of the shoot, but because it is a grotesque and poetic commentary upon European society on the brink of collapse. It is interesting to compare this film with Jean Grémillon's *Lumière d'Eté*, made during the Occupation, about another group of people who carry in their souls the disorganised forces of their own spiritual destruction. The technique of this film, too, turns on the introduction of symbolic situations within an episodic and realistic narrative. The characters drift from one event to another, until it is discovered that each situation becomes a commentary on them and the world they have created. Grémillon's other wartime film, *Le Ciel est à Vous* (the story of an aviator and his wife and the effect their obsession for flying has upon their personal relationships), and the post-war documentary *Le Six Juin à l'aube* (a documentary of great pathos showing the torn-up Norman countryside after the Allied landings), both stress an almost academic and pedestrian desire to be correct and detailed, though underneath this surface effect lies the stir of emotion. Grémillon is undoubtedly an important director.

During the Occupation, French directors were obviously limited for subject-matter, and an urge towards fantasy grew upon many of them. Fantasy is virtually absent from the British film and rare in the American (apart from synthetic dream sequences about the hinterland of the stellar subconscious). Films as different as *La Nuit Fantastique* and *Voyages Surprises* (farce or fantasy?), or most of the productions of Christian-Jaque, Delannoy and Cocteau, depend on themes which are either supernatural or fantastic. Cocteau's calculated legends (*L'Eternel Retour* and *La Belle et la Bête*) both succeeded in bringing folk lore up to date with a modern magic. The first contained many scenes of great atmospheric power (the fight in the bar, and the episode of the dwarf, the lover and the bottle of love-potion), and the second remarkable effects of decor in the haunted castle of the Beast. But the simple passion of the original stories was often lost in the coldness of the technical effects and the grotesqueness of the characterisation.

Les Portes de la Nuit, Marcel Carné's and Jacques Prévert's long-awaited symbolic film, proved to be a culmination to Prévert's ascendancy over Carné, for whom, in the days of *Quai des Brumes* and *Le Jour se lève,* he used to write fine dialogue. The fatalistic philosophy of the poet implies that love and beauty, values understood only by the introspective and sensitive, are envied, hated and destroyed by the evil and powerful, who rule our material destinies. Love and beauty perish, and a mood of melancholy fatalism is all that is left after the forces of evil (themselves distraught by envy of what is good) have exercised their prerogative of destruction. Weighted by literary phrasing, the dialogue of *Les Portes de la Nuit* makes the characters symbolic figures living in a realistic world, the real once more giving emphasis to the unreal, the lovers dancing at night to the ironic tune played by Destiny in a yard full of abandoned statuary and junk.

It is to Georges Clouzot and Claude Autant-Lara that we turn for films closer to the realistic French tradition, though these two directors could hardly be more different. Clouzot's is a harsh realism, an intensification of all that is unpleasant in natures which nevertheless remain strikingly human. The village characters in *Le Corbeau,* the poison-pen film for so long banned because of the pleasure it gave to the Nazis, are not without verisimilitude, though the small community is an unhappy one which has so many unpleasant people in it at one

time. *Quai des Orfèvres,* in spite of the fact that it is intended
for a detective story, has that same close, vivid and bitter
observation of life with its curious triangle situation of the
man and woman pursued by a girl in love with the wife under
the guise of interest in the husband, and the ironic and dis-
passionate detective who cares deeply for the welfare of his
little son, a half-caste, acquired in Africa.

In Claude Autant-Lara France has her most sensitive
director of stories of emotion. His period films, such as
Douce, are exquisite, delicately devised settings for the inconsequent emotions of adolescence, the passions which in oversensitive natures lead to tragedy and self-immolation. *Le
Diable au Corps* is a study of the intense love of a boy and
girl which leads eventually to the girl's death in childbirth after
her marriage to a husband she does not love and pregnancy
due to her true lover. This film became to the French cinema
what *Brief Encounter* was to the British, a film to which one
could turn as a fine example of the treatment of profound
emotion on the screen. Just as *Brief Encounter* depended on
the acting of Celia Johnson, so *Le Diable au Corps* depended
on the acting of Gérard Philippe and Micheline Presle. No
film so dependent on human character could be made without acting of this order, which serves to remind us that the
quality of French films has always depended at least as much
on good acting as on imaginative direction.

7. Germany

Out of the ruined studios of Germany a new and very
national film-production industry began to grow in 1946. The
great UFA Studios (at Neubabelsberg and Johannisthal) lie
in the Soviet zone. The American zone has the Geiselgasteig
and Tempelhof studios, while the British-licensed companies
have to borrow studio space from the American zone or work
out their passage at the few small and scattered studios available in the British zone. The French zone has new studios at
Remagen. The Russians set up a unified production organisation called DEFA; the authorities of the British, American
and French zones prefer to issue film licences to individual
small production units.

All the occupying Powers are sponsoring German film production. Most of the films made in the Western Zones try to escape post-war discontents, though some films have attempted to dramatise them, like the gloomy *Menschen in Gottes Hand* and *Liebe '47*. However, two fantasies, *Der Apfel ist Ab*, the story of Adam's eternal desire for both domestic and profane love, and the superb satiric film on post-war conditions in Berlin, *Berliner Ballade* (directed by R. A. Stemmle), showed imagination and a certain gaiety. Both were very German in style, and showed clearly that production is now well-established artistically, in spite of the scarcity of trained technicians and raw materials.

The first films to be made in 1946–7 under Soviet licence showed a more documentary tendency than those made under British and American sponsorship, but more serious subjects have gradually replaced the first efforts at escapism in the studios of the West. The Russians granted their first licence on May 17th, 1946. Alfred Lindemann became the Chief Producer for DEFA (Deutsche Film Aktien-Gesellschaft). Five films were completed in the first year, and Wolfgang Staudte's *The Murderers are Amongst Us* (first shown October 1946) was the first post-war German feature film. This was a study in war guilt, a theme which has recurred increasingly in later German films. A demobilised Army doctor, obsessed with guilt because he was unable to prevent his Commanding Officer murdering innocent civilians in Poland, degenerates into a drunkard wandering among the dives of ruined Berlin. The officer, on the other hand, has become a prosperous business man with glass in his windows and good food for his devoted family. He is brought to justice, but not before the doctor, self-pitying and demented, has tried to kill him. The doctor's self-respect is restored by the firm action of a girl who has spent the War in a concentration camp and who is determined to reconstruct the life around her as best she can. There was much in this production to remind us of earlier German films, the stress on neurosis, the big close-ups of the doctor with his speeches full of self-pity. But it was an honest film, finely acted and strongly directed, with its backgrounds of serrated ruins making a fantastically patterned skyline at night, and its picture of life in flats full of the endless dust of crumpled plaster.

Other social films followed from DEFA, among them *Irgendwo in Berlin* (*Somewhere in Berlin*), directed by Gerhardt Lamprecht, and dealing with juvenile delinquency; *Freies Land* (*Free Country*), directed by Milo Harbich, a documentary story about land reforms in the Soviet zone, and *Ehe im Schatten* (*Marriage under the Shadow*), directed by Hans Maetzig, a drama of an Aryan husband's attempt to remain united to his Jewish wife during the Nazi period. Staudte's second film was a comedy, *The Strange Adventures of Mr. Fridolin B* (i.e. Mr. John Citizen), a satire on red tape as it affects the ordinary citizen.

After a poor start, one of the licensed companies of the British zone produced the first good film to be made under British sponsorship called *In Those Days* (directed by Helmut Käutner). It was an episodic comedy of a motor-car and its series of owners. Käutner was next associated with a comedy called *Film ohne Titel* (*Film without Title*), starring Willy Fritsch, the famous star of the silent-film period, and showing the reverses of fortune under the Allied bombardment of an art-dealer and a housemaid, who later becomes a privileged person because she is a farmer's daughter.

American-sponsored production was put under the direction of Erich Pommer, who came over from America to take up his duties, full, no doubt, of memories of German film production after the First World War, when the script of *Caligari* was brought to him. Productions under his control include Harald Braun's *Between Yesterday and Tomorrow* (1947), another film on the problem of the Aryan married to a Jewess, and *Lang ist der Weg,* a grim film of the Nazi terror in the Jewish quarter of Warsaw.

Finally, there is Roberto Rossellini's film about a child's sufferings in Berlin, *Germany, Year Zero*. This was sponsored by the French and made by Rossellini with the help of DEFA, the Russian company. Its objective treatment of a situation similar to that of *The Murderers are Amongst Us* (the neurosis being transferred here to a child who poisons his elderly and sick stepfather, and then commits suicide) makes an interesting comparison. Both films are made in the actual surroundings of Berlin; Staudte employs a cast of professional actors, Rossellini uses only one actor (the father) and for the rest uses people he found in Berlin. The difference between the two films goes deeper, however. Rossellini observes and pities, producing an objective study of life under duress with those who succumb to it, those who prey on it and those who just survive it. Staudte makes a psychological drama of his countrymen, stressing the inner conflict of an individual case, feeling his film intensely, subjectively. There could not be a clearer case of two different temperaments revealed through the diverse handling of similar material.

8. *Italy*

During the slow and painful period of the liberation of Italy, stories began to reach England that some very interesting films had been and were being made there. New names, Roberto Rossellini, Vittorio de Sica, Luchino Visconti and others, were mentioned. Then the quick international success of *Roma, Citta Aperta* made the name of Italian cinema, and this isolated example became the herald of a new school of film-making which has proved to be the most promising development in European cinema since the War.

This Italian school has roots which go back before the War. Italy was one of the pioneer countries in the development of film production at the beginning of the century. She was labelled during the twenties as the country that went on producing *Quo Vadis?*, and had taught America the attractions of the spectacular costume film. Italy is still making this kind of pictorial picture, for example *Fabiola* (Blasetti) and *The Last Days of Pompeii*, made for Universalia by the French director Marcel L'Herbier. But the realistic school producing films which get close to the heart of contemporary Italian life also seems to be well established, and its origins in the Italian film go back to the occasional so-called " regional " films of silent days and some of the early work of Camerini and Blasetti during the thirties.

Not all these are what we should call documentary features, in the sense that *Paisa* and *Sciuscia* are. *Roma, Citta Aperta* is a documentary drama, not without a certain melodramatic quality superimposed on the essential truth of its story and the actuality of its location in the streets and tenements of Rome. The same feeling of actuality can be found in

comedies like Blasetti's *Four Steps in the Clouds* (1942) and
Zampa's *To Live in Peace* (1947). Alessandro Blasetti is an
older director whose work goes back to silent days; he has
made every kind of film from the documentary style of his
first films *Sun* (1929) and *Mother Earth* (1930) to "box-office"
pictures and historical films after the style of *Fabiola*. The
whole value of the romantic comedy *Four Steps in the Clouds*
lies in the feeling of reality about the people at the apartment
house and in the train and bus and on the farm, wherever the
flow of the situations takes the leading characters, who are a
commercial traveller in a bad temper and a frightened country-
girl due to have an illegitimate child. This film is made with
a true feeling for human beings, the kind of respect not allowed
in the confections of the commercial cinema working to a
star formula. Similarly, *To Live in Peace* is without doubt as
exaggerated a portrait of Italian village life as *La Femme du
Boulanger* was of rural France; the first was made round the
talent of the Italian comedian Aldo Fabrizi, and the second
depended on the genius of the French comedian Raimu. But
the result was not a rustic effusion trimmed with studio eccen-
tricity and touched with pawky sweetness, but a natural crowd
of characters full of the stuff of life and the vigour of true
comedy. There is similar vigour in Zampa's *Anni Difficili*,
about an Italian family during and after the Fascist period.

The reputation of the new Italian cinema is, however, based
on its more documentary-style films, such as Vittorio de Sica's
Sciuscia (1945) and *Bicycle Thieves* (1948), Giuseppe de
Santis' *Caccia Tragica* (1947), Luigi Comencini's *Proibito
Rubare* (1948), Luchino Visconti's *La Terra Trema* (1948),
Alberto Lattuada's *Senza pietà* (1948) and *Mill on the Po*
(1949), Renato Castellani's *Sotto il Sole di Roma* (1948) and
the films of Roberto Rossellini, notably *Paisa* (1946).

Most of these films must obviously take their subjects from
the period of Italy's Liberation or from immediate post-war
conditions. There was plenty of material, the perils of resistance followed by the social dislocations of the Allied occupation, the black market, juvenile delinquency and the like.
Vittorio de Sica gave up his career as a film-actor in Mario
Camerini's light comedies to become a director of psychological films such as *The Children Watch Us* (1943), which

featured a child four years old. In 1945 he made *Sciuscia*, the film about the shoeshine boys, children exploited by black-marketeers until they became trained thieves and filled up the juvenile prisons. It is a grim documentary of an impossible task as badly handled by the prison authorities as it could be. The film is spoilt only by a curious symbolic end, but its portrait of juvenile prison life in post-war Rome is unforgettable.

De Sica revealed his full importance with *Bicycle Thieves*, the story of the efforts of an unemployed man, aided by his son, to get back a stolen bicycle on which his future employment depends. The film has the beauty of real humanity shown in a setting which ruthlessly exposes the conditions of the poor.

Caccia Tragica (*The Tragic Chase*) was de Santis' first film; in spite of some looseness in its structure, it gave an effective picture of life in a poverty-stricken agricultural camp after the War. Comencini's *Proibito Rubare* (*Stealing Forbidden*) is the story of a priest who founds a " boys' republic " in Naples for the reclaiming of the delinquent street boys. Comencini came to film-making through journalism and script-writing. Luchino Visconti made his name with the production in 1943 of *Ossessione* (*Obsession*) based, like Renoir's *La Bête Humaine*, on Cain's " The Postman Always Rings Twice," which he adapted to the Italian setting of the Po marshlands used by Rossellini in the last episode of *Paisa*; it contained an extraordinary performance by the actress Clara Calamai as the sexually voracious wife of an Italian inn-keeper. For *La Terra Trema* Visconti went to Sicily, and like Flaherty and Rouquier, made his story of the sea, the countryside and the sulphur mines with the real Sicilians unaided by actors.

Alberto Lattuada, established as an important director by *Il Bandito* (1946), took up the difficult theme of miscegenation for *Senza Pietà* (*Without Pity*). Johnny Kitzmiller, the American Negro actor seen in *To Live in Peace*, plays a coloured sergeant in love with a white Italian girl; the story shows the problems and suffering that follow. In *Sotto il Sole di Roma* Renato Castellani tells the story of a boy faced with the post-war conditions of life in Rome. Two other directors of importance belonging to the realist school are Aldo Vergano, whose film *Il Sole sorge ancora* (*The Sun Always Rises*) made in 1946 excited wide comment on its technique by the critics, and Francesco de Robertis, naval officer and former playwright, who made in 1940 *Uomini sul Fondo,* a film about men in the submarine service, followed by a number of other films with naval backgrounds and *La Vita Semplice* (*The Simple Life*), a comedy of the conflict between a Venetian boat-builder and an industrialist.

The work of Roberto Rossellini has done most to make the new Italian cinema known all over the world. Rossellini began his film career as a director of documentary, and worked with Francesco de Robertis, the maker of naval films, on *La Nave Bianca* (*The White Ship*), an indifferent film with a love story set against the background of the naval medical service. His main work began with *Roma, Citta Aperta* (*Open City*) (1945), which was planned before the Germans had left Rome and was made under the most exacting conditions with none of the technical luxuries of normal location and studio production. Touched up with melodrama in the Gestapo scenes (Lesbianism and drugs; piano-playing during the tortures), what really made this film stand out among the many productions about the Underground in Occupied Europe was the sheer authenticity of the street and tenement scenes, and the magnificent acting of Aldo Fabrizi as the priest and Anna Magnani as a housewife involved in the work of the Underground. Both were playing in a new style; Fabrizi was a Neapolitan comedian and Magnani came from the music-halls. Scene after scene in this film gets the full effect of a direct record of events; Magnani receiving the fugitive in her room, her death when she is shot down in the streets, the execution of the priest watched by schoolboys. A similar observation, objective and clear-cold but always compassionate, establishes the tenement life in Rossellini's later film of Berlin, *Germany, Year Zero*.

But *Paisa* is Rossellini's outstanding production in this first period of his career. It is possibly the greatest film to have been made in Europe since the War. Of the seven episodes, so different in content but so remarkably linked by the purposefulness and style of their director, all, except perhaps the first, possess a humanity which distils the poetry out of both the ordinary and extraordinary emotions of human beings. The outrageous comedy of the American Negro military policeman enticed by a small street boy across the ruins of Naples and robbed of his boots whilst he is rolling drunk, an episode full of crazy talk in English and Italian, is followed by the sharp emotions of an Italian harlot who picks up a drunken American soldier whom she remembers too late as the nice boy she welcomed to Rome when she was still a nice girl. Then with an extraordinary sense of delicacy for human contacts and relationships, Rossellini tells the story of three American padres visiting a remote Italian monastery and the shock to the simple Italian brothers when they discover one of their visitors is a Rabbi and another a Protestant priest.[1] The last episode is almost wordless: the manœuvres of partisans, R.A.F. boys and an American soldier through the enemy-infested Po marshlands, beginning with the unforgettable sequence of the labelled body of a Partisan drifting down the current of the river until it is rescued silently and hurriedly by comrades lurking in the tall reeds. *Paisa* should take its place among the rarer works of the cinema when the time comes to see it in historical perspective.

9. *America*

It is easy to lose count of the genuine achievement in American cinema whilst sitting through the enormous output of formula films designed, like the novels and magazine stories from which so many of them derive, to make entertainment as easy a function as possible. The many highly individual directors in America (Chaplin, Ford, Capra, Hitchcock, Wilder, Lang, Wyler, Kazan, Dymtryk, Huston, Welles), some individual on their own account and some when encouraged by producers like Louis de Rochemont, the late Mark Hellinger and Dore Schary make sufficient films to uphold the honour of Hollywood.

Ford, with *My Darling Clementine, Tobacco Road* and *The Fugitive,* has not added to his already high standard, though each of these films was a work of individuality. *Tobacco Road,* based on Erskine Caldwell's depressing study of a group of destitute and degenerate tobacco growers of the South, was an artificial actors' piece, a series of situations designed to give unpleasant characters rope to be unpleasant. *The Fugitive*

---

[1] For a fuller account of this episode from *Paisa* see my essay in "The Experimental Film" (Grey Walls Press), p. 53, and review of the film in the British Film Institute's Record series.

was a film of a higher order, though censorship restrictions could hardly allow the portrait of Graham Greene's whisky-priest, with the intense spiritual conflict behind it, to be developed to the full. The Mexican backgrounds, however, gave full play to Ford's love for strong scenic effects. *My Darling Clementine* was the best of this group, slow, tense, and yet sometimes as gay as the lanky seriousness of Fonda would allow, a beautifully timed film with a wonderful climax.

Hitchcock, with *Spellbound,* a psychiatric melodrama containing a pretentious dream-sequence by Salvador Dali, and *Notorious,* another psychological melodrama, turned his great talent to the fashionable neurotic subjects which held the cinema in thrall after the War. Films like *Spellbound* are dangerous, because they give star-value to neurosis, and make the delicate processes of mental healing appear a scarifying affair, with the psychiatrist often a madman himself, like that old figure of melodrama, the mad inventor. Anatole Litvak outdid all the psychiatric films with *The Snake Pit,* a brilliant study of a patient's sufferings in an American mental institution.

Capra continued his whimsical demonstrations of obstinate human goodness in *It's a Wonderful Life,* a beautifully acted film spoilt by the intrusion of a very eccentric angel to help the hero clean up the community. Fritz Lang's *Scarlet Street* was again remarkably well directed and acted, a model of the art of creating tension; the film was so good that the end had to be an anti-climax on the obvious grounds of censorship. Disney, on the other hand, who used to be one of the real individualists of the American cinema, seems to allow his studio now to get the upper hand of imagination with too much technical pretentiousness: the old Disney is almost invariably drowned with noise, vulgarity and tricks.

John Huston, who was formerly a screenwriter, has emerged during the past few years as an important director. Films like *The Maltese Falcon, The Treasure of Sierra Madre* and *They Were Strangers* possess three great virtues, a sense of background environment, a sense of tension in their dramatic or melodramatic structure, and a great sense of human character. It is unfortunate that Huston sometimes over-plays these virtues until they become tricks or weakness.

An interesting development in Hollywood has been the

tendency for well-known stars and writers to become producers and directors. Dudley Nichols made a slow, serious film, *Sister Kenny,* with Rosalind Russell producing and starring; Robert Montgomery carried the subjective camera to its logical conclusion (which is its death in the almost total elimination of the hero from the screen) in his own film *The Lady in the Lake.* Orson Welles made a technically interesting if somewhat pretentious film *The Lady from Shanghai,* with Rita Hayworth starring alongside himself.

Under an entirely different heading comes Hans Richter's remarkable feature-length experiment *Dreams that Money Can Buy,* which he has produced partly in colour with the assistance of the artists Fernand Léger, Max Ernst, Marcel Duchamp, Alexander Calder and Man Ray, with music by several composers including Darius Milhaud. Each artist contributes in his own style a dream in colour as part of a network of dreams fitted into a fantastic frame-story about a seller of dreams. The film caused a sensation when it opened in 1948 in New York.[1]

The most hopeful sign in Hollywood has been the rise of a new realistic school of cinema parallel to similar work done by European directors. Initiated by progressive working producers like de Rochemont, Schary and Adrian Scott, films like *Crossfire, The House on 92nd Street, 13 Rue Madeleine, Boomerang, Gentleman's Agreement, The Naked City* and *The Best Years of Our Lives* (the latter directed by William Wyler for Sam Goldwyn) have appeared around 1946-7. Whereas *The House on 92nd Street, 13 Rue Madeleine* (both directed by Henry Hathaway for Louis de Rochemont) and *The Naked City* (directed by Jules Dassin with the late Mark Hellinger producing) were record-films with sensational war and crime stories distinguished by their documentary treatment, the other films introduced, to a varying degree, a hard core of American social problems. *Boomerang* (directed by Elia Kazan for Louis de Rochemont) started with a murder, but turned the attempt at its solution into a study of political rigging in a small American town: the dilemma facing the

---

[1] There is a considerable amateur *avant-garde* movement at work in America. A history of its development is given by Lewis Jacobs in " Experimental Film " (Grey Walls Press).

hero of this film, played by Dana Andrews, was an acute moral problem of a kind liable to strike at the conscience of any member of the audience. *Crossfire* (Edward Dymtryk) launched into anti-Semitism, followed by the over-dramatised *Gentleman's Agreement*. Then came a number of realistic crime films, harsh, vivid, laconic and even sometimes poetic in their feeling for the essentials of character and situation, including *The Window* (Ted Tetzlaff), *Force of Evil* (Abraham Polonsky), *They live by Night* (Nicholas Ray), *Body and Soul* (Robert Rossen), *Cry of the City* (Robert Siodmak), *Act of Murder* (Michael Gordon), *A Street with No Name* (William Keighley) and *The Set-Up* (Robert Wise).

The Best Years of Our Lives, lengthy, garrulous, sentimental, amusing, satiric, using every skilful device known to excite tears and laughter, is none the less a rich documentary portrait of American life and temperament. This is its true value, quite apart from the skill with which the characters are handled and their environments represented, like the bank official's apartment, the store and the field of derelict aircraft. Like Capra's films, *The Best Years of Our Lives* is human to the point of overheating, though this may be an observation due to the over-cool temperament of an Anglo-Saxon observer. Even so, this film has been the subject of suspicion, during the investigations in 1947, of left-wing influences, said to be rampant in Hollywood films. The undemocratic way the investigations were conducted by the Congressional Committee led to a bad press in America and the rest of the world. The danger of the indictment of men like Scott, Dymtryk and the screen-writers Albert Maltz (of *The Naked City*) and Dalton Trumbo, is that the fear of handling socially controversial subjects will lead to the destruction of the realistic school so soon after its birth. Mervyn Le Roy, director of *I am a Fugitive from a Chain Gang*, is quoted in " Sight and Sound " (No. 65, p. 33) as saying: " The screen is under attack from all sides at the moment. The best thing it can do is to settle for what critics call escapist entertainment until the storm blows over."

Above and apart from all these controversies, Charles Chaplin (no longer Charlie) works on his rare films, retaining his British nationality after a lifetime in Hollywood. *Monsieur*

Verdoux merged farce and the macabre in a bitter satire against the violence and acquisitiveness of contemporary society. A pacifist, he condemns war, claiming that if nations can take life in order to protect their persons and property, so, morally speaking, can the individual. In *Monsieur Verdoux* he created the microcosm of contemporary society in the form of one man who, faced with ruthless dismissal from his work in a bank, gaily and skilfully robs and destroys a number of women in order to preserve his little home and his faithful wife and child. Once these beloved ones are destroyed by a social catastrophe, he fatalistically gives himself up to justice, and dies with bitter comments on his lips. In the foreground of this satire, which is not far removed from that of Swift, Chaplin introduces his old clowning and sleight of hand by-play before murder. *Monsieur Verdoux* is the most extreme film Chaplin has made, his bitterest comment on the way of the world, the little man taking his revenge for the wrongs society has done to humanity and justice. He plays this new figure superbly, blending farce with drama. Whether his view of life is correct or not, in no film has he expressed it so openly or with such courage, for it is hardly likely that his popularity could be increased through such a film. But, like Bernard Shaw before him, it is likely that the survival of his reputation is above the transitory rise and fall of mere popularity. For Chaplin possesses the surety of his acknowledged genius.

10. *Britain*

British film production reached the climax of its dilemma in 1948. Production costs for a first-feature film averaged £220,000. Cinema attendances were down on the immediate post-war peak of over 30 million a week; the loose money in the public pocket had been drained off. An order went out for retrenchment: films had got to cost less and earn more. Retrenchment of costs might not do much harm; but retrenchment in taste, which is what the " earn more " clause in effect meant, was surely in the long run false economy. There will always be, it is true, a basic audience of many millions for competent films made to formula, but it is the little extra value, if only on the grounds of mere novelty, that increases the cinema queue. A quarter of the people in Britain virtually never go to the pictures. Only an increased quality in values can convert a reasonable proportion of these people into film-goers.

In spite of constant changes and re-groupings among British feature-making units as between Rank, Korda, American or independent sponsorship, the units themselves often remained stable in their key personnel. Films continued to possess the hall-mark of their production-style: Ealing, Gainsborough, Cineguild, Individual, Archers, Charter, Wilcox's and Korda's personal productions retained a continuity of treatment, whether the results were good or indifferent as film-making. What had to be kept in mind increasingly by them all was that their job depended on entertaining the largest possible audiences (overseas as well as at home), and that it rested on them individually as artists how far the flag of their personal artistic standards had to be hauled down in the process. It is sufficient to say that 1946 to the summer of 1949 was a period in which the flag generally was lowered to half-mast in the public interest (it seems), in spite of the production of a number of films which, either wholly or in part, possessed quality, such as *The Rake's Progress, Mine Own Executioner, Theirs is the Glory, So Well Remembered, Men of Two Worlds, Hue and Cry, Fame is the Spur, Brighton Rock, They Made Me a Fugitive, Good Time Girl, Great Expectations, Oliver Twist, Odd Man Out, I Know Where I'm Going, A Matter of Life and Death, The Red Shoes, School for Secrets, The Overlanders, Hamlet, Passport to Pimlico, Kind Hearts and Coronets, Whisky Galore, The Queen of Spades, Scott of the Antarctic, The Small Back Room, The Small Voice, The Fallen Idol, The Third Man* and *The Elusive Pimpernel*. As against these titles, some 150 other films of feature-length were released, not mentioning the disgraceful quota " interest " films of half an hour's length or more, and the field of documentary proper to which feature-length films like *School for Danger* and *Children on Trial* belong.

On the other hand, the technical and incidental artistic capacities of the studios were shown off to excellent effect. Everyone commented on the colour of *Men of Two Worlds* and the Archers' films, the montage of *Odd Man Out* and the Cineguild pictures, the decor of *Oliver Twist, Black Narcissus* or *An Ideal Husband,* the music of Alwyn, Walton or Vaughan Williams.

Unfortunately, the superficial excellences of too many otherwise indifferent films cost tens of thousands of pounds to achieve; in fact, the technical neurosis tended to increase as the quality of the stories declined.

The old urgency had gone. Technique was no longer the servant: it had become the master. Put Rossellini's rough picture *Open City* or Jiri Weiss's *Stolen Frontiers* against the British films of 1946–8, and how many of them do not appear like faded leaves painted in exquisite detail by a lady in Cornwall. Put *Le Diable au Corps* or our old achievement *Brief Encounter* against them, and how few of them seem to possess a memorable character the urgency of whose problems really mattered to both the film-maker and his audience. No amount of technical or subsidiary artistic excellence, of colour, decor, montage or music can make up for our indifference to artificial characters placed in situations which do not call for our real concern. Emotion had gone: the films grew cold. It is always strength of emotion which holds an audience down in its seats.

A shortage of actors, too, does not help the situation. The few good artists, both of star and supporting rank, are worked to death till we are over-familiar with their features and voices and find it difficult to lose their too familiar identities in the illusion of the part they are playing. The younger newcomers for the most part are an empty-faced lot, victims of grooming before the attraction of an unusual personality has had any chance to develop, if indeed it was there at all when they were first selected for the screen. The art of film-acting depends to a great extent on the suggestion of personality, the hidden qualities which at any moment in a performance are seen to emerge, through the eyes, through the smile, or a movement of the head or body. Few of our stars possess these hypnotic characteristics which fascinate a susceptible audience; few screen stories in any case allow for the emergence of such qualities in the human personality. The better Continental pictures usually gain the praise they do from British critics and film-goers precisely because they stress the importance of the human personality in both their stories and their acting.

During the War the remedy for spiritual and emotional atrophy was at hand, and the impressive series of war films was the result. It is more difficult nowadays, with no common subject to which film-makers can turn with a certainty of drawing on the public emotion. *In Which We Serve,* like *The Best Years of Our Lives* and *Open City,* had all the trump-cards in the pack lined up in its favour. But if the larger-scale causes of human emotion have now disintegrated or changed, the emotions themselves remain the same. Yet few films go straight for these emotions without in some way or other emasculating or turning them synthetic in the process. The star-system, though it may sell tickets, dehumanises stories. For few of the stars of Britain or America have strong or impressive or even fascinating personalities. They show no evidence of having lived widely or suffered deeply or even spontaneously enjoyed themselves. How can they therefore re-create strong drama or gay comedy on the screen? They and their promoters are too concerned with the mannequin and show-girl aspect of the business; the Americans can beat us all hands-down in this cul-de-sac of film-making.

The more exceptional pictures are none the less made. *Odd Man Out,* though it never explained the political motivation of the hero or the sexual dilemma of the girl, had magnificent acting and a quality of presentation which brought the spectator right into the action. *Great Expectations* had a brilliant opening and a freshness of style lacking in *Oliver Twist,* though the latter was more tightly knit in the general development of its episodic story and was brilliantly rather than movingly presented. The characters of Dickens, so dependent on the vigorous personality of their author, tend to become eccentric types on the screen, adapted to the limitations of our small number of regular character actors. The Powell-Pressburger pictures were technical feats of distinction which tend to force their characters into the pattern of a preconceived treatment: there was no valid reason why the poet-airman who admired Donne should dream so synthetic a heaven, and no valid reason why the ballet-dancer should commit suicide except that it made a neat parallel with the theme of her ballet. The studies in ballet rehearsal in *The Red Shoes,* however, are among the best work in recent British cinema. *Fame is the Spur, So Well Remembered* and *Men of Two Worlds* suffered from over-length, with the result that the genuine interest of their central problems lagged dramatically. *Brighton Rock, Good Time Girl* and *They Made Me a Fugitive* were the best-made of the violent school in post-war British films; *Good Time Girl* was the nearest to a documentary treatment of the problem of juvenile crime, while *Brighton Rock,* though it had pace and style, suffered from modifications of the religious problem which is the heart of Graham Greene's book and weakened the character of the girl.

Until recently, comedy was the weakest branch of British script-writing. *The Rake's Progress* possessed a genuine irony, and Peter Ustinov's domestic comedy in *School for Secrets* was caustic and amusing, provided we had not to accept these scientific figures of fun as the inventors of radar. While *Vice-Versa* was a partly successful *tour de force* in burlesque, *Private Angelo* was less successful because Ustinov changed the character of Linklater's Italian hero. Ealing Studios has brought out a number of good comedies, *Hue and Cry* and *Passport to Pimlico*, both semi-realistic fantasies written by T. E. B. Clarke, *Kind Hearts and Coronets,* a mock-heroic comedy based on a fantastic series of murders, and *Whisky Galore*, about having no whisky at all.

The Overlanders was in a class apart; though its characterisation tended to be weak, it was rich in Australian prospecting, opening up new themes and localities for film-making in the future. *Hamlet* showed up more acutely than *Henry V* all the problems of reducing the dramatic verse of Shakespeare to the intimacies of the film-camera: it was impressive and dignified, at times strikingly beautiful and cinematically effective (in the play-scene, for instance), but it suffered mortally from its truncations, while Olivier's interpretation of the character lacked the dramatic warmth he gave to Henry, a far less passionate character, but one more easily active and suitable for the screen.

There were other films released during this period which were important, including *Scott of the Antarctic*, a film beautiful for its colour and its music, but deficient in characterisation, owing to the difficulty of dramatising famous people, the war films *Men of Arnhem* and *The Captive Heart*, and Thorold Dickinson's best film *The Queen of Spades*, remarkable for the creation of atmosphere through design, photography and editing and for the acting of Edith Evans. *The Small Back Room*, an essay in realism by Michael Powell and Emeric Pressburger, was equally successful as a comedy of character and as a study of wartime Whitehall. To these should be added Carol Reed's *The Fallen Idol* and *The Third Man*, the first for its studied and effective direction of the child actor Bobby Henrey, and the second for its brilliant characterisation.

Lastly, there is the development of the Rank Organisation's production of films for children which has resulted in some excellent small-scale feature films like *Bush Christmas* (made in Australia) and *The Boy who stopped Niagara* (made in Canada). It is to be hoped that the absurdity which makes it illegal to employ children of school age in films in this country will soon be put right with proper safeguards for the children's welfare. Meanwhile, it forces a great deal of this valuable experimental production to be undertaken abroad. Several of the films, however, have been sufficiently good to appear as second features in normal cinema schedules, and to add considerably to the quality of the programme as a result. This branch of British production is becoming more of a credit to us as time goes on.

What it comes to is that the talent and the opportunities are present, but there remains a rooted fear of the distributor and the public. Actually, there is nothing like a challenge to stir everyone up and sell the tickets. So, since ticket-selling is the livelihood of the film-maker, all we need is the challenge.

11. *The Documentary Film*

The post-war expression of documentary all over the world has been one of the more exciting and positive phases of the awkward years of peace. It has produced its problems, and the voices of frustration have been loud. But the films have been made by the hundreds, and a new attitude to the uses of documentary is observable in many countries. The film has no longer to fight for recognition as a medium of public welfare and education. Broadly speaking, documentary films are produced under three kinds of sponsorship—State, industrial and private. The second kind of sponsorship can come either from within the film industry itself (such as the Rank

Organisation's sponsorship through G.B. Instructional and *This Modern Age* Series) or from other industries interested in promoting films about their work and its relationship to world welfare (such as film sponsorship by the gas, oil, chemical and air transport industries). The third kind of sponsorship derives from the old system of dependence on the rich patron or the promotion of individual films by cultural organisations. In extreme cases the film-maker scrapes some money together and makes his film out of shoestring resources. From whatever source the money may come, in countries all over the world films are being made about our human activities which, properly preserved and understood, will be a priceless record of twentieth-century life for the historians and scientists of the future.

The problems of State sponsorship have been interminably argued. The best film-makers are artists, and they revolt against the demands and delays of Government offices. On the other hand, State sponsorship is the only form of sponsorship through which the full range of the film's public service can be realised. This was emphasised by Grierson in articles which appeared in " Documentary 47 " and " Sight and Sound " No. 66, when he took charge of film production for the Central Office of Information in 1948. He urged documentary film-makers in Britain to bring their imaginations into play within the orbit of the State film service and the subjects most immediately required in the public interest, rather than to indulge in æsthetic frustrations which were for the most part without real creative significance.

UNESCO has endeavoured to superimpose a form of co-ordination upon the various kinds of documentary film promotion which so many different countries have either adopted by plan or evolved spontaneously. In 1947–8 it carried out a survey of the technical film-needs of twenty-nine countries, including many devastated during the War. It planned (because it had no money to sponsor them directly) schedules of film subjects required for international distribution, and requested a wide range of countries to undertake the production of those particular subjects for which each one was specially qualified. (For example, Britain could promote a film on cleaned pictures, or the development of mass radiography, America on soil conservation or prefabrication, and so on). UNESCO set up advisory committees in many countries to promote this work and urge sponsors of all kinds to adopt the needed subjects as part of their production programme. UNESCO has been condemned as a madhouse of theorists and as a nest for sinecures, the less scrupulous nations sending to act as their officials either political time-servers or playboys anxious to spend their salaries on nights in Paris. Whatever the possible shortcoming of officials and departments, UNESCO represents an important idea which ranges from the high-level aim of the interchange of the cultural currency of the nations to the more easily defined routine tasks of measuring the physical needs of the less privileged countries in primers, wireless sets or film-stock, and endeavouring to arrange for those needs to be met.

Another factor in international documentary is the foundation of the World Union of Documentary in 1947. The Union (with Basil Wright as its first President) issued an important Declaration after an initial meeting in Brussels. Documentary was defined as follows:

" By ' Documentary ' is meant the business of recording on celluloid any aspects of reality, interpreted either by factual shooting or by sincere and justifiable reconstruction, so as to appeal either to reason or emotion, for the purposes of stimulating the desire for and the widening of human knowledge and understanding, and of truthfully posing problems and their solutions in the sphere of economics, culture and human relations."

(" Documentary Film News," August 1948, p. 89.)

Other important sections of the Declaration are:

" The indispensable rôle of documentary in the fields of information and education and in the communication of ideas makes it necessary for the documentary workers, not only to state the problems exactly, but also to guide the public towards the solution of these problems.

" In this task, it is the responsibility of every documentary worker to master the technique and artistic potentialities of the documentary film, so that art and technique are fused with the social purpose of documentary.

" The documentary film has established itself as a form of film art. It has a profound influence on feature films in all countries. This influence will certainly continue. In particular, documentary film workers should engage in all activities designed to secure the full and unfettered expression of social, economic and cultural life through the medium of film.

" The principal tasks confronting documentary workers are as follows: the fight against the enemies of peace and democracy; national, racial and economic oppression and religious intolerance; poverty and disease, illiteracy, ignorance and other social evils; and the fight for peace and reconstruction; independence of subject peoples; free intellectual and cultural expression; dissemination of knowledge, not at present available to all.

" Documentary film workers will collaborate with all international organisations working for the principles enumerated above."

The many festivals of documentary and scientific films held in Britain, France, Czechoslovakia, Belgium and elsewhere have enabled us to see each other's productions on a sufficient scale to realise the quality and individual styles of documentary film-making evolved in over twenty countries. Hundreds of films have been completed since the end of the War.

It is more difficult to summarise the achievement of countries where private sponsorship is the chief form of production than that of countries where some kind of total plan is in operation. France, for example, has produced a large number of films, impressionist, ironic, realistic according to the feeling of their makers. (Many of them are listed by Ernest Borneman in " Documentary 48.") They represent a much wider artistic variety than British documentary, but certainly less social purpose. Nicole Vedrès compiled *Paris 1900* with a witty and imaginative mixture of the factual and burlesque films of the first fifteen years or so of French cinema. She has managed to reflect an epoch from the sparse and flickering survivals of the first silent period. Jean Grémillon's *Le Six Juin à l'aube* is steeped in melancholy, the recollections of Normandy as it was and the realities of invasion and liberation; ostensibly it is a documentary of the Normandy campaign, but framed in a poem of the land loved by a native, for Grémillon is a Norman. Rouquier's *Farrebique* also has this peasant quality of love of the earth, a nostalgia for the fundamental and simple living of men and women whose job is to grow crops under the great and clouded sky. Roger Leenhardt has made the first satisfactory film on the history of the film apparatus in *La Naissance du Cinéma*. Many films have been made about French artists, notably *Matisse* and *Rodin*. The most brilliant and elaborate example of this new technique in art appreciation which uses the resources of the cinema is Paul Haesaerts' and Henri Storck's Belgian film study of Rubens (described in detail by the writer in " Sight and Sound," No. 67). The scientific films of Painlevé and Comandon will be discussed later. French stylishness is variously represented in all these films, as it is in the wonderful underwater journeys *Epaves* and *Paysages du Silence* (Cousteau), Rouquier's short film *Le Tonnelier,* Yannick Bellon's *Les Goëmons* and the curious mime-film *La Rose et la Réséda* made by André Michel and derived from a Resistance poem by Louis Aragon.

Several countries stand out in documentary production – including Russia, Denmark, Italy, Canada and Czechoslovakia. Russia has a large planned output of State-sponsored documentary, mostly recording the progress of the various Soviet republics. An important branch of Soviet production lies in scientific documentary. Denmark has developed on a small scale the State-sponsorship of factual films on lines similar to Britain: her 1948 Catalogue has a hundred titles covering social services, architecture, social propaganda, agriculture, health, biology and so on. Some two-edged films were produced during the Occupation, such as *The Corn is in Danger,* where somehow the squeaky-voiced corn-weevils get themselves identified with the Nazis.

Sweden has no State scheme of sponsorship and so her documentaries have more of the quality of *avant-garde* experiments. The outstanding work is by Arne Sucksdorff and Gosta Werner. Werner's film, *The Sacrifice,* a gruesome reconstruction of a Stone Age appeasement to the gods by human blood, in which the atmosphere of tension and panic is worked up by extraordinary rhythms of the cutting and the musical score, was one of the discoveries of the 1948 Edinburgh festival. Sucksdorff's films (*People in the City, A Divided World* and other films mainly about the open countryside) are rhythmical experiments of imaginative distinction, creating an atmosphere similar to that of lyrical poetry.

Czechoslovakian documentary enjoys State sponsorship with planned production and exhibition, and allowance is therefore made for the social and educational subjects typical of the production of Britain, Canada and Denmark. The Czechs are remarkable on an international level for their puppet and cartoon films which possess a style unique to themselves, with no signs of the influence of Disney or Pal.

Poland is developing realistic and documentary film production, especially on scientific subjects. *The Last Stage*, directed by Wanda Jakubowska, is an example of Polish work in the realist feature film and gives an unequalled picture of life in a concentration camp during the War made by a woman who was herself a prisoner in Auschwitz. Yugoslavia, too, has started to produce feature films, many about Yugoslav life in wartime.

In Germany documentary production has been sponsored by the Film Section of British Information Services. Young film-makers such as Peter Schnabel and Rudolph Kipp are making fine films, like the *Report on the Refugee Situation* and *Rosinenbomber,* a strikingly well-photographed film about the Berlin airlift.

When John Grierson left Canada and eventually came to Europe to work first at UNESCO and now at the British Central Office of Information, Ross McLean became Canadian Film Commissioner. Canada, like Britain, has maintained her State-sponsored film production since the War, and many of her films have for some years been distributed in Britain by the M.O.I. and its successor the C.O.I. More recently her experimental films, including the Mental Mechanism series (*The Feeling of Rejection, The Feeling of Hostility*) which dramatise the bad mental habits that some unfortunate people acquire in the course of their upbringing and social contacts, the witty colour-patterns designed by Norman McLaren and created without the use of a camera, and such unique films as *The Loon's Necklace*, a legend played in Canadian-Indian masks, have been added to the more usual documentaries of social explanation which are the staple output of the Canadian

film organisation. Canada sets great stock by her theatrical
as well as her non-theatrical distribution: her success in
achieving this is a real step forward in the use of the film as
a public information service. Australia founded its National
Film Board on the model of Canada in 1945, whilst New Zealand has produced a weekly theatrical factual and news film
since 1939. South Africa has yet to establish State production. India and Pakistan, however, seem to be establishing
film-making on a more permanent basis than hitherto.
Planned production of documentary is also beginning in
Poland and Yugoslavia.

Italian documentary is led by the work of Luciano Emmer
and Enrico Gras, whose carefully photographed and edited
reconstructions of the narratives within the works of artists
like Giotto, Carpaccio and Bosch are so imaginatively done
that, with Roman Vlad's music, they constitute a new branch
of film-making. Emmer's regional films of Italy, such as *Isole
della Laguna*, combine close observation with a poetic treatment. But it is the art and architecture of Italy that appeals
most to her documentary film-makers.

American documentary in any usual sense of the term is
almost non-existent through lack of sponsorship. Occasionally a sponsor will appear or private finance is subscribed
and films as widely different as Flaherty's *Louisiana Story* or
the psychological film *The Quiet One* are made. Much
American factual film-making is carried out directly on
16 mm. and distributed non-theatrically; hundreds of educational and "interest" films are created annually by producers like the "Encyclopædia Britannica." Also the Film Section of U.N.O. is sponsoring the production of films on international themes in America and other countries.

The use of the film as a recording instrument and tool for
scientific experiment is not new, and since the War it has been
developing rapidly. The Congress of the International
Scientific Film Association held in London in the autumn of
1948 showed some fifty films from fifteen countries, including
Australia, Austria, Belgium, Canada, Denmark, France,
Great Britain, Poland, the U.S.A. and U.S.S.R. It is important
to differentiate here between three uses of the film, for the
popular exposition of scientific subjects, for the demonstration

of technical subjects to specialised audiences (for example, a surgical operation or a job in precision engineering), and for actual research where the motion-picture camera becomes part of the laboratory apparatus revealing new knowledge to the scientist. By the use of high magnification, and quickened or slowed motion (motion can be speeded by three thousand times, whilst action lasting, say, three months can be contracted to, say, three minutes) the camera can reveal the processes of life and growth in the plant and animal worlds, and the behaviour of small masses observed under scientifically controlled conditions. The late Percy Smith, Jean Painlevé and Dr. J. Comandon have become outstanding in this field, but many scientists have produced remarkable studies of animal and insect life, not forgetting Pudovkin's own early film made with Professor Pavlov called *The Mechanics of the Brain* (1925). Among spectacular phenomena filmed are the behaviour of micro-organisms under surgical operation conducted by special micro-instruments made by Comandon, transparent fresh-water animalculæ by Storch of Vienna, the gigantic leaping flames of the sun's surface by Leclerc and the curious under-water life photographed by Cousteau.

The development of British documentary during the first three years of peace has been a matter of consolidation rather than extension into new uses. The work of the Colonial Film Unit, with its simple but skilful demonstration of hygiene, agricultural methods and other aspects of African citizenship reconstructed and acted by the Africans themselves, has now reached the stage that African film technicians are being trained to make their own films. The patient work of George Sellars during and since the War has led to this new achievement. These films have evolved a technique suitable for the limited visual experience of the less-developed Africans.

We have seen that the sponsorship of British documentary, whilst being mainly official, is by no means entirely so. Documentary, as distinct from those " interest " films designed solely to stir the casual curiosity of limp minds, has been sponsored by the J. Arthur Rank Organisation in the series known as *This Modern Age,* an excellent and responsible monthly study of some aspect of world affairs, and in documentaries such as Jill Craigie's *The Way We Live.* The remarkable feature-length study of the history of atomic research by G.B. Instructional called *Atomic Physics* is also a product of commercial sponsorship. Various industrial undertakings, notably the oil and chemical industries, are continuously sponsoring films in Britain, like I.C.I.'s series on Anæsthesia and the Shell Film Unit's *How an Aeroplane Flies* and *The Cornish Engine*.

The feelers of experiment are, however, noticeable in certain groups of British documentaries. The instructional film is developing its technique carefully. *24 Square Miles* is a long film based on a social survey undertaken by the Agricultural Economic Research Institute in Oxfordshire; it illustrates the facts and problems of rural life impartially, but in such a way as to promote organised group discussion afterwards as a necessary part of the film. While *The Story of Printing* and *Day and Night,* the latter in colour, are very clear examples of simple explanation of complex subjects to junior audiences, *Instruments of the Orchestra* is a film subtly scored by Benjamin Britten so that each instrument is demonstrated in a continuous development of the composition : this film is both stirring as well as instructional.

A particularly interesting group of films are those which use naturally recorded observations and interviews of children or adults for the purpose of studying human behaviour. Starting with Geoffrey Bell's brilliant series on personnel selection for the Army (no one who has seen it will forget the interview between an Army psychiatrist and a potential officer in this series), the candid camera has done a great deal for the study of child behaviour in *Children Growing Up with Other People* and *Children Learning by Experience*. Another interesting film in popular psychology was *Your Children and You* on parental as distinct from child behaviour for once in a way. The Crown Film Unit's *Children on Trial* made a moving drama out of the responsibility of the community to a boy who is an habitual thief and later of the boy himself to the community once his personal problem (as distinct from that with his family) is solved.

New treatments of subjects usually taken the hard dull way were shown in *Chasing the Blues* (a gay extravaganza on industrial welfare), *Dover '47* (which satirised the conventional travelogue in order to get behind the real conditions of a town which suffered in the War), and above all in the witty social cartoon series featuring the character Charley made by John Halas and Joy Batchelor. Here at last is a genuine, fresh, well-designed and pioneering series of cartoons without any debt to Disney: Charley is a British type, simplified but without sentiment.

There remain, lastly, the films which have reconstructed places in Britain and abroad, films like *North-east Corner, A City Speaks, Five Towns, A Cumberland Story* and *Waverley Steps* at home, and *Three Dawns to Sydney, Cyprus is an Island, A String of Beads, The Bridge, Voices of Malaya* and *Daybreak in Udi* abroad. Paul Rotha's *The World is Rich* is necessarily a universal film, arguing with all his pungency and technical adroitness the need to foster the earth's food supplies. Ralph Keene's films introduce a poetic atmosphere: the poet Laurie Lee has assisted the beautiful photography of his films made in Cyprus and Assam with some of the best commentaries heard in recent British documentary, commentaries which it is interesting to compare with Dylan Thomas's greatly debated but much more pretentious verse for the film *Our Country*. The poetic film has not been common in British documentary: *Song of Ceylon* still remains unsurpassed, though John Eldridge, working at the time for Greenpark, has made two impressionist films, *Three Dawns to Sydney*, a series of impressions of the countries which lie on the route of a plane flying from London to Sydney, and *Waverley Steps*, a study of life in Edinburgh. These films are among the most encouraging made since the War.

Britain's collective documentary achievement is still first in the world, since the use to which the films are put, their distribution and exhibition, is as outstanding a piece of organisation as the film production itself. Documentary, whether utilitarian, imaginative, explanatory or poetic, must in all cases be brought to the right audiences everywhere. Otherwise it rapidly becomes an *avant-garde* flower trying to grow in an empty pot without soil to feed its living roots.

12. *Film Studies*

In this book I have attempted a study of the film on the high level of values which its best work and its potentialities warrant. There is now no question of its influence and importance in many branches of modern life, in art, entertainment, education, technology and science. Gilbert Cohen-Séat, founder of the French scheme of film studies called Filmologie, in which University teachers and students are encouraged on an international scale to undertake, mostly voluntarily in their spare time, the examination of the film medium from the strictly philosophical and psychological standpoints, has stated that in his view the invention of motion pictures will become as important to the development of civilisation as the invention of printing.

The Universities, however, still seem to require time to take this new medium of expression into full account from an æsthetic and social point of view. There is no lack of interest in the film as a kind of artistic by-product causing important social disturbances, but the moment the æsthetic and social values of the cinema are discussed, everyone, including the most learned of us, becomes an amateur and dilettante. It is true that certain American Universities have departments of film studies, but these concentrate almost entirely on vocational courses for future film technicians, not unlike those in the various Film Schools and Institutes in some European countries. Certain Universities and University Colleges of this country study the use of visual aids in education, always including the film, and organisations such as the Universities Film Council, the British Psychological Society and the Scientific Film Association encourage academic interest in the film, but these interests are concerned almost entirely with the use of the cinema in technical education and scientific research, and do not therefore study the wider issues which so badly need the attention of professional planned research.

The three main branches of film studies are: first, the historical and æsthetic (this is, the detailed study of the history of the film and the development of its art and technique); second, the social and economic aspects of the film, taking into account its psychological influences on the public and its growth and significance as an entertainment industry, and thirdly, its importance as a new educational medium. Work in the first two fields continues to be undertaken only by individual students, and it is notorious how few in number are the genuinely valuable and reliable books on film history and æsthetics. The film in relation to the social sciences is largely a matter of guess-work, or, in a few instances, of casual research conducted for a short while by isolated individuals and organisations. There is no permanent, scientific investigation being undertaken anywhere into the numerous social and psychological problems which are involved in the weekly exhibition of standardised commercial film entertainment to hundreds of millions of people of all ages and nationalities all over the world. The social repercussions of this entirely new factor in civilisation are being allowed to pass virtually unquestioned, except by critics in search of a little sensational copy for the newspapers or by the observers employed on occasional semi-official enquiries initiated through a survey or questionnaire.

The film trade itself and governmental departments of commerce publish miscellaneous statistics of film production, distribution and exhibition, but such figures need verification and co-ordination over a period of time to be of permanent value in the study of the industry as a whole. This work can be done only by carefully trained, full-time students who have learned something of the meaning and significance of all these sensational figures with their streamers of noughts.

The influence of the film has received more consistent attention in the case of children than of adults. This is because children are more accessible than adults, and the avidity with which they rush off to the pictures at all hours of the day and night has startled educationists into studying this hypnotic rival to homework and organised games. The Children's Film Clubs offer obvious chances for controlled field-work by students of the social sciences. The Payne Fund studies, undertaken nearly twenty years ago in America, and the recent researches undertaken here in Britain by J. P. Mayer, by Mary Parnaby and Maurice Woodhouse, by Birmingham University, and by the officials of the Children's Film Department of the Rank Organisation, are all producing useful results. Little comparable material is available about film influences on adolescents and adults, though organisations like Mass Observation have compiled some data on the cinema, and Wartime Social Survey (working for the Ministry of Information) and

Social Survey (working for the Central Office of Information)
have both published some very thorough statistics of cinema
attendance in Britain during and since the War.[1]

Britain is a most suitable country for the fuller development of film studies. It has a cinema-attendance figure as
high as that of any country in the world, not excluding
America. It has as long a history of film-making and film-
going as America and France, the other two outstanding
countries with a pioneering film industry in the nineties of last
century. Owing to the predominance of American productions in our cinemas for a full generation, the international
influences of the film can begin to be observed. A strong
tradition of documentary film-making going back for twenty
years gives us a prolonged experience of the use of the film
in education and public information, a service which is not confined merely to this country, but which has, for example, done
pioneer work in the education of backward races in Africa,
which alone offers considerable possibilities for the research
worker. Finally, the presence of organisations such as the
British Film Institute, with its fine library of international film
books and journals, and the more recent British Film
Academy, offers to the student some, at any rate, of the background material he will require to begin his work.

It seems likely that the example set by serious voluntary
students both inside and outside our Universities, together
with the researches undertaken by the staff-members of the
Institute and the Academy, will finally persuade one or other
of the Universities to found a permanent Department of
Motion Picture Studies to co-ordinate this complicated work
and to train people to undertake it. It is not inconceivable
that the film industry itself would assist in some of the
financial outlay. However the foundation of such a Department finally comes about, the work most obviously needs
doing, and the results of its various research projects would be
of the greatest interest and importance. It will be interesting
to see which of our Universities is the first to take up the
challenge and set to work.

[1] A summary of these and other comparative figures is given on
pp. 239–240.

Additional

1. *The Cinema Audience in Britain*

Reprinted from " Further Education," Vol. I, No. 8, by kind permission of the Editor.

THE Social Survey Organisation undertook during 1943 an enquiry into the cinema-going habits of the British public. This report was published by the Ministry of Information. During 1946 a second survey was completed, and the report on this survey was published in 1947 by the Central Office of Information (2s. 6d.). This second survey, written by Kathleen Box, is based on a double set of enquiries, the first made in March, and the second in October 1946. The methods used are described as follows:

> " In both enquiries samples of the adult civilian population were interviewed. In the first enquiry quota sampling was the method used, representative numbers of individuals who had left school being selected from different sex and occupation groups. Workers were interviewed at their places of work, and housewives and the retired and unoccupied at their homes. In the second enquiry individuals were selected at regular intervals from the Maintenance Registers for those aged sixteen and over and were visited and interviewed at their homes. In both cases appropriate numbers of interviews were allotted to each of the twelve Civil Defence Regions, and people living in towns of different sizes and in rural areas were represented in their due proportions."

The first sample covered about 2,000 and the second about 3,000 cases.

The salient figures might be selected and summarised as these:

(1) 24 per cent. of adults never go to the cinema; 32 per cent. of adults go to the cinema at least once a week; 13 per cent. of adults go more than once a week; 5 per cent. of children never go to the cinema; 65 per cent. of children of school age go to the cinema at least once a week.

(2) 69 per cent. of the age group 16–19 years go to the cinema at least once a week; 57 per cent. of the age group 20–29 years go to the cinema at least once a week; 62 per cent. of the cinema audience are under 40 years of age as against 45 per cent. of the population. Women are rather in the ascendancy in the average cinema audience.

(3) 70 per cent. of cinema-goers (i.e. those who go at least once a month) go regularly: two-thirds of this percentage select between different cinemas in their area, one-third of this percentage go regularly to the same cinema whatever the programme; 30 per cent. of cinema-goers only visit the cinema because they want to see a definite film; 70 per cent. of the mothers of children who visit the cinema regularly find out what films their children are going to see.

(4) The total expenditure of the civilian population of Great Britain on cinema-going is rather over £100 million a year. (The Monopoly Report of 1944 gave this figure as about £110 million and the White Paper on National Income and Expenditure 1938–46 gave the 1946 figure as £121 million. The average price paid for a seat by adults is 1s. 9d.

(5) 40 per cent. of factory, clerical and distributive workers go to the cinema at least once a week. Professional and managerial workers go less frequently. Half of those retired or unoccupied never go to the cinema. Working-class children go to the cinema more frequently than middle- or upper-class children.

These facts are of the greatest interest, and are open to varying degrees of interpretation. There is space here for only a few of the main points which occur to me.

First, about a quarter of the adult population never go to the cinema. These include a large proportion of the older persons. People over 50 years of age represent 36 per cent. of the population, but only 18 per cent. of the cinema audience. This proves that we have not yet reached the stage when the whole of the population has been brought up against the background of a firmly established national cinema-going habit. (In 1914 the estimated weekly attendance was only 7 million weekly as against 22 million in 1939 and 30 million today.) When the younger generation of the 'thirties and 'forties becomes the older generation of the future, no doubt the cinema attendance of the aged will be found to be much higher. After all, only 5 per cent. of the children of today are not cinema-goers.

I have found, after lecturing extensively on the film, that although there is widespread interest in the cinema among professional people and those engaged in educational and social welfare, a large proportion seldom see films at all. They say they are far too busy, and quite a few, judging from their tone, regard cinema-going as a patent waste of time. The prestige of the film-society movement, which has doubled itself since the war, counteracts this attitude to a certain degree, but at a time when it is imperative that the better kind of film should meet with the active support of all intelligent and responsible people, it is wrong that an influential section of this public still regard all films as childish. Quite often these people take the chair at leactures about the cinema!

On the other hand, it is plain that the youthfulness of the average film audience has become highly influential on the policy of film producers. Youth is depressed by tragedy, elated by hope, regards love as a great and mysterious adventure, and desires life to be exciting without involving much reflection. The films which are most successful at the box-office as those which ceaselessly feed these attitudes with their happy endings, culminating in marriage after a series of quick-moving, thrilling adventures. Films which reflect the values and problems of maturity (e.g. the *real* problems of marriage, of careers, work and public life, of social evils and abuses, and real problems of individuals living in the new age of scientific invention and political strife) tend not to be good box-office, because a greater part of their emotional values and excitements lies outside the experience of younger people. If, however, older people increase in numbers in our cinemas, their maturer demands will begin substantially to influence the box-office, provided they are prepared to exercise discretion in their choice of films.

On the matter of choice of films, the Social Survey makes an interesting statement.

" It is clear that more of the younger than the older people go to the cinema regularly, choosing which of the cinemas available they will go to according to the films that are showing. Older people more frequently stick to the same cinema and more of them do not go regularly, but only go when they want to see the films that are on. In other words, younger people tend to make sure of getting some entertainment regularly, exercising choice within a limited field, and older people tend to forgo entertainment unless it is of the type they require. There is, however, also a substantial proportion in all groups, ranging from 19 per cent. of frequent cinemagoers in the youngest group up to 31 per cent. in the oldest, that go to the same cinema regularly, exercising no choice whatsoever."

Considering the present imperfect state of education in this country, this is encouraging. In effect, larger numbers of people select their films (if only within a narrow field) than accept them blindly. It is commonly assumed that the reverse is the case.

In the matter of expenditure, a few figures will help us to see the cinema-going habit in due proportion to other national amusements. Mark Abrams, in the course of a most interesting article in the *Contact* volume " Britain Off Duty," gives us the following comparative figures from various sources on annual expenditure:

Cinema-going—£121 million (30 million seats sold in a peak week).

Dance hall admissions—£15 million (3 million admissions weekly).

Wireless licences—£9 million.

Dog-track gate money—£8½ million (1,350,000 admissions weekly).

Football gate money—£3 million (1,110,000 admissions weekly).

Football pools—£40 million (11 million coupons submitted weekly during the season).

Newspapers—£50 million.

Magazines—£26 million.

Gambling on horse-racing—£315 million (gross turnover: net expenditure £30 million).

Gambling on greyhound racing—£210 million (gross turnover: net expenditure £16 million).

Gambling with gaming machines—£10 million (gross turnover: net expenditure £2 million).

To these figures may be added those for theatres and music-
halls. Their annual turnover is £13 million. The annual
audience for the theatre is in the neighbourhood of 31 million
(one-fiftieth part of the cinema's annual audience) and that
for the music-halls 85 million.

There can be little doubt that we are a pleasure-loving
nation, but of all the mass-audience amusements, the cinema
takes pride of place.

2. Why, not start a Film Society?

There is no reason why not.

The first decision to make is the scale upon which the proceedings are to be run. You can either start a Film Society
on 16 mm. substandard (which is cheap) or by gathering a
membership large enough to be able to hire a cinema on a
Sunday afternoon. Or you may be lucky enough to live in a
town where some college or institution has a 35-mm. installation.

The second decision is one of objective. Is the society to
cater for a limited interest (for example scientific or religious),
or for the widest possible interest, taking all types of film for
its province? Once these decisions have been taken a small
executive committee should be formed to initiate the necessary
publicity for membership. The executive committee should not
be so large that it can never meet, or so small that it is not
representative of a variety of educational and social interests.
It should contain a representative of each of the chief social
bodies, like the teaching profession and the trade unions, which
can help through their own organisations to build up a reliable
membership. The committee should contain an accountant, or
someone with training in figures, to act as treasurer, a person
of organisational experience to act as secretary, and at least
one person with knowledge of films and projection. If the
society is to meet in a cinema, the manager of the cinema
selected should be on the committee; his help, if sympathetic,
can be invaluable. The chairman should have enough personality to stop discussions on montage.

Taking a substandard society first, it should be assumed that
a good programme, with a feature film, cannot be assembled for

under about six pounds. A person or organisation should be found (in a college, institute or school in the first place) in possession of a 16 mm. sound projector (and a sound projectionist). A certain sum should be allowed off the revenue to put aside for projector spares and for servicing the machine. Allowance should also be made for the printing or duplicating of tickets and other publicity, and for the use of a hall.

It is best to sign on one hundred and fifty members before launching out too far. Sound films are expensive to hire though many documentaries can be obtained free. It is worth while to spare no pains to make your first shows successful in programme, presentation and audience. Good audiences attract better. Substandard shows for a shilling or one-and-six a performance will attract a wide audience if the programmes are good and well put over, and the building where they are shown is easily accessible by public transport.

Do not forget there is no legal hold over a substandard film show. No licence is necessary; but it is always as well to use a hall licensed for dances and meetings, with good seating and marked exits at the rear. The hall should be good acoustically (get advice if you are not sure). The screen should be mounted as high as possible so that the picture is clear above the heads of all the audience when seated. Stewards with torches are essential.

By now the potential Film Society will probably be in touch with the Federation of Film Societies, which will give advice on all points connected with general organisation and finances, claims for exemption from Entertainments Tax and the problem of film selection. Tax exemption can be claimed for *bona fide* film societies working either on substandard or in a cinema. More details about the Federation will be given later.

Second, the Public Cinema Film Society. It is essential for the Executive, when it has its objective defined, to meet the Trade with a view to finding a sympathetic manager. Choose, if possible, a cinema of small capacity yet centrally placed, such as a news theatre. If you are to hold your membership, the situation of the cinema is in the end of greater importance than its capacity. The Society can easily be confined to the balcony of a large cinema. Choose a house which does not open too early on Sunday evenings. Sunday afternoon is the best time to open. The manager will explain the complexities of the extension of the Sunday-opening licence.

This licence may cause you and the manager a battle with the Licensing Bench. It is well to find out the mood of the Bench on the subject, and if necessary the mood of the Watch Committee. A friendly town councillor is of great assistance here: so is a broad-minded pillar of the Church. You must be prepared, along with the manager, to fight for your Sunday-opening rights before the Licensing Bench. Whatever their attitude, remember they are the servants of the State, not its masters.

The work of the Film Society movement has now been centred upon the Federation of Film Societies, which has its headquarters at the British Film Institute, 164 Shaftesbury Avenue, W.C.2 (Scotland has its own Federation, with head-quarters at Film House, 6/8 Hill Street, Edinburgh; it works in association with the English and Welsh Federation in London). The Federation levies an annual subscription of £1 per hundred members of the subscribing society. For this it gives full advice on constitutional and legal points, publishes a Bulletin, which includes film reviews, and pamphlets of use to film societies, arranges standard rental charges for films with the trade, assists in the organisation of lectures and books films for member societies. Film Societies should also join the British Film Institute, whose publications (including the " Monthly Film Bulletin," numerous pamphlets and the monthly journal " Sight and Sound ") are of importance. Other regular publications include " Sequence," " Documentary Film News " (publishers Film Centre, 34 Soho Square, W.1) and the annual Pelican " The Cinema " replacing " Penguin Film Review." Other organisations with which Film Societies should keep in touch include the Scientific Film Association, 34 Soho Square, London, W.1.

It is best to form a Film Selection Sub-Committee of three or four knowledgeable members of the main Executive Committee. Their job will be to draw up provisional programmes well ahead of the Society's season in consultation with the Federation. In addition to the Federation's publications, it is absolutely essential they should possess the Catalogues of as many film libraries as possible. There are about sixty of these, mainly in London. The Federation will provide a list, but here are a few of the more important libraries:

British Instructional Films, Ltd., Mill Green Road, Mitcham, Surrey. (*Entertainment, Educational and General Interest films on 16 mm.*)

Butcher's Film Service, Ltd., 175 Wardour Street, W.1. (*Entertainment and General Interest films on 16 mm.*)

Central Film Library, Imperial Institute, S.W.7. (*Library of E.M.B., G.P.O., M.O.I. and C.O.I. films.*)

C.W.S. Film Department, Transport House, Smith Square, S.W.1. (*Distributors for the Soviet Film Agency and other sources.*)

Dawn Trust Film Library, The Studio, Aylesbury, Bucks. (*Entertainment, General Interest and Religious films.*)

French Film Delegation, 27 Queen Anne Street, W.1. (*French documentaries.*)

Film Traders, Ltd., 167 Oxford Street, W.1. (*Selection of Continental films, some on 16 mm.*)

Gaumont British Film Library, 1 Aintree Road, Perivale, Middlesex. (*Large selection of Entertainment and General Interest films on 16 mm.*)

Ron Harris, King Street, Maidenhead, Berkshire. (*Entertainment and General Interest films on 16 mm.*)

John King, Film House, East Street, Brighton, 1. (*Entertainment and General Interest films on 16 mm.*)

M.G.M., 16 mm. Department, 1 Belgrave Place, S.W.1. (*Entertainment and General Interest films on 16 mm.*)

March of Time, 4 Dean Street, W.1. (*March of Time Series available on 16 mm.*)

National Film Library, 4 Great Russell Street, W.C.1. (*Feature and Documentary films of historical and artistic interest.*)

Soviet Film Agency, 5 Kensington Palace Gardens, W.8. (*Lists contain important Russian feature and documentary films.*)

Wallace Heaton, Ltd., 127 New Bond Street, W.1. (*Entertainment and General Interest films on 16 mm. and 9·5 mm.*)

Wigmore Films, Ltd., 35 Beaufort Gardens, Brompton Road, S.W.3. (*Entertainment and General Interest films on 16 mm.*)

Finally, keep your members together by an inclusive charge for, say, a six-month season based on your estimated overheads, with a good margin. The film world is not an easy world to handle, and mistakes can and do happen. There will be heart-aches and headaches, and a reserve local programme should be kept in readiness should film despatch at any time let you down. A reserve substandard projector is also a comfort.

A well-organised Film Society is one of the greatest pleasures there is, and a definite addition to the social life of any community; from it can branch out all types of cultural activity, discussion groups, W.E.A. classes on the film, even film-making groups working on substandard documentary during the summer when it is not advisable to run large-scale film performances. The Society can acquire a library, or work in conjunction with the local town library, ensuring that all new film books are added to the shelves. A large Film Society can run branches on substandard for specialised interests—such as health, education, science, religion and travel. A small group, carefully organised, can be developed into a large and flourishing society filling a cinema at two successive performances.

The purpose of a Film Society is to give a critical audience a chance to select its own films from sources all over the world, and so to free itself from the limitations of the programmes run for profit in the commercial cinemas. Its programmes supplement those shown publicly, which in practice are entirely, or almost entirely, British and American films. The film is a highly international art, and Film Society programmes should emphasise this in the range of their selection. Nor should the artistic development of the film from the historical point of view be overlooked: though *Birth of a Nation* may not appeal to the full membership of a society, there is every reason why it should be shown at a special meeting where it can be introduced in proper perspective and its importance in the history of the cinema demonstrated. The aim of a Film Society is to develop the appreciation of the cinema by showing good films of every kind from every source available. Only by the constant exhibition of such films can we develop large numbers of people with any real sense of the film's place in modern art and its importance to modern civilisation.

3. *Film Archives*

By Ernest Lindgren

(*Deputy Director of the British Film Institute and
Curator of the National Film Library*)

There are few things more ephemeral than a commercial film.
At one moment, it seems to be showing everywhere, and the
next moment it has disappeared for good and lives only in the
memory of those who have seen it. Occasionally under pressure of circumstances films may be commercially reissued, but
this is not a practice which the film industry follows enthusias-
tically. Yet from time to time films appear which one would
afterwards like to see again and which would bear reshowing.
To see D. W. Griffith's *Birth of a Nation* or Eisenstein's *Battleship Potemkin* is still an exciting experience. Moreover, cinematograph film itself is a medium not only for the reproduction
of the appearance and sound of the living, moving world around
us, but also for its perpetuation. It is a new form of historic
document, far exceeding in fidelity and completeness of
impression all previous forms.

It is such considerations as these which lie behind the national
film archive movement. During the last ten years particularly,
national film libraries have sprung up in many countries. In
New York there is the Museum of Modern Art Film Library;
in Paris there is the Cinémathèque Française. In London we
have the National Film Library of the British Film Institute;
and there are similar libraries in the Argentine, Australia,
Belgium, Czechoslovakia, Denmark, Holland, Italy, New
Zealand, Poland, Sweden, Switzerland, Uruguay and the
U.S.S.R. All these libraries have similar objects: to preserve
cinematograph films either as examples of film art or historic
documents, or both; to make such films available to interested
students in their own countries; and to facilitate the exchange
of such films, and information concerning them, between one
country and another. It is perhaps the second of these objects
which will be of the greatest general interest.

Many who have followed Dr Manvel through this survey will
be impressed with the power of the cinema as a social force
and with the need to improve the quality of film production;

but they will equally be impressed by the highly complex and powerful organisation of the cinema industry, and may well wonder whether there is anything ordinary people can do within the realm of practical politics to achieve this end.

The only effective solution is a long-term one: to educate film audiences. The man who pays his shilling at the box-office is the one who can order any tune he wants from the apparently all-powerful pipers of the film industry—if only there are enough of him. People, and especially young people, must be shown that intelligent and informed criticism can increase their delight in film-going; it can make the films they see, not so much the short-lived opiate of the escapist, as works to be selected, enjoyed, discussed, remembered and in some cases to be seen again.

The ripples stirred by the pioneer work of the film societies have spread in ever-widening circles until now even teachers and administrators of education, whose attitude in the past has generally been one of academic aloofness, are beginning to show a lively interest. The claims of film appreciation as a new subject, at least in the fields of continued and adult education, are beginning to be heard. The British Film Institute is anxious to encourage film appreciation; it is the function of the National Film Library to provide material for its study.

Primarily, the purpose of the Library is to preserve films and film records of historical value. Because celluloid film and its thin coating of photographic emulsion are, on any long-term view, extremely fragile, the originals in the Library cannot be projected on to the screen; for this purpose copies have to be made. This means that by an unfortunate necessity much of the Library's collection is momentarily submerged, held in trust for the future.[1]

A number of films, however, selected for their value as illustration material for appreciation courses in schools and for historical programmes for film societies, have already been copied, and 16 mm. and 35 mm. prints can be obtained through the Library's Lending Section at moderate hiring fees. In some cases composite films have been specially edited from selected excerpts. "A Catalogue of the Lending Section," with brief

[1] Except for the individual student who can look at films on a movieola.

historical and technical notes, can be obtained from the Film
Institute. The Film Institute has also published pamphlets on
the study of film appreciation, which suggest various ways in
which the subject may be approached, and include lists of
recommended books. Beyond this we welcome the enquiries
of those who want assistance on any particular problem. The
Lending Section, in short, is that part of the National Film
Library " open to the public "; and we are anxious to do all
we can to ensure that they enjoy the most fruitful use of it.
The pamphlets referred to above can be obtained for 7½d.
each, including postage, on application to the British Film
Institute, 164 Shaftesbury Avenue, London, W.C.2.

Many films mentioned in this book can be obtained on 16 mm.
stock. The chief titles include *Nanook of the North* (Flaherty),
The Cabinet of Dr. Caligari (Wiene), *The Last Laugh* (Murnau),
Berlin (Ruttman), *The Battleship Potemkin* (Eisenstein), *Mother*
(Pudovkin), *The General Line* (Eisenstein), *The Ghost that
Never Returns* (Room), *Turksib* (Turin), *The Italian Straw Hat*
and *Le Million* (Clair), *The Blue Angel* (von Sternberg),
Kameradschaft (Pabst), *Song of Ceylon* (Wright), *The Plow
that Broke the Plains* and *The River* (Lorentz), *The Atone-
ment of Gosta Berling* (Stiller), *Earth* (Dovzhenko), *La
Passion de Jeanne d'Arc* (Dreyer), *The Birth of a Nation* and
Intolerance (Griffith). The composite film covering the history of realist cinema, *Film and Reality*, made by Cavalcanti
for the National Film Library, is strongly recommended, since
it includes sequences from many of the pre-war films mentioned in the section on Documentary.

The Library has also produced a group of films in which
well-known film critics are given the opportunity to analyse
and comment on important films of their choice. In the first
three of the series, Mr. Jympson Harman analyses the editing
of a scene in *Great Expectations,* Miss Dilys Powell comments on *The Overlanders* and Mr. Basil Wright analyses *Odd
Man Out.*

Book List

N.B.—Books marked * are indispensable

1. FILM HISTORY

A MILLION AND ONE NIGHTS. Terry Ramsaye. Simon and
Schuster, 1926. A discursive but fascinating history of
silent cinema written from the American point of view.

*LE CINEMA SOVIETIQUE. Léon Moussinac. N.R.F., Paris,
1928. An excellent account of the early period of Soviet
cinema, based on personal investigation.

*THE FILM TILL NOW. Paul Rotha. Cape, 1930. A fine and
very detailed account of the achievement of the silent
cinema. Revised edition with Richard Griffith, Vision
Press, 1949.

CELLULOID. Paul Rotha. Longmans, Green and Co., 1931.
A sequel to the above, entering upon the sound film.

A HISTORY OF THE MOVIES. B. B. Hampton. English edition,
Noel Douglas, 1932. History primarily of American
Cinema. Well illustrated. Recommended.

*DOCUMENTARY FILM. Paul Rotha. Faber and Faber, 1936.
Revised edition, 1939. An important historical record of
documentary, with an evaluation of its achievement.

MOVIES FOR THE MILLIONS. Gilbert Seldes. Batsford, 1937.
A very readable account of the chief trends of the cinema
from an historical angle, with the emphasis on American
film.

*HISTORY OF THE FILM. Bardèche and Brasillach. Translated
and edited by Iris Barry. Allen and Unwin, 1938. An
interesting and important history from the French point of
view. Revised edition, André Martel, Paris, 1949.

THE FILM ANSWERS BACK. E. W. and M. M. Robson. Bodley
Head, 1939. A spirited defence of the American film for
its healthy sociological content as contrasted with the
decadence of European cinema.

*HISTOIRE DE L'ART CINEMATOGRAPHIQUE. Carl Vincent.
Editions du Trident, Bruxelles, 1939. A detailed history

of the film from the beginnings to about 1937. Recommended.

*THE RISE OF THE AMERICAN FILM. Lewis Jacobs. Harcourt Brace and Co., New York, 1939. This is undoubtedly one of the few very good books on the film, but naturally limited to the achievement of America, with occasional references only to European cinema. It is both lively and authoritative. It takes the various periods of the development of American film, deals first with the economic issues of the industry, next with the work of important directors who developed the art of the film, and closes with a survey of the period from the point of view of the social content of the films both good and bad.

*GEORGES MÉLIÈS, 1816–1938. Maurice Bessy and Lo Duca Prisma, 1945. A lavishly illustrated study of the early French director of theatrical fantasies in film. Contains many examples of Méliès' own treatments and scripts.

*IMAGES DU CINEMA FRANÇAIS. Nicole Vedrès. Les Editions du Chêne, Paris, 1945. A survey of the development of French cinema largely by means of stills grouped under types of film, such as Burlesque, Comedy, Horror films, "La Condition Humaine," etc. An interesting and unusual book.

PRESENTING SCOTLAND: A FILM SURVEY. Norman Wilson. The Edinburgh Film Guild, 1945. A short but excellent survey of the history of the documentary presentation of Scotland, with proposals for the founding of a documentary school in Scotland itself.

*THE INDEX SERIES OF THE BRITISH FILM INSTITUTE. These monographs on and indexes of the works of distinguished directors, with historical and critical data, are important as contributions to the supply of definitive information about leading directors. The series includes the names of Méliès, Griffith, Chaplin, Lang, Flaherty, Lubitsch, Richter, Dovzhenko, Ford, Murnau, von Sternberg, Hitchcock and Pudovkin.

THE BRITISH FILM YEARBOOKS. Peter Noble. British Yearbooks. These annual surveys of the British film contain lists of the personnel of the Industry, the films of the year, and a number of articles by various well-known film-makers and critics.

*THE FACTUAL FILM. O.U.P., 1946. One of a series of reports prepared for the Arts Enquiry by a group of anonymous experts and sponsored by the Dartington Hall Trustees in association with the Nuffield College Reconstruction Survey. Covers the development of documentary in Britain, and contains recommendations concerning the economic reorganisation of the British film industry.

TWENTY YEARS OF BRITISH FILM. Michael Balcon. H. Forsyth Hardy, Ernest Lindgren and Roger Manvell. Falcon Press, 1946. A fully illustrated survey of the development of British feature and documentary film, 1928–45.

*L'INVENTION DU CINEMA, 1832–1897. Volume One of Histoire Générale du Cinéma. Georges Sadoul. Editions Denoël, Paris, 1946. The most authoritative history of the development of technical experiment and apparatus which led to the invention of the film camera, projector and celluloid stock. Highly recommended.

*LES PIONNIERS DU CINEMA, 1897-1909. Georges Sadoul. Editions Denoël, Paris, 1947. The second volume of Sadoul's history covers the period of Méliès and Pathé in France, and also considers contemporary work done in Britain and America.

*LOUIS LUMIERE, INVENTEUR. Maurice Bessy et Lo Duca. Prisma, Paris, 1948. An authoritative and fully illustrated account of one of the most important single figures in the invention of motion pictures.

LE DESSIN ANIME. Lo Duca. Prisma, Paris, 1948. A fully illustrated history and technique of animated films.

*HISTOIRE DU CINEMA. 1895–1929: Vol. I. Le Cinéma Français 1895-1929. René Jeanne and Charles Ford. Robert Laffont, 1947. The first of four volumes of a comprehensive film history, far more detailed than any other work except Sadoul's, in comparison with which it is more popular in treatment.

*DER FILM ALS WARE. Peter Bächlin. Burg-Verlag, Basle, 1945. A history of the world film industry and an analysis of its economy. A shortened version of this important book has appeared in French as "Histoire Economique du Cinéma" (La Nouvelle Edition, Paris, 1946).

THE FILM. Georg Schmidt, Werner Schmalenbach and Peter Bächlin. Holbein Publishing Company, Basle, and Falcon Press, 1948. Using an original lay-out of stills, diagrams and text, this book, originally published in German, demonstrates the æsthetic, social and industrial factors in the cinema. English version prepared in consultation with Roger Manvell.

*FROM CALIGARI TO HITLER. Siegfried Kracauer. Dobson, 1947. A detailed account of the German cinema, 1919–33, written to prove the argument that national tendencies which culminated in Hitler can be traced in the cinema of this period.

FIFTY YEARS OF GERMAN FILM. H. H. Wollenberg. Falcon Press, 1947. A volume in the National Cinema Series edited by Roger Manvell. Written with emphasis on the historical and social development of the German film. The book contains a large selection of stills.

*EXPERIMENT IN THE FILM. Roger Manvell (Editor). Grey Walls Press, 1948. Essays, historical and æsthetic, by the critics and film-makers Lewis Jacobs (America), Jacques Brunius (France), Grigori Roshal and Roman Karmen (Russia), Ernst Iros and Hans Richter (Germany), and Edgar Anstey, Roger Manvell and John Maddison (Britain), on the development of the experimental and *avant-garde* film in these countries. Contains much historical material not previously recorded.

*THE HISTORY OF THE BRITISH FILM. Vol. I: 1896–1906. Rachael Low and Roger Manvell. Vol. II: 1907–14. Rachael Low. Allen and Unwin, 1948 and 1949 respectively. Sponsored by the British Film Institute, these detailed accounts of the rise of the British film will be completed in four volumes, and will end with the close of the silent-film period. The history is written under the auspices of a Research Committee under the Chairmanship of Cecil Hepworth.

SOVIET CINEMA. Thorold Dickinson and Catherine de la Roche. Falcon Press, 1948. A volume in the National Cinema Series edited by Roger Manvell discussing the contribution of Soviet Russia to the film. Contains the largest collection of Russian stills yet published.

FRIESE-GREENE. Ray Allister. Marsland Press, 1948. A fascinating biography of Britain's pioneer inventor of cinematography, fictionalised in treatment, but based on a careful investigation of the facts.

THE ITALIAN FILM. Vernon Jarrett. Falcon Press, 1950. A volume in the National Cinema Series, this book is a fully illustrated popular history of the Italian cinema.

2. THE ART OF THE FILM

*FILM TECHNIQUE. V. I. Pudovkin. Translated by Ivor Montagu. Gollancz, 1929. New edition, Newnes, 1933. An essential book.

CINEMA. C. A. Lejeune. Maclehose, 1931. A collection of excellent reviews, dealing with many distinguished directors and actors.

SCRUTINY OF CINEMA. William Hunter. Wishart, 1932. Using certain outstanding films as the key to his review of cinema, the author assesses its general achievement up to 1932.

*FILM. Rudolf Arnheim. Faber, 1933. The most complete æsthetic of cinema yet written. Not easy reading on the whole.

FILM CRAFT. Adrian Brunel. Newnes, 1933. The studio and scenario in working dress. A collection of many interesting comments from different participants in the collective film job.

THE PRIVATE LIFE OF HENRY VIII. Lajos Biro and Arthur Wimperis. Edited by Ernest Betts. Methuen, 1934. A complete scenario, nicely cleaned up for the press. But useful and illuminating, as well as entertaining.

*A GRAMMAR OF THE FILM. Raymond Spottiswoode. Faber, 1935. Rather academic in approach, but one of the few competent books on the technique of the film.

FILM ACTING. V. I. Pudovkin. Translated by Ivor Montagu. Newnes, 1935. A later book than " Film Technique," it contains Pudovkin's detailed comments on the work of the Russian actor.

FILM MUSIC. Kurt London. Faber, 1936. Designed rather

for the musician than the layman, but of considerable general interest.

FILM AND THEATRE. Allardyce Nicoll. Harrap, 1936. A fairly elementary textbook of cinema technique by a distinguished historian of the drama.

*MOVIE PARADE. Compiled by Paul Rotha. Studio, 1936. Revised edition by Paul Rotha and Roger Manvell, 1950. A fine collection of stills giving a pictorial history of world cinema in its various branches.

THE CINEMA AS A GRAPHIC ART. Vladimir Nilsen. Newnes, 1936. A Russian cameraman's textbook on the æsthetics of his art.

*GARBO AND THE NIGHT-WATCHMEN. Alistair Cooke. Cape, 1937. Cooke calls this a bedside book. Its bedside manner is limited to keeping the reader awake. Satiric, amusing, caustic comments by American and British critics of distinction and wit.

DESIGNING FOR MOVING PICTURES. Edward Carrick. Studio, 1941. An excellent book on the design and structure of film sets and properties.

*THE FILM SENSE. S. M. Eisenstein. Faber, 1943. Of great importance, but difficult and sometimes perverse to read.

*TWENTY BEST FILM PLAYS, BEST FILM PLAYS, 1943-44, and also 1945. Gassner and Nichols. Crown, N.Y. These three volumes are the beginning of a regular series of annual collections of film scripts edited for the reading public. The first collections contain such important films as *It Happened One Night*, *Rebecca*, *The Grapes of Wrath*, *Little Cæsar*, *Fury*, *The Life of Emile Zola*, *Juarez*, *The Good Earth*, *All that Money can Buy*, *Stagecoach*, *The Miracle of Morgan's Creek*, *The Ox-bow Incident*, *Hail the Conquering Hero*, *The Southerner* and *Double Indemnity*. Introductions on script-writing by Dudley Nichols.

*THE ART OF WALT DISNEY. Professor R. D. Feild. Collins, 1944. An important and detailed, as well as beautifully illustrated volume, the result of a year's academic research in collaboration with the Disney studios themselves. Gives a complete history of the development of Disney's technique of animation, and the organisation of the Studios.

INVITATION TO THE FILM. Liam O'Laoghaire. Tralee, The Kerryman Ltd., 1945. Shows the position of the film in Ireland, with proposals for the development of an Irish industry for the production of features and documentary. An excellent survey of the whole field of the cinema. Well illustrated.

FILM APPRECIATION AND VISUAL EDUCATION. The British Film Institute, 1944. An important collection of papers on all branches of the art and technique of the film with contributions from Thorold Dickinson (Directing), Sidney Cole (Editing), Ken Cameron (Sound), Edward Carrick (Art Direction), W. J. Speakman (Audience Reaction), and several papers on the film in education.

*GRIERSON ON DOCUMENTARY. Edited with an Introduction by H. Forsyth Hardy. Collins, 1946. A well-edited selection of Grierson's brilliant essays on documentary and early reviews of feature films.

CHESTNUTS IN HER LAP. C. A. Lejeune. Phœnix House, 1947. A collection of Lejeune's reviews written since 1936.

*THE ART OF THE FILM. Ernest Lindgren. Allen and Unwin, 1948. The most complete and carefully considered account of the art and technique of the film to have been published in this country. Very highly recommended.

ANATOMY OF THE FILM. H. H. Wollenberg. Marsland Publication, 1947. A guide to motion-picture appreciation intended for the beginner.

LE CINEMA. André Vigneau. Les Lettres Françaises, Cairo, 1945. A carefully considered and illustrated æsthetic and social study of the cinema by the famous French photographer, for a time producer to the Misr Studios in Cairo.

INTELLIGENCE DU CINEMATOGRAPHIE. Marcel L'Herbier (Editor). Editions Corrêa, Paris, 1946. An anthology of French film criticism from its origin to the present day. Of considerable historical interest.

COMPOSING FOR THE FILMS. Hanns Eisler. Oxford University Press, New York, 1948. A devastating survey of the contemporary American film music by a distinguished composer, who analyses the special conditions governing composition for the screen.

THE BOYS' AND GIRLS' FILM BOOK. Mary Field and Maud

Miller. Burke Publishing Company, 1947. An excellent survey of all aspects of film-making (not omitting historical, economic and social considerations) for intelligent older children.

ART AND DESIGN IN THE BRITISH FILM. Edward Carrick. Dobson, 1948. A fully illustrated survey of the work of leading British art directors and designers.

DRAWN AND QUARTERED. Richard Winnington. Saturn Press, 1948. A selection of Winnington's sharp reviews and brilliant satiric drawings of film stars from the period 1943–8.

SCOTT OF THE ANTARCTIC. David James. Convoy Publications, 1948. Written by the film's Arctic Adviser, this book is a model description of the planning and making of a film which involved considerable research and elaborate location work.

FILM FORM. Sergei Eisenstein. Harcourt Brace and Co., N.Y., 1949. A series of essays on film theory, dated 1928 to 1944, selected by Eisenstein himself and edited and translated by Jay Leyda. Eisenstein was a highly imaginative thinker on film aesthetics, often seeming to lack discipline in the consideration of his subject and to fit elaborate theoretical explanations to his own intuitive work as a great creative artist. This volume of essays has all the virtues and all the faults of his critical method.

BRITISH FILM SCRIPTS. Edited by Roger Manvell. Methuen, 1950. The final shooting-scripts of *Brief Encounter, Odd Man Out* and *Scott of the Antarctic* published in association with the British Film Academy.

3. THE FILM AND SOCIETY

THE NEW SPIRIT IN THE CINEMA. Huntly Carter. Shaylor, 1930. A rather pretentious book on sociological lines. But full of useful information.

THE FILM IN NATIONAL LIFE. A. C. Cameron. Allen and Unwin, 1932. " Being the Report of an Enquiry conducted by the Commission on Educational and Cultural Films into the Service which the Cinematograph may render to Education and Social Progress."

MOTION PICTURES AND YOUTH. W. W. Charters. The Macmillan Company, 1933. A summary of the conclusions of the Payne Fund Studies of the effect of motion pictures upon children and youth. Based on evidence collected as early as 1929–33, it still contains valuable data.

THE CENSOR, THE DRAMA AND THE FILM, 1900–1934. Dorothy Knowles. Allen and Unwin, 1934. A history of the effect of censorship on the drama, with an additional section on the cinema.

THE ARTS TODAY. Edited by Geoffrey Grigson. Bodley Head, 1935. Contains an important article, mainly from the social angle, by John Grierson.

SOVIET CINEMA. Voks, Moscow, 1936. A Russian-produced piece of triumphant publicity resulting from the release of *Chapayev* and the birth of the new Soviet Cinema.

THE AFRICAN AND THE CINEMA. L. A. Notcutt and G. C. Latham. Edinburgh House Press, 1937. A remarkable study of the special technique required in the production and projection of films for primitive peoples.

MONEY BEHIND THE SCREEN. F. D. Klingender and Stuart Legg. Lawrence and Wishart, 1937. The financial structure of the British Film Industry, with a less detailed summary of the American industry. Important revelation of vested interests in the film industry of the past.

*CHILDREN IN THE CINEMA. Richard Ford. Allen and Unwin, 1939. An important study of the place of the cinema in child life.

*AMERICA AT THE MOVIES. Margaret Thorp. Yale, 1939; Faber, 1947. Margaret Thorp examines what the American film-goers want, what they get, and how the industry organises them to want what they get.

U.S.S.R. SPEAKS FOR ITSELF. Vol. IV, Culture and Leisure. Lawrence and Wishart, 1941. The short article by Eisenstein on the Russian Cinema should be read for its account of the structure of the Soviet industry.

*HOLLYWOOD. Leo Calvin Rosten. Harcourt Brace, 1941. The result of a three-year investigation conducted by a team of social investigators. An astonishing collection of data about the organisation, finance and personnel of Hollywood. Indispensable, but the facts in this enormous collection are of varying importance and require skilled interpretation. This interpretation is only partly undertaken by the book, which otherwise certainly starts something.

*Tendencies to Monopoly in the Cinematograph Film Industry. Stationery Office for the Board of Trade, 1944. A mine of information concerning the ramifications of the British film industry, especially in relation to the extension of power by the Rank organisation and the relationship of the British to the American film industry during the War.

*Freedom of the Movies. Ruth Inglis. University of Chicago Press (G.B., Cambridge U.P.), 1947. Written as a report from the American Commission on Freedom of the Press, which included the film in its survey. This is an important book on the history of American film censorship and its social implications.

*Essai sur les Principes d'une Philosophie du Cinema. Vol. I. Introduction Générale. Gilbert Cohen-Séat. Presses Universitaires de France, 1946. An outstanding study of the importance of the cinema considered from the strictly philosophical and psychological points of view. This author has founded the international Filmologie movement in association with universities in France and abroad. The occasional review " Filmologie " reports the progress of these studies.

Sociology of the Film: Studies and Documents. J. P. Mayer. Faber, 1946. Half this book consists of the documents resulting from Mayer's interviews and questionnaires and from other material coming mainly from children and adolescents. The author generalises on various film problems resulting from his analysis of this evidence. An interesting and often provocative book.

British Cinemas and their Audiences. J. P. Mayer. Dobson, 1949. The text of this book is mainly extensive essays, some rather self-conscious, many of great interest, written by the readers of " Picturegoer " in answer to the author's queries on the history of their cinema-going and their taste in films.

THE NEGRO IN FILMS. Peter Noble. Skelton Robinson, 1949. This book is a study of the Negro actor especially as he appears in the American film, and the problems involved in the racial interpretation of the Negro in the film.

4. MISCELLANEOUS

FOR FILMGOERS ONLY. Edited by R. S. Lambert. Faber, 1934. A collection of essays on various aspects of cinema, written with the cultural and educational angle in mind. Quick reading.

SECRETS OF NATURE. Mary Field and Percy Smith. Faber, 1934. A book of great interest on the making of nature films.

THE MOVIES ON TRIAL. W. J. Perlman. Macmillan, New York, 1936. A symposium of American opinion on the film. Chiefly sociological.

FOOTNOTES TO THE FILM. Edited by Charles Davy. Lovat Dickson Ltd., 1937. The best of the anthologies of ' aspects.' Highly recommended, though the standard of the articles varies.

WE MAKE THE MOVIES. Edited by Nancy Naumberg. Faber and Faber, 1938. A survey of the chief stages of film-making, with articles by Jessy Lasky, Sidney Howard, Bette Davis, Paul Muni, and Walt Disney. Recommended.

THE CINEMA TODAY. D. A. Spencer and H. D. Waley. Oxford University Press, 1939. A most readable book on the technical side of photography, recording and projecting of films.

PROMISED LAND. Cedric Belfrage. Gollancz, 1939. A study of the development of property in Hollywood; a documentary story delivered from the political left; a terrible indictment of unhindered speculation and exploitation in site and building values in a new community.

CINE-BIOLOGY. J. V. Durden, Mary Field and Percy Smith. Penguin, 1941. A development of the subject of " Secrets of Nature " for Pelican Books.

WORKING FOR THE FILMS. Oswell Blakeston (Editor). Focal Press, 1947. A collection of short essays by experts in almost every branch of film-making on their work. Intended for readers contemplating a career in films.

BRITISH FILM MUSIC. John Huntley. Skelton Robinson, 1947. An invaluable reference volume on British film music composers.

REPORT OF THE COMMISSION ON TECHNICAL NEEDS IN PRESS, RADIO AND FILM. Two Volumes, UNESCO, Paris, 1947 and 1948. The official survey of the post-war technical needs of countries, including Belgium, Czechoslovakia, France, Denmark, Italy, Greece, the Netherlands, Norway, Poland, Yugoslavia, Mexico, Venezuela, China, India and Pakistan. Full of important statistical information.

THE USES OF THE FILM. Basil Wright. Bodley Head, 1948. A short but acute survey of conditions governing motion-picture production in Britain.

INFORMATIONAL FILM YEAR-BOOK. Albyn Press, Edinburgh. An annual directory to the British documentary movement.

5. PERIODICALS

KINEMATOGRAPH WEEKLY. One shilling weekly. An excellent illustrated record of trade feeling from the exhibitors' angle. Contains all the news about new films, with reviews, publicity, etc.

DOCUMENTARY FILM NEWS. Should be taken by everybody interested in the welfare of cinema, its cultural value, its use for propaganda. Published by Film Centre, 34 Soho Square, London, W.1.

MOTION PICTURE HERALD. Quigley Publications, New York. Weekly. The most important American exhibitors' journal. Full of news from the American angle.

L'ECRAN FRANÇAIS. Paris. Weekly. An independent journal on the cinema in France.

SEQUENCE. An occasional journal on the art of the film, giving careful reviews of the work of outstanding directors.

DOCUMENTARY. An annual brochure published by the Albyn Press, Edinburgh, in connection with the Edinburgh Festival. Gives useful surveys of international documentary production.

LA REVUE DU CINEMA. Edited by Jean-George Auriol. A post-war revival of the outstanding French review on the art of the film. Highly recommended.

HOLLYWOOD QUARTERLY. Published under the sponsorship of the University of California, this is a fine academic journal devoted to the art of the film.

BIANCO E NERO. Published by the Centro Sperimentale di Cinematografia, this is the outstanding Italian journal devoted to film studies.

THE CINEMA. An illustrated Pelican volume of studies on all aspects of international cinema, edited by R. K. Neilson Baxter, H. H. Wollenberg and Roger Manvell. Published annually, and replacing "Penguin Film Review."

THE PUBLICATIONS OF THE BRITISH FILM INSTITUTE, 4 Great Russell Street, London, W.C.1. The Institute's regular publications can be subscribed to separately, and include the journals "Sight and Sound" and "The Monthly Film Bulletin," indispensable both for criticism and record.

Fifty Years of Films

THIS List, compiled during 1949, represents some of the more representative work in the general development of the film, but not all. Space precludes it from being comprehensive, and it is confined almost entirely to the work of American, British, French, German, Italian and Russian directors. It should be noted that only a *selection* of films is given for most directors.

ABBAS, ACHMED
  Children of the Earth, 1946
ALEXANDER, DONALD
  Our School, 1941
  Life begins Again, 1943
ALEXANDROV, C. V.
  Jazz Comedy, 1934
  The Circus, 1936
  Volga-Volga, 1938
  The Bright Path, 1941
ALEXEIEF, G.
  Night on the Bare Moun-
    tain, 1934 (with Parker)
ALLEGRET, MARC
  Voyage au Congo, 1927
  Lac aux Dames, 1935
  Sans Famille, 1936
  Orage, 1937
  Entrée des Artistes, 1938
ALLEGRET, YVES
  Dedée d'Anvers, 1948
  Une si Jolie Petite Plage,
    1948
  Manèges, 1949
ANDRIEVSKY, A.
  Robinson Crusoe, 1946
    (Stereoscopic)
ANGER, KENNETH
  Escape Episode, 1946
  Fireworks, 1947

ANNAKIN, KEN
  We of the West Riding,
    1946
  Holiday Camp, 1947
ANSTEY, EDGAR
  Granton Trawler, 1934
  Housing Problems, 1935
    (with Arthur Elton)
  Enough to Eat, 1936
ANTONIONI, MICHELANGELO
  Nettezza Urbana, 1948
ASQUITH, ANTHONY
  Shooting Stars, 1928
  Underground, 1928
  Cottage on Dartmoor, 1928
  Tell England, 1930
  Dance Pretty Lady, 1932
  Pygmalion, 1938 (with Les-
    lie Howard and Gabriel
    Pascal)
  French without Tears, 1939
  Freedom Radio, 1941
  Quiet Wedding, 1941
  Cottage to Let, 1941
  We Dive at Dawn, 1943
  Demi-Paradise, 1943
  The Way to the Stars, 1945
  The Winslow Boy, 1948
  THE BROWNING VERSION, 1951.
AUTANT-LARA, CLAUDE
  Fait-Divers, 1927

CALEF, HENRI
Jericho, 1945

CAMERINI, MARIO
Rotaie, 1930
Gli Uomini che Mascal-
zoni, 1932
Il Cappello a tre Punte,
1934
Daro un Millione, 1936
Ma Non e une Cosa Seria,
1936
Il Signor Max, 1937
Molti Sogni per le Strade,
1949

CAMPOGALLIANI, CARLO
Montevergine, 1939

CAP, FRANTISEK
Men without Wings, 1946

CAPRA, FRANK
American Madness, 1932
Lady for a Day, 1933
It Happened One Night,
1934
Mr. Deeds Goes to Town,
1936
Lost Horizon, 1937
You Can't Take it with You,
1938
Mr. Smith Goes to Washing-
ton, 1939
Meet John Doe, 1941
Why we Fight Series
(Service Films), 1943
Arsenic and Old Lace, 1944
It's a Wonderful Life, 1947

CARNE, MARCEL
Jenny, 1935
Drôle de Drame, 1937
Le Quai des Brumes, 1937
Hotel du Nord, 1938
Le Jour se Lève, 1939
Les Visiteurs du Soir,
1942
Les Enfants du Paradis,
1944
Les Portes de la Nuit,
1946

CASTELLANI, RENATO
Un Colpo di Pistola, 1942
Sotto il sole di Roma,
1948

CAVALCANTI, ALBERTO
Rien que les Heures, 1926
En Rade, 1927
La P'tite Lili, 1928
Le Petit Chaperon Rouge,
1929
Coalface, 1935 (with Grier-
son)
We Live in Two Worlds,
1937
Film and Reality, 1942
Greek Testament, 1943
Dead of Night, 1945
(in part)
They Made Me a Fugitive,
1947

CENTRAL NEWSREEL STUDIOS
(Moscow)
Leningrad Fights, 1942
Defeat of the Germans near
Moscow, 1942
One Day of War, 1943
Story of Sebastopol, 1943
Story of Stalingrad, 1943
69th Parallel, 1943
The Partisans, 1944
Drive to the West, 1944
Justice is Coming, 1944
(Kharkov Trial)

CHAMBERS, JACK
Night Shift, 1942
Power for the Highlands,
1943
The Bridge, 1946

CHAPLIN, CHARLES
Keystone Films, 1914
Tillie's Punctured Romance,
1914
Essanay Films, 1915
The Champion, 1915
The Tramp, 1915
Carmen, 1916

DE SICA, VITTORIO
Maddalena, Zero in Condotta, 1940
Un Garibaldino al Convento, 1942
I Bambini ci Guardano, 1943
La Porta del Cielo, 1944
Sciuscia, 1945
Ladri di Bicicletti, 1949

DICKINSON, THOROLD
Spanish ABC, 1938
Gaslight, 1940
The Prime Minister, 1941
Next of Kin, 1942
Men of Two Worlds, 1946
The Queen of Spades, 1948

DIETERLE, WILHELM
The Last Flight, 1932
Fog over 'Frisco, 1933
The Story of Louis Pasteur, 1936
The Life of Emile Zola, 1937
Blockade, 1938
Juarez, 1939
Dr. Ehrlich's Magic Bullet, 1940
This Man Reuter, 1941
All that Money can Buy, 1941
Portrait of Jennie, 1949

DISNEY, WALT
Alice in Cartoonland, 1923
Steamboat Willie, 1928
Skeleton Dance, 1929
Snow White and the Seven Dwarfs, 1938
Pinocchio, 1940
The Reluctant Dragon, 1941
Fantasia, 1941
Bambi, 1942
Dumbo, 1942
Victory Through Airpower, 1943
Saludos Amigos, 1944
The Three Caballeros, 1945

DONSKOI, MARK
(With R. Perelstein)
The Childhood of Maxim Gorki, 1938
Out in the World, 1939
My Universities, 1940
The Rainbow, 1944
Unconquered, 1945
The Village Teacher, 1949

DOVZHENKO, A.
Zvenigora, 1928
Arsenal, 1929
Earth, 1930
Ivan, 1932
Aerograd, 1935
Shors, 1939
Liberation, 1940
The Battle for the Ukraine, 1943
Life in Blossom, 1947

DREVILLE, JEAN
La Cage aux Rossignols, 1944
La Ferme du Pendu, 1945
La Bataille de l'Eau Lourde, 1947

DREYER, CARL TH.
(Commenced direction Denmark. Worked in Sweden, Germany and France)
La Passion de Jeanne d'Arc, 1928
The Adventure of David Gray, 1931
Day of Wrath, 1943

DULAC, GERMAINE
La Fête Espagnole, 1920
Le Diable dans la Ville, 1924
The Seashell and the Clergyman, 1927

DUPONT, E. A.
Variety, 1925 (Supervision Erich Pommer)
Piccadilly, 1928

DUVIVIER, JULIEN
Poil de Carotte, 1932

Great Citizen, 1937–9
The Turning Point, 1946

FANCK, ARNOLD
White Hell of Pitz Palu, 1929
FEHER, FRIEDRICH
The Robber Symphony, 1936
FERNANDEZ, EMILIO
Maria Candelaria, 1946
FEYDER, JACQUES
Thérèse Raquin, 1927
Les Nouveaux Messieurs, 1928
Le Grand Jeu, 1933
La Kermesse Héroïque, 1935
Knight without Armour, 1937
Une Femme Disparaît, 1941
FIELD, MARY MACADAM. 1949.
(Associated with G.B. Instructional since 1927)
They Made the Land, 1938
FISCHINGER, OSCAR
Lichtertantz, 1932
FLAHERTY, ROBERT
Nanook of the North, 1920–21 (released 1922)
Moana, 1923–4 (released 1926)
24 Dollar Island, 1925
White Shadows of the South Seas, 1927–8
Tabu, 1928–9 (released 1931)
Industrial Britain, 1931–2 (with John Grierson)
Man of Aran, 1932–3 (released 1934)
Elephant Boy, 1935–7
The Land, 1939–42
The Louisiana Story, 1948
FLEMING, VICTOR
The Virginian, 1929
Blonde Bombshell, 1933
The Wizard of Oz, 1940

FLOREY, ROBERT
A Hollywood Extra, 1928 (with Slavko Vorkapich)
The Loves of Zero, 1929
FORD, JOHN (began direction 1917)
The Iron Horse, 1924
Arrowsmith, 1935
The Informer, 1935
The Plough and the Stars, 1937
Stagecoach, 1939
Young Mr. Lincoln, 1939
Grapes of Wrath, 1940
The Long Voyage Home, 1940
Tobacco Road, 1941
How Green was my Valley, 1941
Battle of the Midway, 1942
My Darling Clementine, 1946
The Fugitive, 1947
FORDE, WALTER
Rome Express, 1933
For Ever England, 1935
The Four Just Men, 1939
Atlantic Ferry, 1941
Flying Fortress, 1942
FORST, WILLY
Maskerade, 1934
Burgtheater, 1937
FRANCIOLINI, GIANNI
Fari nella Nebbia, 1942
FRANKLIN, SIDNEY
The Good Earth, 1937
FREND, CHARLES
The Big Blockade, 1942
The Foreman went to France, 1942
San Demetrio, London, 1943
Return of the Vikings, 1944
Johnny Frenchman, 1945
Scott of the Antarctic, 1948
FRIC, MARTIN
The Warning, 1947

FRÖHLICH, GUSTAV
  Wege im Zwielicht, 1948

GALEEN, HENRIK
  The Golem, 1920 (with
    Paul Wegener)
  The Student of Prague, 1925
GANCE, ABEL
  J'accuse, 1919
  La Roue, 1920–22
  Napoleon, 1925
GENDELSTEIN, A.
  Lermontov, 1944
GERASIMOV, SERGEI
  The New Teacher, 1939
  The Ural Front, 1944
  Young Guard, 1948
GERMI, PIETRO
  In the Name of the Law,
    1949
GILLIAT, SYDNEY
  (See also Frank Launder)
  Waterloo Road, 1945
  The Rake's Progress, 1945
  London Belongs to Me,
    1948
GORDON, MICHAEL
  Act of Murder, 1948
GREMILLON, JEAN
  L'Etrange Monsieur Victor,
    1937
  Remorques, 1939
  Lumière d'Eté, 1942
  Le Ciel est à vous, 1943
  Le Six Juin à l'Aube, 1946
GRIERSON, JOHN
  Drifters, 1929
  Producer, G.P.O. Unit,
    1933–7; Canadian Film
    Commissioner, 1939–45;
    Producer, Central Office
    of Information, 1948
GRIERSON, MARION
  So this is London, 1934
  For all Eternity, 1934
  Edinburgh, 1935

GRIERSON, R. I.
  Today we Live, 1937 (with
    Ralph Bond)
GRIFFITH, D. W.
  Edgar Allan Poe, 1909
  Judith of Bethulia, 1913
  The Birth of a Nation,
    1915
  Intolerance, 1916
  Hearts of the World, 1917
  Broken Blossoms, 1919
  Way down East, 1920
  Orphans of the Storm, 1921
  Isn't Life Wonderful, 1924
GRUNE, KARL
  The Street, 1923
  At the Edge of the World,
    1926
  Jealousy, 1926
  Waterloo, 1928
GUITRY, SACHA
  Bonne Chance, 1936
  Roman d'un Tricheur, 1936
  Les Perles de la Couronne,
    1937
  Remontons les Champs
    Elysées, 1938
  Ils étaient neuf célibataires,
    1939

HALAS, JOHN
  Train Trouble, 1945
  Old Wives' Tales, 1946
  Handling Ships, 1946
  Charley Series, starting
    1947
  Fly about the House, 1949
HAMER, ROBERT
  Pink String and Sealing
    Wax, 1947
  It Always Rains on Sun-
    day, 1948
  Kind Hearts and Coronets,
    1949
HARBICH, MILO
  Freies Land, 1946

HATHAWAY, HENRY
The House on 92nd Street, 1946
13, Rue Madeleine, 1946
Call Northside 777, 1947

HAWKS, HOWARD
Scarface, 1932
Sergeant York, 1941
Red River, 1946

HEISLER, STUART
The Glass Key, 1942

HENNING-JENSEN, B.
De Pokkers Unger, 1947
Ditte Menneskebarn, 1947

HEPWORTH, CECIL
(Joined industry, 1896)
Rescued by Rover, 1905
Coming thru' the Rye, 1924

HEYER, JOHN
The Valley is Ours, 1949

HITCHCOCK, ALFRED
The Pleasure Garden, 1926
The Lodger, 1926
Blackmail, 1929
Juno and the Paycock, 1930
The Skin Game, 1931
The Man who knew too Much, 1934
The Thirty-Nine Steps, 1935
Secret Agent, 1936
Sabotage, 1936
Young and Innocent, 1937
The Lady Vanishes, 1938
Jamaica Inn, 1939
F o r e i g n Correspondent, 1940
Rebecca, 1940
Suspicion, 1942
Saboteur, 1942
Shadow of Doubt, 1943
Lifeboat, 1944
Spellbound, 1945
Notorious, 1946
Rope, 1949
Under Capricorn, 1949
STAGE FRIGHT 1950

HOCHBAUM, WERNER
Die Ewige Maske, 1935

HOLLERING, GEORGE MICHAEL
Hortobagy, 1936

HOLMES, J. B.
The Cathode Ray Oscillograph, 1934
The Mine, 1936
Merchant Seamen, 1941
Coastal Command, 1942
The Centre, 1948

HOWARD, LESLIE
Pygmalion, 1938
(with Anthony Asquith and Gabriel Pascal)
Pimpernel Smith, 1941
The First of the Few, 1942
The Gentle Sex, 1943
The Lamp still Burns, 1944

HURST, BRIAN DESMOND
Theirs is the Glory, 1946

HUSTON, JOHN
The Maltese Falcon, 1942
The Treasure of Sierra Madre, 1947
Key Largo, 1948
We were Strangers, 1949

INCE, THOMAS H.
Typhoon, 1914

INGRAM, REX
Four Horsemen of the Apocalypse, 1921
Mare Nostrum, 1926

IVENS, JORIS
Rain, 1928
Philips Radio, 1930
New Earth, 1931
Komsomol, 1932
Spanish Earth, 1937
Power and the Land, 1940
Indonesia Calling, 1946

JACKSON, PAT
Health in War, 1940
Ferry Pilot, 1941
Western Approaches, 1944

JAKUBOWSKA, WANDA
 The Last Stage, 1948
JENNINGS, HUMPHREY
 Heart of Britain, 1941
 Listen to Britain, 1941
 The Silent Village, 1943
 The Fires were Started, 1943
 Diary for Timothy, 1946
 A Defeated People, 1946
 The Cumberland Story, 1947

KANIN, GARSON
 A Man to Remember, 1938
 Bachelor Mother, 1939
 The Great Man Votes, 1940
 They knew what they Wanted, 1940
 Tom, Dick and Harry, 1941
 The True Glory, 1945 (with Carol Reed)
KAUTNER, HELMUT
 In jenen Tagen, 1947
 Film without Title, 1948
 Der Apfel ist Ab, 1949
KAZAN, ELIA
 Pie in the Sky (with Ralph Steiner), 1933
 A Tree grows in Brooklyn, 1945
 Boomerang, 1946
 Gentleman's Agreement, 1947
KEENE, RALPH
 New Britain, 1940
 Spring on the Farm, 1942
 Crown of the Year, 1943
 The Crofters, 1944
 Cyprus is an Island, 1946
 A String of Beads, 1947
KEIGHLEY, WILLIAM
 Green Pastures, 1936
 The Man who came to Dinner, 1942
 The Street with no Name, 1948

KIMMINS, ANTHONY
 Mine Own Executioner, 1947
KING, HENRY
 Tol'able David, 1921
 In Old Chicago, 1938
 Wilson, 1944
KIRSANOFF, DIMITRI
 Ménilmontant, 1924
 Brumes d'Automne, 1928
 Mortes Moissons, 1948
KLAREN, GEORGE C.
 Wozzek, 1947
KLINE, HERBERT
 The Forgotten Village, 1944
 My Father's House, 1946
KORDA, ALEXANDER
 The Private Life of Henry VIII, 1933
 Rembrandt, 1936
 Lady Hamilton, 1941
 Perfect Strangers, 1945
 An Ideal Husband, 1947
KULESHOV, LEV
 Red Front, 1920
 Adventures of Mr. West in the Land of the Bolsheviks, 1924
 The Death Ray, 1924
 Expiation, 1926
 The Great Consoler, 1933
 The Siberians, 1940

LA CAVA, GREGORY
 Gabriel over the White House, 1933
 Private Worlds, 1935
 My Man Godfrey, 1936
 Stage Door, 1938
LACOMBE, GEORGES
 Le Pays sous Etoiles, 1945
 Martin Roumagnac, 1946
LAMPIN, GEORGES
 L'Idiot, 1946
LAMPRECHT, GERHARD
 Emil and the Detectives, 1931
 Irgendwo in Berlin, 1946

LORENTZ, PARE
The Plow that Broke the Plains, 1936
The River, 1938
The Fight for Life, 1940

LUBITSCH, ERNST
(Commenced direction 1914)
Dubarry, 1919
Sumurun, 1920
Anne Boleyn, 1920
The Flame, 1923
(Arrived America, 1923)
The Marriage Circle, 1924
Forbidden Paradise, 1924
Lady Windermere's Fan, 1925
The Student Prince, 1927
The Patriot, 1928
The Love Parade, 1929
One Hour with You, 1932
Trouble in Paradise, 1932
The Merry Widow, 1934
Bluebeard's Eighth Wife, 1938
Ninotchka, 1940
That Uncertain Feeling, 1941
To Be or Not to Be, 1942
Heaven can Wait, 1943
Cluny Brown, 1946

LYE, LEN
Colour Box (Dufay), 1935
Rainbow Dance, 1936
Trade Tattoo, 1937
Newspaper Train, 1942
Kill or be Killed, 1943

MACDONALD, D.
Men of the Lightship, 1940
The Brothers, 1947
Good Time Girl, 1948

MACHATY, GUSTAV
Erotikon, 1927
From Saturday to Sunday, 1931
Ekstase, 1933

MACKENDRICK, ALEXANDER
Whisky Galore, 1949

MAETZIG, HANS
Ehe im Schatten, 1947

MALRAUX, ANDRE
Espoir, 1939

MAMOULIAN, REUBEN
Applause, 1930
City Streets, 1931
Love me Tonight, 1932
Dr. Jekyll and Mr. Hyde, 1933
Gay Desperado, 1936

MANDER, KAY
Homes for the People, 1945
24 Square Miles, 1947
La Famille Martin, 1949

MANN, ANTHONY
T Men, 1947

MARCH OF TIME
Commenced 1935

MARX BROTHERS
Animal Crackers, 1932
Horse Feathers, 1933
Duck Soup, 1933
Night at the Opera, 1936
A Day at the Races, 1937
Room Service, 1938
At the Circus, 1939
The Marx Brothers go West, 1941
The Big Store, 1941

MASSINGHAM, RICHARD
They Travel by Air, 1948

MATHIESON, MUIR
Instruments of the Orchestra, 1946

McDONELL, FERGUS
The Small Voice, 1948

McLAREN, NORMAN
Animated films in Canada since 1941

MÉLIÈS, GEORGES
(Commenced work, 1896)
Voyage dans la Lune, 1902

La Fille du Puisatier, 1940

PAINLEVE, JEAN
Le Pieuvre, 1925
Stickleback's Egg, 1925
The Sea-Urchins, 1926
Hermit Crab, 1928
Sea Horse, 1934
The Fourth Dimension, 1938
Vampire-bat, 1945
Freshwater Assassins, 1947
Pasteur (with Rouquier), 1948
Our Planet the Earth, 1948

PALERMI, AMIETO
Napoli d'Atri Templi, 1938
La Peccatrice, 1940

PAL, GEORG
On Parade, 1936
Sky Pirates, 1938
Big Broadcast, 1938
Love on the Range, 1939

PASCAL, GABRIEL
Pygmalion, 1938
(with Leslie Howard and Anthony Asquith)
Major Barbara, 1941
Cæsar and Cleopatra, 1945

PETERSON, SIDNEY
The Potted Psalm, 1947
(with James Broughton)

PETROV, VLADIMIR
Storm, 1934
Peter the Great I and II, 1938-9
Kutuzov, 1944
The Battle of Stalingrad, 1949

PEWAS, PETER
Strassenbekanntschaft, 1948

PICK, LUPU
Shattered, 1921
New Year's Eve, 1924
The Wild Duck, 1926

POLONSKY, ABRAHAM
Force of Evil, 1949

POMMER, ERICH
Vaudeville, 1925 (with E. A. Dupont)
Nina Petrovna, 1929
Vessel of Wrath, 1938

PONTING, HERBERT
With Scott in the Antarctic, 1913

POTTER, H. C.
Hellzapoppin, 1942
The Time of Your Life, 1948

POWELL, MICHAEL
The Edge of the World, 1937
Contraband, 1940
49th Parallel, 1941
One of our Aircraft is Missing, 1942
The Life and Death of Colonel Blimp, 1943
The Volunteer, 1943
A Canterbury Tale, 1944
I know where I'm going, 1945
A Matter of Life and Death, 1946
Black Narcissus, 1947
The Red Shoes, 1948
The Small Back Room, 1949

PORTER, EDWIN S.
The Great Train Robbery, 1903

PREOBRASHENSKAIA, OLGA
Peasant Women of Riazan, 1927

PREVERT, PIERRE
L'Affaire est dans le Sac, 1932 (with Jacques Prévert)
Voyages Surprise, 1947

PROTAZANOV, JACOB
Without Dowry, 1936
Adventures in Bokhara, 1943

PTUSKO
The New Gulliver, 1934
The Stone Flower, 1947

PUDOVKIN, V. I.
  The Chess Player, 1925
  Mother, 1926
  Mechanics of the Brain, 1926
  The End of St. Petersburg,
    1927
  The Heir to Jenghiz Khan
    (Storm over Asia), 1928
  Life is very Good, 1930 (re-
    made as A Simple Case,
    1932)
  Deserter, 1933
  Victory, 1938
  Minin and Pozharsky, 1939
  Twenty Years of Cinema,
    1940
  General Suvorov (with M.
    Doller), 1941
  Feast at Zhirmunka, 1941
  In the Name of the Father-
    land, 1943
  Admiral Nakhimov, 1946
  Zhukovsky, 1949

RADVANYI, GEZA
  Somewhere in Europe,
    1949
RAY, MAN
  Le Retour à la Raison, 1923
  Emak Bakia, 1926
  L'Etoile de Mer, 1928
  Le Mystère du Chateau du
    Dé, 1929
RAY, NICHOLAS
  They Live by Night, 1948
REED, CAROL
  Laburnum Grove, 1936
  Bank Holiday, 1938
  The Stars look Down, 1939
  Gestapo, 1940
  Kipps, 1941
  The Young Mr. Pitt, 1942
  The Way Ahead, 1944
  The True Glory, 1945 (with
    Garson Kanin)
  Odd Man Out, 1947

The Fallen Idol, 1948
  The Third Man, 1949
REINIGER, LOTTE
  The Adventures of Prince
    Achmed, 1926
  The Adventures of Dr. Doo-
    little, 1930
  Carmen, 1933
  Papageno, 1935
  Galathea, 1935
RENOIR, JEAN
  Une vie sans joie, 1924
    (Second version: Cather-
    ine, 1927)
  La Fille de L'Eau, 1924
  Nana, 1926
  Charleston, 1927
  La Petite Marchande
    d'Allumettes, 1928
  Le Tournoi, 1928
  La Chienne, 1931
  La Nuit du Carrefour, 1932
  Boudu sauvé des eaux,
    1932
  Toni, 1934
  Madame Bovary, 1934
  Le Crime de M. Lange,
    1935
  La Vie est à Nous, 1936
  Les Bas-fonds, 1936
  La Partie de Campagne,
    1936–7
  La Grande Illusion, 1937
  La Marseillaise, 1938
  La Bête Humaine, 1938
  La Règle du Jeu, 1939
  This Land is Mine, 1943
  The Southerner, 1945
RICHTER, HANS
  First Scroll-film, 1919
  Rhythm Series, 1921–5
  Ghosts before Breakfast,
    1928
  Dreams that Money can
    Buy, 1944–8
RIEFENSTAHL, LENI
  The Blue Light, 1933

The Olympic Games, 1938

RILEY, RONALD
Steel, 1945

ROBISON, ARTHUR
(Commenced direction about 1917)
Warning Shadows, 1922
Manon Lescaut, 1926
The Student of Prague, 1936

ROOM, ALEXANDER
Bed and Sofa, 1927
The Ghost that Never Returns, 1929

ROMM, MIKHAIL
The Thirteen, 1937
Lenin in October, 1937 (with D. Vassiliev)
Lenin in 1918, 1939
Girl No. 217, 1944
V. I. Lenin, 1949

ROSHAL, GREGORI
Petersburg Night, 1934
Artamonov and Sons, 1941
Song of Abai, 1945
Academician Pavlov, 1949

ROSMER, MILTON
The Great Barrier, 1937

ROSSELLINI, ROBERTO
La Nave Bianca, 1941
Roma, Citta Aperta, 1945
Paisa, 1946
Germania, Anno Zero, 1947–8
Amore (Vox Humana and The Miracle), 1948
La Macchina Ammazzacattiva, 1949
Terra di Dio, 1949

ROSSEN, ROBERT
Body and Soul, 1947

ROTHA, PAUL
Contact, 1933
Rising Tide, 1934
Shipyard, 1935
The Face of Britain, 1935
The Fourth Estate, 1939
Roads across Britain, 1939

World of Plenty, 1943
Land of Promise, 1945
A City Speaks, 1948
The World is Rich, 1948

ROU, ALEXANDER
The Magic Fish, 1938
The Little Humpbacked Horse, 1941

ROUQUIER, GEORGES
Farrebique, 1946

RUGGLES, WESLEY
Cimarron, 1930

RUTTEN, GERALD
Dood Water, 1934

RUTTMANN, WALTHER
First Abstract film, 1921
Berlin, 1927
Toenende Welle, 1928
The Melody of the World, 1930
Dusseldorf, 1937

SAGAN, LEONTINE
Mädchen in Uniform, 1931

SANTELL, ALFRED
Winterset, 1936

SAVILLE, VICTOR
I was a Spy, 1933
South Riding, 1938

SEASTROM, VICTOR
The Exiles, 1922
He who gets slapped, 1924
The Wind, 1928

SENNETT, MACK
(Started own production, 1912)

SERVICE FILM UNITS
Siege of Tobruk, 1942
Malta G.C., 1942
Desert Victory, 1943
Naples is a Battlefield, 1944
Tunisian Victory, 1944
The True Glory, 1945
Burma Victory, 1945

SHANKAR, UDAY
Kalpana, 1948

SHAW, ALEX
    Under the City, 1934 (with Arthur Elton)
    Airmail, 1935 (with Arthur Elton)
    The Future is in the Air, 1937
    Five Faces, 1938
    Penicillin (with Kay Mander, 1945)
SHUMLIN, HERMAN
    Watch on the Rhine, 1943
SIODMAK, ROBERT
    Phantom Lady, 1944
    The Spiral Staircase, 1946
    Cry of the City, 1948
SJÖBERG, ALF
    Frenzy, 1944
SMART, RALPH
    Bush Christmas, 1947
SMITH, PERCY
    Began filming 1908
    Worked with Bruce-Woolfe on Nature films, 1921–44
SNEJKO-BLOTSKAIA, A.
    Little Hunchback Horse (Cartoon), 1949
SOLDATI, MARIO
    Piccolo Mondo Antico, 1941
    Fuga in Francia, 1948
STAUDTE, WOLFGANG
    The Murderers are Amongst Us, 1946
    Die Seltsamen Abenteuer des Herrn Fridolin B., 1948
STEINER, RALPH
    (with Willard van Dyke)
    The City, 1939
STEKLY, KAREL
    The Strike, 1947
STEMMLE, R. A.
    Berliner Ballade, 1949
STILLER, MAURITZ
    Arne's Treasure, 1919

    The Atonement of Gosta Berling, 1924
STORCK, HENRI
    Borinages, 1933 (with Ivens)
    The World of Paul Delvaux, 1947
    Rubens, 1948
STRAND, PAUL
    Manhattan (with Charles Sheeler), 1921
    Pescados, 1935
    Native Soil, 1949
STURGES, PRESTON
    The Great McGinty, 1940
    The Lady Eve, 1941
    Christmas in July, 1941
    Palm Beach Story, 1942
    Sullivan's Travels, 1942
    The Miracle of Morgan's Creek, 1943
    Hail the Conquering Hero, 1945
SUCKSDORFF, ARNE
    Rhythm of a City, 1947
    A Divided World, 1947
    The Open Road, 1948

TATI, JACQUES
    Jour de Fête, 1949
TAYLOR, DONALD
    Lancashire at Work and Play, 1934
    Citizens of the Future, 1935
    Our Country, 1945 (with John Eldridge)
TAYLOR, JOHN
    The Smoke Menace, 1937
    Dawn of Iran, 1938
TENNYSON, PEN
    The Proud Valley, 1940
TETZLAFF, TED
    The Window, 1948
    Johnny Allegro, 1949
THARP, GRAHAME
    Airscrew, 1940

INDICES

These Indices give only the main references to their subjects which occur on pp. 13–250.

INDEX OF FILM TITLES

INDEX OF NAMES

INDEX OF MAIN SUBJECTS

PELICAN BOOKS

A 126

FILM

ROGER MANVELL